Minority-Dominant Relations

A Sociological Analysis

Minority-Dominant Relations

A Sociological Analysis

F. JAMES DAVIS

Professor of Sociology
Illinois State University

AHM Publishing Corporation
Arlington Heights, Illinois 60004

The table on page 177 is reprinted from *Assimilation in American Life: The Role of Race, Religion, and National Origins* by Milton M. Gordon, copyright©1964 by Oxford University Press, Inc. Reprinted by permission.

The table on page 197 is reprinted from *Population* by William Petersen, copyright©1961 by The Macmillan Publishing Co., Inc. Reprinted by permission.

Contents

TWO

PATTERNS OF ACCOMMODATION

T̄H̄R̄ĒĒ

THE ASSIMILATION OF GROUPS

FOUR

ACTION TOWARD EQUALITY

14   Dilemmas of Change: Goals and Means   **285**

to the memory of

ARNOLD M. ROSE

friend of minorities,
friend of sociology,
who left us too soon

Preface

Students of minority-dominant relations need a careful, balanced, understandable synthesis of the wide-ranging data and theoretical issues. Such a framework makes it possible to interpret research results, descriptions of detailed experiences of particular groups, more extended theoretical analyses, and strategies and processes of change. It provides perspective for a wide variety of social action, policymaking, professional, administrative, and scholarly concerns. The framework developed in this book is sociological, but the relevant source materials cut freely across the disciplines. Historical continuities are emphasized, especially in twentieth-century America, and frequent comparisons are made with minority situations in other societies. Perspective is hard to come by, and historical and comparative materials are invaluable.

American blacks justifiably receive major attention, but other race groups are included, along with national and religious minorities, and women. The parallels between women as a minority and other groups are often striking. Groups that receive only limited attention are the aging, the handicapped, and deviant groups, partly because they have not been studied much as minorities and partly for lack of space. Attitudes of prejudice are related to the central emphasis on patterns of discrimination. The focus is on the interaction between minority and dominant groups, and thus on power relations, ideologies, and conflict. Change, and minority strategies for accomplishing it, are stressed more than in most general texts on minorities.

At a time when many white sociologists were abandoning minority-dominant relations as a specialty and developing other interests, in the early 1970s, I made the decision to move in the opposite direction. I returned to this early and long-standing interest in a troubled, but exciting, time. Sound knowledge of intergroup relations requires contributions from members of both minority and dominant communities, and of students who are marginal to both. Valuable new data and interpretations have emerged from the efforts of minority scholars in recent years, and the challenge of this sometimes tumultuous interest has never been greater. Many aspects of discrimination and prejudice in the dominant community have been neglected or only partly understood, and minority persons lack satisfactory access, just as researchers from dominant groups encounter barriers in studying minority communities. The problems are those of the national community and the world. We are all a part of the main.

Anyone who has attempted a synthesis of the scope represented by this book knows the overwhelming sense of obligation for the work of many people to whom acknowledgement must be given only in footnotes and lists of references. I am grateful to two of my departmental colleagues for their help—to Barbara Sherman Heyl for valuable comments on the entire manuscript and to Dorothy Lee for reactions to selected chapters. Ernest Campbell reviewed the manuscript carefully and gave me the benefit of numerous comments and questions. It is a pleasure to thank Mrs. Alberta Carr for the contributions that only a superb, experienced manuscript typist can make. I remain grateful to my wife, Lucile, for the kind of constant understanding and support that no author has the right to take for granted.

F. J. D.
August 1977

ONE

BASIC CONCEPTS AND PROCESSES

1

Minorities in Human Societies

Repeatedly in human history, groups that are physically or culturally different, or both, have come into contact with each other. Although other groups have sometimes been accepted and considered interesting or even exciting, more often they have been seen as unwanted competitors, disturbers, or feared enemies. Conflict has been frequent and, more often than not, the ensuing relationships have been unequal. Racial and cultural contacts have typically resulted in relationships between minority groups and their reciprocal: dominant or majority groups.

MINORITY GROUP DEFINED

The following definition, used in this book, was stated by Louis Wirth:

> We may define a minority as a group of people who, because of their physical or cultural characteristics, are singled out from others in the society in which they live for differential and unequal treatment and who therefore regard themselves as objects of collective discrimination.[1]

In this definition a minority is seen as a group that is discriminated against—that is, one that is subjected to differential and unequal treatment. It is a subordinate or dominated group—therefore, one that is relatively powerless. Differential treatment requires some kind of visibility, which may be based either on physical or cultural traits. Culture becomes apparent in such traits as language, gestures, food customs, rituals, and religious symbols. And, says Wirth, a minority is not just a category of people with some common traits, because the unequal treatment they receive produces or enhances a sense of group identity. This sense of identity varies in degree, and does not necessarily foster active protest.

A minority group in this sense may be small in numbers, or large. Only when other factors are held constant is group size nicely correlated with power. Large groups may be dominated effectively, sometimes by groups that are smaller. In the Union of South Africa the dominant whites (largely of Dutch and English origin) are only about one-fifth of the population, yet they have strongly dominated the blacks and the "coloureds" (mixed peoples). The large Roman Catholic population in the United States was for a long time subjected to marked discrimination. Many small religious groups are discriminated against, as illustrated by the Jews, and by Jehovah's Witnesses or other fundamentalist sects. Other small religious groups, such as the Episcopalians and the Unitarians, occupy prominent places in the dominant community. Large or small in numbers, a minority group is small in the power to control its own status in society.

If an extremely small group or coalition monopolizes political, economic, and other institutional power in a society, it is useful to employ such terms as *power elite* and *subjugated masses* rather than dominant and minority groups.[2] The assumption is that the elites behave toward all other people essentially alike, rather than according differential treatment to various physical and cultural groups. Where societal power is more widely distributed, characteristically there are numerous minorities and several dominant groups. The term *dominant community* is used to refer to all groups participating in a pattern of discrimination against a particular minority.

RACIAL AND CULTURAL MINORITIES

Until the 1970s the sociological study of minorities was limited almost solely to racial, national, and religious minorities. Racial traits in scientific usage are physical; the term *race* is used to refer to certain biological traits that enable mankind to be divided into rough, overlapping categories. Racially mixed peoples must be included among racial minorities, since they are distinguishable in their physical appearance from the dominant groups. Racial minorities usually are identifiable by shared cultural or subcultural traits, at least to some degree, as well as by physical characteristics. Racial and cultural traits are often confused, as we shall see in Chapter 6.

National and religious minorities are cultural groups. National minorities—such as the Irish, Swedish, or Italian peoples—share a common cultural heritage, the major identifying traits of which are language, mode of dress, folk behavior, and sometimes religion. A different language or dialect is not essential, but usually it is the chief criterion.[3] National groups of immigrants in the United States have experienced much discrimination in their efforts to climb the status ladder.

Religious groups share either a total cultural pattern for community life or a *subculture,* which means a set of beliefs and practices that are congruent with the general cultural pattern in some respects but which also include distinctive elements. When cultural or subcultural groups are subjected to differential and unequal treatment they are minority groups. Both sectarian groups and established denominations, including the Roman Catholic Church, may be discriminated against. In the United States both Christian and non-Christian groups have experienced minority status.

Although a group may have more than one distinguishing trait, the dominant community usually responds to one as the most salient. For instance, Italians in the United States have usually been seen as a national group rather than as a religious minority, while Irish Catholics have been treated more as a religious than as a national group. East Asian peoples in the United States, although they could be identified as national or religious minorities, have usually been perceived as racial groups.[4]

The term *ethnic group* will be used in this book to mean a group with a sense of identity based on loyalty to a very distinctive cultural pattern.[5] The group may have real or assumed common ancestry,[6] but this is not essential to the definition used here. National groups, such as Swedish or Polish immigrants in the United States, clearly qualify as ethnic groups. Many religious groups do also, as illustrated by the Jewish people and the Old Order Amish. The term does not seem very applicable to many denominations and sects; they are ethnic only to the degree that their subcultures are distinctive from others. The student should be aware that sociologists often have used the term "ethnic" to refer to cultural or subcultural manifestations of any kind and degree, thus apparently including all religious minorities.[7] Groups that are racially distinguishable may have ethnicity in the more distinctive sense, but not necessarily. The Navajo Indians have retained a high degree of ethnic identity, in contrast to black immigrants in England from Jamaica and Trinidad, who know no other culture than the British.

WOMEN, AGE GROUPS, THE HANDICAPPED, AND DEVIANTS

Racial characteristics are not the only physical traits that may provide a visible basis for differential treatment; sex, age, and physical handicaps may also become the ground for categorical discrimination. To the extent that women, the aged, and the physically handicapped are discriminated against as possessors of common physical characteristics, and regard themselves as objects of such treatment, they are minority groups. The strength of this awareness varies widely, but some sense of group identity is essential if a physical category is to be a human group.

Women as a Minority

In most societies throughout history women have had lower prestige and less power than men, often being little more than male property objects, and their status has usually depended on that of male relatives. Typically their inferior family, economic, political, educational, and religious statuses, and the accompanying traditional roles, have been supported by law. Even where these traditional patterns have been modified, so long as inequalities remain, the social status of women is—like racial status—ascribed at birth. This ascription of status is followed by giving all females the same categorical treatment, regardless of individual capabilities and interests. The result is the channeling of girls and women into marriage and family roles, and restricting them to certain kinds of work outside the home and to a limited system of rewards.[8]

Industrial-urban forces have facilitated a long-range trend from a patriarchal to an equalitarian family system, and throughout much of the twentieth century ours has been semipatriarchal. This means much variation and ambiguity, but generally a moderated, controversial, and changing pattern of male control.[9] Increased need for educated white-collar workers early in the century began a massive movement of women into low-paying clerical jobs.[10] The women's movements of the nineteenth century in the United States culminated at least in some legal changes, including the right to vote, granted in 1920 in the Nineteenth Amendment to the Constitution.

Important economic gains for women made during and after World War I were lost in the 1930s, as the traditional male heads of households were given priority in allocating the scarce jobs and payroll dollars. During World War II there were some occupational advances again, when women were needed for war production and other jobs; but many of these gains were temporary. At the end of the 1960s, following some major legal advances concerning the employment of women and a period of militant racial protests, a multifaceted women's liberation movement rapidly achieved national attention, support, and influence. The successes have been tempered by setbacks, including the continuing failure to get the Equal Rights Amendment to the United States Constitution ratified by the necessary three-fourths of the state legislatures.

Dramatic changes in the status of women in a few years' time, coupled with the determined push for a great deal more change toward the goal of equal status with men, have aroused or lent heat to a host of sharply debated issues, examples of which are day care centers, abortion, grounds for divorce, premarital and extramarital sexual relations, and the token numbers of women in law, judgeships, medicine, dent'stry, business administration, and in important elective and appointive political offices. Some issues now being taken seriously would have seemed absurd a few years ago, such as exclusion of women from the priesthood, equal funding for women's athletics, the legality of all-boys' choirs in public schools, and the fitness of women to hold the office of president of the United States.

This partial listing of issues associated with the drive for equal status for women suggests the fundamental and complex nature of the pattern of social relations between the sexes. Despite all the changes to date and the great differences between the position of American women and those of much of the rest of the world, substantial inequality of status remains, and to reduce it requires a great many more changes in the attitudes, ideas, and daily habits of both males and females. Alternative new norms for male-female relationships are being explored, and much excitement and anxiety, movement and countermovement, are to be expected.

Patterns of accommodation between the sexes reflect basic values in the society. Underlying the searches for new norms are at least relative shifts in priorities of value, including the shift from the ideal that women work away from home only because of economic need to their right to do so because they want to meet other needs;[11] from the sacredness of life in the human fetus to the right of women to control their own bodies; and the very basic shift from the value of marriage and family stability to that of personal welfare and happiness.[12]

The Aging as a Minority

While a case can be made that youth, children, and even the middle-aged experience group prejudice and discrimination, the argument on behalf of the aging is very strong. In the early decades of this century increasing productivity and the consequent rising level of living resulted in the dream of retirement from a lifetime of work, a concept that facilitated the development of retirement pension systems and in 1935 the passage of the basic Social Security Act. The status of retired persons was envisioned as respected and secure, as would befit those who had earned rest and pleasant leisure-time activities. Instead, the realization of mass retirement has been associated with a lowered social status for "senior citizens," involving economic insecurity and patronizing discrimination. Older workers typically are not evaluated as individuals, and compulsory retirement at a fixed age is justified by such stereotypes of them as nonproductive, rigid, and prone to accidents, absenteeism, and turnover. Employers with pension plans avoid hiring persons in their fifties. Company costs for workmen's compensation and accident and disability insurance are increased by hiring women over forty or men over forty-five.[13]

Economic insecurity not only makes other activities difficult, but it symbolizes a low overall social status. It has become rare for the nuclear family to make room for, or to help support, a grandparent. The general assumption seems to be that when people reach the age at which employment typically ends they no longer wish to be active in family affairs, in labor unions, in professional associations, in leadership roles in a lodge or church, or in wider community activities. Attempts by the aging to combat the economic and other discriminatory practices against them, such as political effort toward legislation banning discrimination in hiring based on age, have had limited success to date. However, such organized actions and the sense of identity with other aging people seem to be on the increase.

The Physically Handicapped as a Minority

Persons with physical handicaps are expected to play restricted roles in the community, and thus are usually so marginal and obscure that they are almost invisible. They must learn to play the roles of the sick to which society assigns them,[14] and not aspire to normal roles that are closed to them. Instead of being evaluated on their individual merits for jobs and other social positions, they encounter special treatment based on stereotypes of their abilities and interests. When handicapped groups become vocal and support political action on their behalf, they often protest against established programs of help on the ground that the policies reflect stereotypes and channel them into a limited range of opportunities. Societal pressure is heavy for the handicapped to support themselves, yet systematic discrimination works against this very goal.

Agencies that deal with the blind, for example, typically emphasize probable success in getting employment, and they limit their clientele to those who fit stereotypes involving youthful hopes and education for particular kinds of work. Most agencies for the blind compete for the educable youth and employable adults, but ignore services to children with multiple handicaps and to the elderly blind. More than two-thirds of the blind are elderly, and many could profit from rehabilitative efforts to improve their performance in family, work, and other roles, but one estimate is that at least nine-tenths of the agencies withhold such services. Both public and private funds for aid to the blind are plentiful, but agency policies restrict services to a fairly small proportion of the blind population and channel the chosen clients into a limited, safe, "successful" range of opportunities.[15]

Deviant Behavioral Groups as Minorities

In order for deviants to constitute a minority group, even to a limited degree, there must be a sense of identification with a group that shares a deviant culture or subculture and that is subjected to illegitimate treatment by the dominant community. Legitimate treatment, whether by legal agencies or other means, is action generally considered in the society to be appropriate and justified.[16] Social control of specific deviant acts is usually accepted as legitimate, but generalized harassment and exploitation of a deviant group are not. Also illegitimate is the denial of opportunities for equal treatment when deviant individuals attempt to "go straight." Deviant groups as varied as the mentally ill, alcoholics, prisoners, youth gangs, and communes may all experience such discrimination.[17]

Persons who have committed felonies experience societal punishment that continues indefinitely when they encounter continuing police harassment, job discrimination, and the inability to regain civil rights.[18] The Gay Movement of recent years consists of efforts toward decriminalization and other actions designed to protect homosexuals from being "shaken down" by the police and by youthful gangs, and from being discriminated against in employment.[19] Prostitutes' unions have been organized in a number of cities to combat harassment and exploitation by the courts, by landlords, businesses, doctors, lawyers, and especially by the police. These unions are demanding that proper procedures be followed in court actions against prostitutes, that males be included in laws against prostitution, that customers be arrested as well as prostitutes, and ultimately that prostitution be decriminalized at least to misdemeanor status, or fully legalized and zoned. Many programs for helping such groups as ex-alcoholics, ex-prisoners, and ex–mental patients are designed to erase the stigma, and thus to facilitate equal opportunities for jobs and other social statuses.

MEASURING GROUP STATUS AND DISCRIMINATION

Comparing different groups on indexes of particular aspects of well-being—such as income, employment, amount of education, or health—provides measures of group status. Rather than attempting to combine such measures to obtain an index of the general status of a group, the usual procedure is simply to use the individual measures to document overall generalizations. For example, using an Index of Dissimilarity to analyze United States Bureau of Census data on income, occupation, and education, two researchers concluded that American blacks gained significantly on whites in these respects from 1959 to 1969.[20] Another measure showed the black gains in income during the 1960s to be slight.[21] Using an Equality Index, two other investigators reported that blacks made considerable gains on whites from 1940 to 1968 in income, education, occupation, weeks worked per year, housing, and mortality.[22] Despite these gains, the remaining inequalities were great by 1970.[23]

Such measures of inequality of group status are very often cited as indirect evidence of discrimination against minorities, but care must be exercised in making this inference. A group's current status in some particular respect, such as health, has also been a product of the group's overall position in the social structure. This general status may have been affected significantly by discriminatory practices, of course. Immigrant groups have usually entered a new country at a low status level, for instance, and discrimination adds to the difficulty of improving it. Even if discrimination is minimal or absent, a group with limited education, skills, money, and political power cannot realize equality of status at once.[24] Yet, under certain conditions, groups can make significant gains in status in the face of considerable discrimination against them. Thus changes in the indexes of inequality do not necessarily indicate corresponding increases or decreases in the amount of discrimination being practiced.

Whenever possible, then, measures of unequal status need to be supplemented by evidence of acts of discrimination, as direct as possible. Some differential and unequal treatment is highly visible, such as enforcing legal requirements for segregated public facilities. At the other extreme are subtle forms of discrimination that are screened from public view, and unrecorded, such as secret agreements not to rent or sell housing to certain groups. Descriptions of individual acts of discrimination are valuable evidence, but the question of how representative they are needs to be answered as well as possible.

MINORITIES IN THE UNITED STATES

The European settlers quickly established a pattern of domination of the nominally sovereign native American Indian "nations," but not until they were totally defeated did the latter become a legal minority. In 1871, with the establishment of the reservation system, the surviving Indian peoples became wards of the United States government. Census estimates at that time indicated less than half a million Indians, compared with nearly a million when Columbus discovered America. Around 1900 there were only about a quarter of a million, and by 1970 the number had grown to a little above three-quarters of a million.

Immigrants came primarily from Great Britain and elsewhere in Northern Europe for over two and a half centuries, then around the turn of this century the volume from Southern and Eastern Europe greatly accelerated, adding a large number of new ethnic minorities. Many white immigrant groups have occupied minority group status and have seemed well assimilated by the third generation, Protestants from Northern Europe often by the second. Today, except for the Puerto Ricans, second-generation immigrants are often not classed as minorities and even most of the first-generation groups (foreign-born) are omitted by some students. In 1970, 4.7 percent of the population were foreign-born, and 11.8 percent had at least one foreign-born parent.[25]

Roman Catholics, constituting about one-fourth of America's population, are America's largest minority except for women; but many students no longer count Catholics because of the marked decline in discrimination against them in recent decades.[26] The *American*

Jewish Yearbook estimate of the number of Jews in the United States in 1970 was over six million.[27] Religious minorities include a great many Protestant sects, mostly small ones, and followers of many other faiths. If Roman Catholics are omitted, blacks are the largest minority group except for women, their over 22½ million people in 1970 making up 11.1 percent of the population of the United States.[28]

Most of the people counted in the census as "negro" actually are racially mixed, with negroid genes outnumbering the caucasoid ones, and with some from the American Indians. Most of this amalgamation took place during slave times, as we will see in Chapter 6. (See Chapter 5 for the definition and classification of the races.) The United States Census takers follow the traditional Southern definition of a negro as anyone who has any visible trace of black ancestry or who is known as a black in the community. Clearly, if the government defined race in terms of the predominance of actual racial traits (which is roughly the practice in Latin American nations), considerably fewer people would be classed as black. Census workers count what is considered socially significant, so they follow the South's and the country's social definition of race.

Migration of blacks to cities and out of the South was heavy in the 1920s and has been again ever since the early 1940s. From 1940 to 1970 more than four and a half million blacks moved out of the South, so that by 1970 more were living outside than inside the region. In 1910 one-fourth of all American blacks lived in urban areas, but by 1970 four-fifths did.[29] Blacks are now more urban than whites are, and are especially concentrated in the large, central cities. The usual move in recent years has been from a Southern city to a Northern one. To dramatize the situation, more blacks now live in Chicago than in the entire state of Mississippi, and more are in the New York City area than in any Southern state.

Many Mexican Americans are racially visible, since the vast majority are Mestizo, a mixture of Mexican Indians with Spanish or other whites.[30] However, since the dominant whites (Anglos) perceive Mexican Americans mainly as a cultural rather than a racial minority, the latter are identified by census takers as people of Mexican national origin, and included in the broader Spanish-speaking category. Mexican Americans were approximately tied with Jews in size among other minorities in the United States in 1970, with over six million people.[31] By March 1975, the number of Mexican Americans had grown to over six and two-thirds million.[32] The Jewish people in the United States had long been heavily urban; and, by 1970, 85 percent of the Spanish-surnamed population in the Southwestern states lived in urban areas. Next in size in 1970 came the Puerto Ricans with around a million and a half, and all other groups had less than one million. In declining order of size, the remainder includes American Indians, peoples of Cuban,

Japanese, Chinese, and Filipino descent,[33] and many still smaller groups.

MINORITIES IN A WORLD OF NATION-STATES

Minority-dominant issues have been prominent around the world in recent decades, and in debates in the United Nations the references to the Declaration of Human Rights have been frequent. The Soviet Union illustrates the ethnic diversity and tensions in today's world. About half the population of the vast Soviet Union are Russians; the rest consists of somewhere around one hundred (depending on the system of classification used) national groups of varying sizes. The count was closer to two hundred a century ago. There is racial variation, and fear of the "yellow peril."[34] There is a great variety of languages, although schoolchildren learn Russian along with their own tongue. The Soviet policy is to encourage a considerable degree of cultural pluralism as a means of facilitating loyalty to the central government, but the long-range goal appears to be assimilation (Chapter 10). Most of the ethnic groups live in their own officially recognized territories and their nationalism is tolerated so long as it is not "excessive." Hostility to religion militates against ethnic identity, and so also does industrialization. Jewish culture and identity are discouraged both by the antireligion and anti-Zionist policies, yet anti-Semitism is formally defined as a crime. The anti-Zionist policy prohibits Jews from emigrating to Israel.[35]

European colonial occupation of much of the world involved patterns of domination of native peoples, with continuing consequences today. The new African states have boundaries determined by colonial administrators, and the 1968–1970 civil war in Nigeria (the Biafran rebellion, of the Ibo peoples) is but one example of the lack of correlation between boundaries and ethnicity.[36] Colonial populations were typically small and temporary, but some of them came to stay as permanent settlers and grew in size, as in the Union of South Africa, Australia, and Latin America.

The South African system of *apartheid* (pronounced apart-hate, and meaning apartness) has been a heated international issue for decades. The whites have controlled the residence, movements, and occupations of the nonwhite four-fifths of the population, using repressive measures and officially justifying them with a racist ideology.[37] The educated blacks and "coloureds" are caught between Western ideals of achievement and the realities of their low statuses. Tight police surveillance, supplemented by terrorism, has been used to keep the nonwhite groups in their ascribed statuses. Recent concessions and official consideration of more equalitarian alternatives have led to non-violent demonstrations designed to hasten further changes, without much apparent success.[38] In 1976 a series of more violent outbursts took place in the larger cities, with the loss of several hundred lives, mostly those of the minority peoples.

The end of both world wars brought strong international support for the principle of the self-determination of peoples, yet the redrawing of boundaries and the establishment of a host of independent new nation-states have created as many new minority-dominant situations as they have resolved. Even the smallest countries have their inter-group tensions and conflicts. The cold war has aggravated many minor-ity-dominant problems, such as those between the overseas Chinese and the dominant peoples of Thailand, Indonesia, and other countries of Southeast Asia. International conflicts have produced many political refugees, creating minority issues and adding to the ones associated with voluntary migration. The Communist countries of East and Southeast Europe continue to worry about their ethnic divisions, in-cluding the resistance to assimilation by over a million Gypsies, nearly one-third of them in Czechoslovakia.

The numbers and statuses of Jews in Arab countries were sharply lowered by the establishment of the state of Israel, which also created the Palestine Arab refugees,[39] and by the subsequent Arab-Israeli con-flicts. The Arabs who remained in Israel became a minority, and the Oriental Jews (North African and Asian) have complained about being discriminated against by the European Jews who are politically and economically dominant in Israel.

When the Indians were pressured to leave by the government of newly independent Kenya during the 1960s, Great Britain faced the dilemma of choosing between immigration controls and treating all citizens of the Commonwealth as if they were British citizens. The legislative decision in 1968 was to restrict the colonial immigration sharply, and also in 1968 the Race Relations Act was passed to provide for fair treatment of immigrants already residing in Great Britain. Immigrants from Commonwealth areas had been encouraged in order to meet a labor shortage, and many black workers have come from the Caribbean and from Africa, along with many dark-skinned caucasoids from Pakistan and India. Settling mostly in slums in London, but also in other industrial cities in Great Britain, these groups have had severe housing problems and have met discrimination.[40]

These illustrations are but a small sample of the world's minority-dominant situations today, and it should be noted that the historical record shows that minority problems extend far back in time. Women, the handicapped, and deviant groups have also experienced minority status in other places and times, but the aged have fared well in nearly all traditional societies. The emphasis in this book is on American minorities, but some reference to those in other countries will help keep our patterns in perspective and help prevent oversimplified and provincial conclusions.

MINORITY-DOMINANT RELATIONS
AS SOCIAL ISSUES

Although group prejudice and discrimination have been among the major dilemmas of the modern world, rising to a peak of attention in the United States since the mid-1950s, they do not automatically distress the society in which they occur. Minority-dominant relations evidently become social issues only under certain conditions. In fact, situations of extreme oppression have often been much less controversial than have semiequalitarian ones. Since minorities have less power to control the relationships, and also to control the mass media of communication and other agencies of public discussion, discrimination does not become an important social issue unless the dominant community becomes upset about it. Some sociologists find it useful to limit the definition of a social problem to major public issues,[41] but it is not necessary to accept that in order to highlight the conditions under which minority experiences become and continue to be major issues in society.

The first essential for the emergence of a social issue is that a social condition, such as group discrimination or drug addiction or environmental pollution, contradicts the *value priorities* held by enough people in the dominant community to provoke widespread discussion and proposed actions toward alleviating or eliminating it. *Value beliefs specify the way people believe things should be.* If value consensus becomes very high the support for mobilizing efforts to eliminate the condition becomes very strong, so that the issue ceases to be social and becomes a purely technical (means-ends) one. Instead, if other value priorities are in conflict with those that condemn the social condition, the debate continues about what the goals ought to be. And if agreement on the goals is reached but there are value disagreements over the means to use in reaching the goals, as in the debate over the use of violent means, the social issue remains unresolved.

Even when there are no controversies over values, there may be disagreement over the relevant existential (reality) beliefs. While values reveal the way persons or groups think things ought to be, *existen-*

tial beliefs indicate the way people think things are. Existential beliefs may be concerned with the existence or the causes of the condition, or with proposed steps toward its reduction or elimination. Thus, a social issue will continue if there are significant disagreements over either the value priorities or the existential beliefs, or both. Some political and other groups in the dominant community have more influence than others in the processes of public discussion and decision making, so the probability of any faction's having its value priorities and existential beliefs implemented in social norms depends on its relative power position.

Values and Minority Issues

What American values are threatened by widespread discrimination against physical or cultural groups? In a classic study of racial segregation in the Deep South, the "American Dilemma" was said to consist of a conflict between discrimination and the basic democratic values of equal opportunity, liberty, fraternity, and democratic participation in government.[42] This dilemma is as old as the country, since a compromise on slavery was written into the Constitution, providing that slavery could continue but that the slave trade could be ended after two decades.[43] Abigail Adams pointed out to her husband John, later the second president, the incongruity between declaring all men equal and denying freedom to blacks. Just before the Declaration of Independence was signed, she also appealed to her husband to support full legal, political, and educational rights for women, an appeal that failed.

Two related values threatened by group discrimination are a healthy economy and the effective use of the abilities of all persons in society. Limiting an entire group to certain kinds of work means failure to utilize its full range of talents, and there is evidence that this reduces the real incomes of both minority and dominant groups.[44] The presence of danger from the outside, as in wartime, increases the general concern about the labor force. But, quite aside from crises, efficient use of resources is an important American value.

Good international relations is a value threatened by criticism of group discrimination in the country. In recent decades the United States, the Soviet Union, and the Union of South Africa have been foremost among the recipients of criticism for their treatment of minorities—in United Nations forums, by foreign students,[45] and in the world press. When in 1956 Autherine Lucy, the first black ever admitted to the University of Alabama, was subjected to rioting and finally dismissed, offers came from the Norwegian Students Association to pay for her education at the University of Oslo; and the Danish students made a similar offer. The greater the concern for the country's international image, the more influence such incidents have on public discussion of minority issues.

The value of the well-being of the individual, including good physical and mental health, is threatened by group discrimination. Minority peoples often have high rates of ill health, crime, alcoholism, drug addiction, suicide, and other individual casualties. Finally, peace and order are threatened by intergroup tension and violence, with costs both in dollars and in lives.

The above values come into conflict with those values in the dominant community that are protected by discrimination against minority groups, such as control of the most prized businesses, occupations, and professions, ownership of choice property, symbols of class status, control of government at all levels, control of public facilities, and membership in exclusive private organizations, including churches. Pride in and loyalty to one's group, including its ideas of the good and the beautiful, are also valued. Another suggestion is that dominant groups come to value their sense of group superiority. And actions aimed at improving minority status may be opposed as threats to peace and order.

When dominant communities and whole societies are in conflict over the priorities of value in intergroup relations, it is important to seek out evidence of the conflict rather than to assume a monolithic consensus of values underlying a pattern of institutionalized discrimination. This is extremely important in estimating the possibilities and probabilities of change. Often various groups in the dominant (and also the minority) community disagree on value priorities; persons within groups disagree with each other; and there are often conflicting values within the person.

Existential Beliefs and Minority Issues

Disagreement over existential beliefs keeps issues about minority-dominant relations alive even if there is substantial agreement on the relevant priorities of value. Even if there is a strong agreement that equal educational opportunity is an important value, for example, disagreement over the existential belief that racial groups are biologically unequal in their learning potentials results in dilemmas of policy. There is a wide range of beliefs about physical and cultural groups and about interaction between them. Many of these beliefs about reality are highlighted in Chapter 3 in the discussion of stereotypes and other aspects of prejudice. In Chapter 5, the role of existential beliefs in ideological justifications of discrimination is discussed.

TOPICS EMPHASIZED IN THIS BOOK

The groups given the greatest attention throughout the book are racial, national, and religious minorities. Women receive considerably more emphasis than it was possible to devote to the aging, the handicapped, and deviant groups. Attitudes of prejudice are included in the analysis (especially in Chapter 3), but the greater emphasis is on the patterns and processes of systematic discrimination against groups. Minorities in the United States are emphasized, but, in order to put our own experience into perspective, comparisons are frequently made with those in other societies.

Social conflict and group power are treated in Chapter 2, but are also emphasized throughout the book as central elements in patterns of group domination. It is assumed that power is distributed in quite different ways in different times and places, and that in the United States it is dispersed unequally but not monopolized by a small, elite group. The process of conflict is related to various forms of accommodation among groups, including patterns of segregation and the acceptance of subordinate status (Part II). Some attention is also given to the other outcomes of group conflict (Chapter 2). Assimilation is analyzed but not assumed to be the inevitable, or even the most common, outcome of group interaction (Chapters 9 and 10). The role of both value and existential beliefs is stressed, especially as components of prejudice and of ideologies used to justify either existing patterns or proposed changes. Racist beliefs are compared with scientific beliefs about the human races (Chapter 5).

Part of Chapter 7 and all four chapters in Part IV are devoted to social change in intergroup relations, especially to protest and to social movements designed to bring about more group equality. The public discussion of minority issues is part of this treatment, and the central focus is on the initiatives for and the processes of change. While this is a heavier stress than has often been placed on resistance to inequality and to strategies and processes of change, the emphasis is warranted by the realities of protest and change in minority-dominant relations.

FOOTNOTES

Footnotes refer to the list of references at the end of each chapter.
1   Wirth, 1945, p. 347.
2   Schermerhorn, 1970, p. 13.
3   Miroglio, 1969.
4   Marden & Meyer, 1973, pp. 45–46.
5   Berry, 1965, p. 46.

6 Schermerhorn, 1970, p. 12; Francis, 1976, p. 6.

7 Gordon, 1964, pp. 27–29.

8 Epstein, 1976, pp. 416–32; Myrdal, 1944, pp. 1073–78; Hacker, 1951; deBeauvoir, 1952, pp. 122–31.

9 Winch, 1963, pp. 81–84; LeMasters, 1957, pp. 29–33.

10 Huber, 1972, pp. 338–39.

11 Epstein, 1976, pp. 422–23.

12 Davis, 1970, pp. 151–52.

13 Barron, 1961, Ch. 4.

14 Scott, 1969, pp. 14–38, 71–89.

15 Scott, 1969, pp. 50–52, 56–70.

16 Weber, 1947, pp. 124–32, 152–53, 324–27.

17 Sagarin, 1971, Ch. 1.

18 Kuehn, 1971.

19 Hacker, 1971; Kameny, 1971.

20 Farley & Hermalin, 1972.

21 Villemez & Rowe, 1975.

22 Palmore & Whittington, 1970.

23 Shin, 1976.

24 Lieberson & Fuguitt, 1967.

25 U.S. Bureau of Census, 1970. P. C. (1)-C1, Table 68.

26 Greeley, 1972.

27 *American Jewish Yearbook,* 1970, p. 354.

28 U.S. Bureau of Census, 1970. P. C. (1)-B1, Tables 59 & 60, pp. 292–93.

29 U.S. Bureau of Census, 1972, p. 15.

30 Newman, 1973, pp. 71–72.

31 U.S. Bureau of Census, 1970, P. C. (1)-B1, Table 97, p. 403 .

32 U.S. Bureau of Census, 1976, Table A.

33 U.S. Bureau of Census, 1970, P. C. (1)-B1, Table 60, p. 293.

34 Isaacs, 1975.

35 Hunt & Walker, 1974, Ch. 3.

36 Hunt & Walker, pp. 18–19, 263–95.

37 Van den Berghe, 1965; Turk, 1967.

38 Kuper, 1965.

39 Khouri, 1970.

40 Hunt & Walker, 1974, pp. 302–14.

41 Davis, 1970, pp. 15–25, 47–48.

42 Myrdal et al., 1944, Chs. 1 & 2.

43 Hunt & Walker, 1974, p. 332.

44 Becker, 1971.

45 Davis, 1961, pp. 50–51; 1971, p. 34.

REFERENCES

Barron, Milton L.
1961   The Aging American. New York: Thomas Y. Crowell Co.

Becker, Gary S.
1971   The Economics of Discrimination, 2nd Edition. Chicago and London: University of Chicago Press.
Berry, Brewton
1965   Race and Ethnic Relations, 3rd Edition. Boston: Houghton Mifflin Co.
Davis, F. James
1961   "American Minorities as Seen by Turkish Students in the United States." Sociology and Social Research 46 (October): 48–54.
1970   Social Problems: Enduring Major Issues and Social Change. New York: The Free Press.
1971   "The Two-Way Mirror and the U-Curve: America as Seen by Turkish Students Returned Home." Sociology and Social Research 56 (October): 29–43.
de Beauvoir, Simone
1952   The Second Sex. Trans. and ed., H. M. Parshley. New York: Alfred A. Knopf, Inc.
Epstein, Cynthia Fuchs
1976   "Sex Roles," Ch. 9 in Robert K. Merton and Robert Nisbet, Contemporary Social Problems. New York: Harcourt, Brace, Jovanovich, Inc.
Farley, Reynolds, and Albert Hermalin
1972   "The 1960's: A Decade of Progress for Blacks?" Demography 9: 353–70.
Francis, E. K.
1976   Interethnic Relations: An Essay in Sociological Theory. New York: Elsevier.
Gordon, Milton
1964   Assimilation in American Life: The Role of Race, Religion and National Origins. New York: Oxford University Press.
Greeley, Andrew M.
1972   "American Catholics—Making It or Losing It?" Public Interest 28 (Summer): 26–37.
Hacker, Helen Mayer
1951   "Women as a Minority Group." Social Forces 30 (October): 60–69.
1971   "Homosexuals: Deviant or Minority Group?" pp. 65–92 in Edward Sagarin (ed.), The Other Minorities. Waltham, Massachusetts: Xerox College Publishing.
Huber, Joan
1972   "Ambiguities in Identity Transformation: From Sugar and Spice to Professor." Notre Dame Journal of Education 2 (Winter): 338–47.
Hunt, Chester L., and Lewis Walker
1974   Ethnic Dynamics: Patterns of Intergroup Relations in Various Societies. Homewood, Illinois: The Dorsey Press.
Isaacs, Harold R.
1975   Idols of the Tribe. New York: Harper and Row.
Kameny, Franklin E.
1971   "Homosexuals as a Minority Group," pp. 50–65 in Edward Sagarin (ed.), The Other Minorities. Waltham, Massachusetts: Xerox College Publishing.
Khouri, Fred J.
1970   "Arabs in Exile." Trans-Action 7 (July-August): 52–55, 58–61.

Kinloch, Graham C.
1974   The Dynamics of Race Relations: A Sociological Analysis. New York: McGraw-Hill Book Co.
Kuehn, William C.
1971   "Ex-Convicts Conceptualized as a Minority Group," pp. 277–88 in Edward Sagarin (ed.), The Other Minorities. Waltham, Massachusetts: Xerox College Publishing.
Kuper, Leo
1965   An African Bourgeoisie. New Haven, Connecticut, and London: Yale University Press.
Lieberson, Stanley, and Glenn V. Fuguitt
1967   "Negro-White Differences in the Absence of Discrimination." American Journal of Sociology 73 (September): 188–200.
LeMasters, E. E.
1957   Modern Courtship and Marriage. New York: The Macmillan Co.
Lind, Andrew W.
1969   Hawaii: The Last of the Magic Isles. London: Oxford University Press.
Marden, Charles F., and Gladys Meyer
1973   Minorities in American Society. New York: D. Van Nostrand Co.
Miroglio, Abel
1969   "Revue de Psychologie des Peuples." The Ethnic Region 24, 3 (September): 252–83.
Myrdal, Gunnar, assisted by Richard Sterner and Arnold M. Rose
1944   An American Dilemma. New York: Harper and Bros.
Newman, William M.
1973   American Pluralism: A Study of Minority Groups and Social Theory. New York: Harper and Row.
Palmore, Erdman, and Frank J. Whittington
1970   "Differential Trends Toward Equality Between Whites and Nonwhites." Social Forces 49 (September): 108–17.
Sagarin, Edward
1971   The Other Minorities. Waltham, Massachusetts: Xerox College Publishing.
Schermerhorn, Richard A.
1970   Comparative Ethnic Relations: A Framework for Theory and Research. New York: Random House.
Scott, Robert A.
1969   The Making of Blind Men. New York: Russell Sage Foundation.
Shin, Eui Hang
1976   "Earnings Inequality Between Black and White Males by Education, Occupation, and Region." Sociology and Social Research 60, 2 (January): 161–72.
Turk, Austin F.
1967   The Futures of South Africa. Social Forces 45 (March): 402–12.
United States Bureau of the Census
1970   Census of the Population 1970. Washington, D.C.: U.S. Government Printing Office.
1972   The Social and Economic Status of the Black Population in the United States, 1971. Washington, D.C.: U.S. Government Printing Office.

1976   Current Population Reports: Population Characteristics Series P-20, No. 290, February 1976. Washington, D.C.: U.S. Government Printing Office.

Van den Berghe, Pierre L.
1965   South Africa: A Study in Conflict. Middletown, Connecticut: Wesleyan University Press.
1967   Race and Racism. New York: John Wiley and Sons.

Villemez, Wayne J., and Alan R. Rowe
1975   "Black Economic Gains in the Sixties: A Methodological Critique and Reassessment." Social Forces 54, 1 (September): 181–93.

Weber, Max
1947   The Theory of Social and Economic Organization. Trans., A. M. Henderson and Talcott Parsons; ed., Talcott Parsons. New York: Oxford University Press.

Winch, Robert F.
1963   The Modern Family, Revised Edition. New York: Holt, Rinehart and Winston.

Wirth, Louis
1945   "The Problem of Minority Groups," in Ralph Linton (ed.), The Science of Man in the World Crisis. New York: Columbia University Press.

2

Group Contact and Interaction

In this chapter minority-dominant relationships are seen as social interaction between groups, and as dynamic rather than fixed. Attention is focused on group conflict, and on the importance of the connections between group power, conflict, and accommodation, including patterns of institutionalized discrimination. Assimilation is seen as but one, not an inevitable, ultimate outcome of group interaction. The more drastic outcomes of group conflict—voluntary emigration, expulsion, and genocide—are illustrated at some length, since the remainder of the book is devoted to interaction between groups that remain in contact. First, before turning to group interaction, let us note the operation of the factors that bring culturally or physically different groups into social contact.

SOURCES OF GROUP CONTACT AND INTERACTION

The first three sources of group contact and interaction discussed below are involved in the creation of racial and cultural minorities. The fourth accounts for additional cultural contacts, and the fifth for interaction between physical groups other than races.

1. Immigration

Racial and cultural groups meet when one migrates into the territory of the other. When this is involuntary, as in slavery or political refugee situations, the immigrants become the minority. When the population movement is voluntary, the relative amounts of power determine whether the immigrants or the natives become dominant. In the United States the native Indians were dominated by the settlers from Northwest Europe, whose descendants in turn dominated the later immigrant groups.

During World War II, the German armies created some thirty million refugees—from Poland, the Ukraine, the Baltic states, the Netherlands, Belgium, and elsewhere. Many millions of these involuntary migrants never returned home, thus becoming minorities in the countries of arrival, just as countless Chinese who fled from the Communist regime in China in 1948 or later have never gone back. Among new refugee groups since midcentury are the Hungarians who escaped after the unsuccessful uprising in 1956, Cubans who fled from the Castro takeover in 1959, and the Vietnamese who left after the end of the war in 1974.

2. The Shifting of Political Boundaries

Racial and cultural minorities have been both created and eliminated by the shifts in political boundaries that have attended the endless conquests of history. Some of these changes in group status in other parts of the world have been noted in Chapter 1, but new minorities also resulted from the expansion of territory in American history. As the frontiers moved westward new Indian tribes were encountered, along with considerable numbers of the French. The United States acquired the Hispanos (Spanish settlers, chiefly in New Mexico) with the territory taken from Mexico in the War of 1846.

The principle of self-determination for national groups was adopted after World War I as the solution to Europe's minority problems. The once large Hapsburg and Turkish empires were reduced to the nation-states of Austria and Turkey, and eleven new states were created out of territories formerly belonging to those empires and to

Germany and Russia. But there were still many more national groups than there were nation-states, so the new boundaries only created new minority-dominant relationships. For example, the new federal kingdom of Yugoslavia emerged after several centuries of Austro-Hungarian and Turkish domination. The Serbs have been dominant, but there are four other major national groups with strong identities. The major religious split was between Roman Catholicism and Eastern Orthodoxy, with a sizeable Muslim minority. In the post–World War II Socialist Federal Republic of Yugoslavia the conflicts have continued, ethnic loyalties vying strongly with class interests.[1]

The United Nations has strongly embraced the principle of self-determination, and dozens of new nation-states have been established since World War II, most of them in formerly colonial areas. Some of these new countries have been noted in Chapter 1. Racial and cultural group tensions are the rule in these new states, even some of the smallest ones, often producing violent conflicts. Programs of technological development often bring changes in patterns of stratification, thus adding to intergroup tensions.

A massive minorities problem was created when Great Britain withdrew from India in 1947, after partitioning it on the basis of religion. Pakistan (East and West) was separated off to become an independent Islamic state from predominantly Hindu India. War ensued over the control of Kashmir, and during 1947 approximately eleven million people crossed the new borders in a mass transferral of Hindus to India and Muslims to Pakistan. Pakistan still has Hindus, and Muslims constitute by far India's largest religious minority. East Pakistan had linguistic and other ethnic, economic, and political differences with the 1,000-mile-distant West Pakistan,[2] and in 1971 India helped the former to win its independence—as Bangladesh, or Bengal Nation. India has fourteen major language groups and numerous smaller ones, so its problems of intergroup relations are very complex.

3. Shifts in Political Power

Sometimes the ascendant group loses its controlling power and a former minority becomes politically dominant, thus reversing the minority and dominant group roles. In Algeria the much smaller French population dominated the Arabs and Berbers for 132 years, until independence was won in 1962, after which most of the French moved to France. In 1976, after over a decade of heavy international pressure, the white government of Rhodesia began negotiating to turn over control to the far larger black population. Surprising as it may seem, Prime Minister Vorster of the Republic of South Africa joined Great Britain and the United States to bring the heaviest pressure on the Rhodesian white government to take the decisive step. Colonial groups have tended to relinquish control and leave when the costs and risks become heavy, but permanent settlers stay in power as long as they can and attempt to retain as many advantages as possible when they are compelled to relinquish their dominance.[3]

Power shifts affect the statuses of all groups in a stratified pattern, not just those at the top and the bottom. Under British control in Kenya the immigrants from India occupied the position of marginal traders, not treated as equals by the British but granted more privileges than were the native Kenyan groups. When independence came in 1963 the restrictions imposed on the Indians by the new government were much heavier than those placed on the British. Much the same thing had happened to the Chinese minority after 1946 when the Philippines became independent from the United States. Newly independent peoples, especially when they are striving hard for economic development, have tended to limit sharply the opportunities of their alien minorities.[4]

4.   The Emergence of New Cultural Groups

The emergence in society of groups with distinctive beliefs and practices creates new cultural contacts. The new subculture justifies the group's ways and gives it a sense of identity. The greater the differences are from the dominant cultural pattern the greater are the resulting tensions and the tendency of the new group to isolate itself in order to protect its members and its way of life. Deviant subcultural groups, such as drug users, homosexuals, and skid row "winos" should be included among cultural groups that may receive discriminatory treatment.

Sectarian groups reject at least some of the beliefs and practices of their parent groups and pursue their own visions of religious truth. Protestantism has been especially prone to both fundamentalist and liberal sectarian splits, which ecumenical leaders struggle to offset. When sects reject a large share of the culture of the dominant community, especially when the beliefs require violation of laws or strong community customs, they tend to become separatist. Thus the Mormons made their nineteenth century moves westward when the reactions to their practice of polygyny became too threatening, and attempted in then isolated Utah to establish political autonomy. When a sect makes peace with the dominant community on key issues, it develops patterns of accommodation that change it from a sect to a denomination. The Mormons were compelled to follow this path when their isolation broke down and federal law was imposed to make polygyny unconstitutional.

Political movements that succeed in creating new parties or other politically distinct groups are very often seen as a threat by the established order. Such groups characteristically have a set of beliefs that justify their specific goals and activities; thus they often have a visible subculture. In many countries the concept of minority refers mainly to political groups and in some, such as France, the freedom of voluntary associations of all types is sharply restricted to prevent them from gaining political power. Although this is an alien view in the United States it was in this spirit that the Communist Party was outlawed in 1954. Deviant behavioral groups are often repressed at least partly because of the belief that their rejection of some of society's norms reflects more total alienation, even support for overt rebellion, as when hippie styles of life have been identified with political revolution.

5. Biological Differentiation, Other Than Race

The biological fact of sexual difference creates possibilities for differential social treatment, including ascription of one sex to a subordinate status. The biological fact of being born at different times results in the possibility that a particular age group may be assigned a minority status. Physical handicapping, whether due to genetic factors, accidents, or diseases, may result in systematic discrimination against groups of the handicapped. Variation in sex, age, and physical condition occurs within the same families and communities, yet patterns of minority-dominant accommodation parallel those of racial and cultural groups, often including elaborate and rigid systems of segregating females, age groups, and the handicapped. When the origins of such patterns lie far in the past, people have considered them to be natural, and have perpetuated systematic forms of group discrimination without defining them as such.

MINORITY-DOMINANT RELATIONS
AS SOCIAL INTERACTION

Members of physical and cultural groups act and react toward each other in terms of shared meanings or symbols, so minority-dominant relations involve what sociologists define as *social interaction.* If the primary aim is to understand the give and take of this *meaningful mutual influencing* of groups, attention cannot be centered on the minority community alone, nor solely on the dominant community. The attitudes, values, and beliefs, the history, customs, institutions, and the sense of identity of both minority and dominant groups must be taken into account in efforts to understand the interaction between them. Concentrating on specific situations helps keep the focus on the interaction, and to illuminate the conditions and consequences of particular patterns of intergroup relations.[5]

Group Goals and Competition

Groups that are influencing each other's chances of reaching the same scarce rewards may be unaware of this interaction. When groups become conscious that they are directly affecting each other's success in getting jobs, housing, or other scarce objectives, yet continue to concentrate their attention on the goals, the process is conscious competition, or rivalry. Since rivalry involves conscious anticipation and communication about the moves of the other group, it is a social process. It frequently produces tensions, so intergroup relations are typically characterized by overt or latent conflict rather than by peaceful rivalry.[6]

Since so much of our attention must be centered on actual and potential conflict, we should note that intergroup relations are not universally hostile. When colonial and native peoples have met, for instance, there has often been a period of curious excitement about the other group, and peaceful trade. Relations have often continued to be cooperative when the native group has had an agricultural surplus or other goods to trade or sell, and subsequent exploitation of their labor has often been accepted calmly.[7] As we shall see in Part II, patterns of relatively peaceful minority-dominant accommodation may continue for long periods of time. However, even the most stable patterns may be undermined, and then latent conflicts become overt.

Intergroup Conflict

Conflict occurs when groups aim at least some of their actions against each other rather than limiting themselves to direct efforts to compete for desired goals. The greater the degree of group rivalry for education, space, community status, or any scarce values, the greater the probability of tensions and of resort to conflict. Much of group competition is for jobs, housing, land, welfare, or other economic rewards. Job competition and conflict are increased either by a reduction in the number of jobs or by an increase in the number of migrants into an area. The incidence of conflicts increases in times of economic depression or recession when minority groups characteristically have the highest rates of unemployment, and often are pushed out of even the less desirable jobs. In addition to conflicts over economic goals there are those over the rewards of group status (prestige, honor, and privilege) and over group power.[8]

For a given level of competition the likelihood of conflict is associated with the *directness* of the rivalry. Groups may be aware that they are affecting each other's chances, but tensions increase as indications of the competition become more obvious and more frequent. The Westward Movement in America increased direct contact with Indian tribes and highlighted the contest for control and use of the land. Increased contacts between urban groups in unemployment offices, union hiring halls, or welfare offices are pointed reminders that the groups are economic rivals.

It would appear in situations such as these that an increase in *numbers* in a minority group is associated with both the amount and directness of rivalry between them and the dominant community. The relationship between minority group size and discrimination is evidently not a simple, linear one, however; and it also operates in combination with group identity and other variables. Group size is important in intergroup conflict and status relations, but its effects must be assessed with care.[9] When more than one sizeable minority is present in a metropolitan area, the relative size of a group affects its income and occupational chances.[10]

Intergroup conflicts vary in intensity all the way from mild verbal exchanges to total mobilization to eliminate the other group from competition. Minor forms of conflict may occur quite frequently, but more total forms exhaust resources and participants and are thus intermittent. The more intense the conflict the more likely it is to take violent forms, designed to inflict severe punishment on the other group, or to force it to emigrate, or even to eliminate the group from existence. We shall be concerned with the conditions under which both dominant and minority groups are most likely to engage in violent intergroup conflict, and in general it will be apparent that either group becomes more prone to use violence when its status is lowered or seriously threatened by a sudden disruption of the group's expectations for the relationship.

Group Power, Conflict, and Institutionalized Discrimination

Groups differ in *power*, which means *the ability to determine the outcomes of group interaction.* The concept of minority-dominant relations implies group differences in power, since dominant groups are able to subject minorities to unequal treatment. When tensions rise in minority-dominant interaction and conflicts occur, the dominant community is more likely to control the outcome because it has more power.

Power relationships also affect the chances of the outbreak of intergroup conflicts. For example, overt conflict is very likely when an object of intergroup competition was originally possessed by the weaker group, as was the case in many parts of the South during the Great Depression when white workers sought unskilled jobs previously held by blacks. Or, the absence of powerful third parties in situations of intense group competition increases the probability of conflict and of violent actions by the dominant group. Frontier clashes with the American Indians illustrate this, and also the point that extreme violence by the dominant group is likely when it cannot make economic profits from the minority and when the imbalance of power is very great.[11]

When a dominant group succeeds in restricting a minority's access to one goal, the latter's success in achieving other goals is often reduced.[12] For example, restriction of access to informal group contacts or the denial of equal educational opportunity both tend to limit economic and political opportunities. The generalizing of dominant group power promotes patterns of *institutionalized discrimination,* which means *systematic discrimination through the regular operations of societal institutions.* All the members of dominant groups, including those who personally do not discriminate and who do not favor the system, receive the benefits of institutionalized discrimination against minorities.[13]

Some brief examples will help clarify the effects of institutionalized discrimination. The median family income of American blacks in 1971 was $6,400, just 60 percent of the median white income of $10,670. When blacks and whites were doing the same work in 1971, the average black received $1,200 a year less. Whites have more desirable jobs, better housing, and lower rates of unemployment and poverty.[14] Whites also have had psychological, prestige, and sexual gains from institutionalized discrimination.[15] When women do either professional or factory work similar to that of men, in the United States as well as in other countries, they are paid less for it.[16]

Despite the realities of institutionalized discrimination, however, in many situations there are limits to the generalizing of the dominant group's power. Otherwise all minority-dominant relationships would inevitably escalate to patterns of power elites *versus* subjugated masses. The amount of the imbalance of power between minority and dominant groups varies widely, is influenced by many factors, and is therefore subject to shifts. A group's size affects the power it is able to wield; but there are many other variables, and even small groups may become powerful if they have sufficient economic resources, unity, organization, coordination with other groups, community prestige, access to the mass media and to political decision makers, and other advantages. Articulateness in expressing ideas that justify the group's actions increases group power, especially when the ideology can be linked successfully with widely held values and beliefs, and disengaged from unpopular ones.

The dominant community in a complex society consists of a maze of interest groups—occupational, political, educational, recreational, and others—and these varied groups may and often do disagree on minority issues. The power of individual interest groups and also of shifting coalitions of groups varies with factors such as those suggested above, and also with the relevance of the group's interests to whatever public issue is being discussed. Thus institutionalized discrimination, while advantageous to all members of the dominant community, may not be defended by many of its members when there is determined action to change the pattern.

Outcomes of Intergroup Conflict

VOLUNTARY EMIGRATION   In order to avoid discrimination and conflict, minorities sometimes decide to end the contact by moving out of the territory. Groups of religious dissenters who left the European countries where they had experienced persecution were prominent among both earlier and later streams of American immigrants, and many of the groups came voluntarily to gain religious freedom. Some of the same groups encountered harassment in their new home and moved again, westward, or sometimes to other countries. The painful choice so often faced by sectarian groups has been either to leave or to begin the compromising that leads to denominational status. A denomination is institutionalized, and thus accommodated to other community institutions.

When a minority of any type is subjected to severe control measures, or to threatened or actual physical violence, the question may arise as to whether a decision to emigrate is voluntary or involuntary. In nineteenth century Russia the czars encouraged pogroms and other extreme measures to force the Jews to convert to Christianity, to emigrate, or to die.[17] During the 1930s, Hitler began the program of increasing harassment of the Jews, designed in part to get them to emigrate. Such harassment, especially when linked with a deliberate policy of putting pressure on a group to emigrate, seems less like voluntary emigration than it does mass expulsion.

EXPULSION   Entire minority groups have been expelled from the territory many times in human history, often when voluntary emigration, efforts at annihilation, forced assimilation, or other dominant group policies have failed.[18] Thus Henry VIII expelled the Gypsies from England, and in the seventeenth century France drove out its Protestants (the Huguenots). In 1492, frustrated over its efforts to convert its Muslim Arabs (Moors) and its Jews to Christianity, Spain expelled both groups. The (superficially) Christianized Arabs who remained suffered heavy discrimination, and they too were expelled in 1609, harshly and with great loss of life.

American history also provides examples of mass expulsion. In 1838 the governor of Missouri issued an order expelling the Mormons from the state. The removal of the Cherokee Indians to Oklahoma took place after gold was discovered on their land, and the Georgia legislature passed an act in 1829 expropriating a large portion of the Cherokee lands. The Cherokees were peaceful, prosperous, settled, and agricultural; they had schools, and were on their way to becoming a literate people, with the aid of Sequoya's alphabet. They appealed to President Jackson and to the United States Supreme Court, but both of these supported the federal Indian Removal Act, designed to expel all Indians from lands east of the Mississippi. Federal troops and hostile civilians moved in and burned and looted Cherokee homes, seized cattle, and drove the Cherokees into stockades. Then "The Trail of Tears" began, during which probably four thousand or so died out of the more than ten thousand Cherokees who made the forced journey.[19]

The expulsion of peoples has happened repeatedly in the twentieth century, often on a massive scale. In 1915 the embattled Turkish empire, fearful of military threats from its minorities, ordered mass marches of the Armenians toward the Russian border area. Most of the survivors fled to Russia, or to the Middle East, Europe, or the United States.[20] The 1919 invasion of Turkish territory by Greece, Great Britain, and other Allies was repelled, and in 1922 over a million Greek residents fled to Greece. In 1924 the new nation-state of Turkey legalized this wartime expulsion, and the treaty required that over half a million Turkish Muslims be expelled from Greece and Bulgaria to move to Turkey.[21] Previously we have noted the much larger population transfer at the time of the partition of India to create Pakistan in 1947. Strong coercion is required to get a great many of the people to leave their homes and suffer hardships in order to facilitate such political exchanges of populations, despite the prospect of avoiding minority status in a country where one's own ethnic group is dominant.

The federal removal of Japanese Americans from the West Coast states during World War II is an instance of expelling an entire minority group from one area and relocating them elsewhere in the country because of a presumed political and military threat. Although they were a comparatively small minority (about 130,000) they were fairly concentrated, and after the Japanese bombing of Pearl Harbor the false rumors of Japanese American espionage and sabotage aroused much public hostility. Two-thirds of the group were American citizens by birth, yet the belief spread that not one of them could be trusted to be loyal to the United States rather than to Japan.[22] This reasoning was not applied to Americans of German or Italian descent, and the commanding officer of the Western Defense Command—General J. L. DeWitt—

advanced a racist argument before committees of the United States Congress and elsewhere. He contended that Japanese Americans have not intermarried much, and that the loyalty of all members of this undiluted "enemy race" is suspect, regardless of pieces of paper that indicate American citizenship. He also argued that the Japanese had to be relocated to protect them from American mobs.[23]

The federal government supported General DeWitt, and in February 1942, President Roosevelt signed the executive order that defined areas from which "enemy aliens" must be removed, and ordered the building of ten relocation camps in California, Arizona, Idaho, Wyoming, Colorado, Utah, and Arkansas. (The Japanese Americans in the Hawaiian Islands were not affected.) The evacuation of the first ten thousand was voluntary; then it became compulsory, for all persons with as little as one-eighth Japanese ancestry. The evacuation began in March 1942, and by November of that year over 110,000 West Coast Japanese were relocated behind barbed wire fences. Many later got work permits in nonprohibited areas, or permits to attend high schools or colleges, and many of the young men served in the armed forces after a 1943 order permitted it. The ban on living in the West Coast areas was ended in 1944; forcible detention in the camps ceased in January 1945; and the camps were closed in 1946. Some Japanese Americans have since moved to other regions of the country, but the majority have returned to the West Coast.[24] They have been only partially compensated for the great financial losses they suffered,[25] and there is no adequate way to measure the loss of homes, personal possessions, and especially the personal shock and the disruption of families.[26]

The Soviet Union took similar action during World War II against eight of its minorities who lived in sensitive border areas, abolishing eight ethnic territorial units and deporting large numbers of these peoples to far areas of the country. Five of these eight territorial republics were finally reestablished in 1957.[27] (Soviet assimilationist policies are treated in Chapter 10.) Such drastic actions may not seem surprising for a totalitarian state, but the wartime relocation on the presumption that all Japanese Americans were potentially guilty of disloyal acts violated basic American liberties.

GENOCIDE   *The deliberate extermination of an entire racial or cultural group* has been attempted many times in human history, sometimes successfully.[28] The first Dutch settlers on the Cape of Good Hope in South Africa perceived the native Bushmen as contemptible subhumans, and tried to annihilate them.[29] The nineteenth century British colonists on the island of Tasmania considered the aborigines to be wild animals, and after seven decades the group was completely exterminated.[30] The native peoples of the Americas had no immunity to a number of European infectious diseases, and sometimes bacteriological warfare was deliberately practiced. For instance, the Portuguese in Brazil planted clothing removed from smallpox victims in Indian villages as one means of exterminating those natives who resisted Portuguese settlement.[31]

After a few years of peaceful barter the unstated but predominant colonial policy toward Indians in the United States was genocide, and this continued until the twentieth century. All of the thirteen colonies paid bounties for Indian scalps,[32] and a frequent tactic was to promote antagonism between tribes to get them to kill each other. Whole tribes eventually were decimated and their remaining numbers forced to move west. Treaties guaranteed that all land west of the Mississippi would belong to the Indian tribes forever, but determined warfare followed whenever Indians resisted the gold rushes or frontier settlement that took place west of the Mississippi. More than once federal armed forces made punitive raids and misrepresented the facts about alleged provocations, and some Union troops deliberately pursued Indians instead of Confederate soldiers during the Civil War. Finally the technologically superior federal armies crushed the last tribal efforts to resist white invasion and domination.[33] When the reservation system began in 1871 the Indian population had been reduced to less than half a million, as compared with an estimate for 1492 of close to a million, and some of the tribes had been annihilated.[34] When the Plains Indians rebelled against the reservation system, one of the war measures used against them was the mass slaughter of their food supply, the buffalo, from 1872 to 1874.[35] By the end of the century there were only about one-quarter of a million surviving Indians.

The term *genocide* was first used at the Nuremberg trials to designate the crimes of the Nazi German leaders who attempted to exterminate the Jewish people, and also the Gypsies, during World War II. Of the close to ten million Jews in Nazi-controlled Europe, it is estimated that approximately six million died. Many were killed by Nazi armies; many others died in the concentration camps of starvation and disease; and great numbers met death in the gas chambers. A part of the program of genocide in the camps was the mass inoculation of prisoners with various diseases.[36] The German railroads were an indispensable part of the process of destruction,[37] an indication of the fact that the entire effort required state approval and the official mobilization of large numbers of people and resources.[38] The ideology that had been developed to support the earlier Nazi actions against the Jews provided the official justification for the "ultimate solution" (see Chapter 5).

The Nazi experience illustrates the view that strong national anxiety about territorial losses can cause a low-status minority to become the target of genocidal policies.[39] Direct conflict over territory can cause this also, especially when the weaker group cannot easily be either expelled or economically exploited, or when it attempts to retaliate against superior force.[40] The American Indians met these latter three conditions of territorial conflict. Genocide is unlikely when both groups are native to the area, when each is powerful enough to injure the other seriously, when the groups agree that they are economically interdependent, or when there are close, multigenerational contacts between the groups.[41]

In 1946 the General Assembly of the United Nations passed a resolution declaring genocide a crime against international law, and in 1951 a detailed United Nations agreement went into effect. This agreement defines genocide as doing one or more of the following things with the intent to destroy all or part of a national, ethnic, racial, or religious group: killing group members, causing serious bodily or mental harm, inflicting conditions designed to cause deaths, preventing births, or transferring children to another group. Nations that have signed this agreement, and this does not include the United States, may request that the United Nations or the International Court of Justice act to prevent or suppress genocidal acts. This machinery has focused international attention on a number of events, such as the alleged Russian deportation of Hungarians to Siberian labor camps after the 1956 uprising in Hungary, and American military actions during the war in Vietnam.

ACCOMMODATION   Intergroup contact comes to an end when the outcome of conflict is expulsion, genocide, or voluntary emigration. For groups to remain in contact there must be some type of *accommodation—the development of working relationships between groups.* Conflict depletes resources, and therefore cannot be continuous. Forces toward accommodation are typically at work while conflicts are taking place, just as forces toward conflict are often at work during periods of accommodation.

States of accommodation vary all the way from very tentative ones, in which latent conflicts may break out at any time, to those that have become highly institutionalized and relatively stable. One way of defining social organization is in terms of patterns of accommodation.[42] Patterns of intergroup accommodation are usually stratified (see Chapter 4), as illustrated by involuntary segregation (Chapter 6), but they may be equalitarian (see Chapter 8). Much of the remainder of this book deals with patterns of accommodation and with efforts to resist and change them.

ASSIMILATION   Although new patterns of accommodation may emerge suddenly, the process of assimilation is necessarily gradual. *Assimilation* is here defined as *the process whereby a group gradually merges with another, thus losing its separate identity.* This includes the loss of pride in whatever distinctive cultural traits the group has had and learning new attitudes and habits in their place.[43] Racial amalgamation (miscegenation) promotes assimilation by eliminating the distinctive physical differences, unless all offspring—regardless of the degree of mixture—are treated as members of the minority race.

The integration of minority groups into the institutional structures of the community facilitates intergroup contacts and may thus promote assimilation. However, a group may become integrated into dominant economic, political, and educational institutions and still retain a large measure of its own family traditions, language, ethnic customs, and even its own neighborhood. A considerable degree of structural integration, in other words, may be associated with *cultural pluralism,* in which groups retain a large measure of their own cultures (see Chapter 8). Conversely, a group may be assimilated culturally to a considerable degree, yet not be very much integrated into the dominant community's institutions, as illustrated by the American black experience.

Minority Status as Dynamic

Racial and cultural relations have rarely been static for long periods in human history, as illustrated repeatedly in this chapter, although there are instances of fairly stable and lengthy patterns of accommodation. The status of a group may rise or fall, sometimes suddenly. The status of Japanese Americans, for example, plunged to a very low point when they were relocated, and rose again after World War II. In later chapters the changes in the status of American blacks will be analyzed.

American Jews had experienced little discrimination before the rapid increase in Jewish immigration from Russia and other Eastern European countries from 1880 on. The sharp increase in anti-Semitism beginning in 1910 seemed to be associated with increased competition for white-collar jobs. After World War I, when antiforeign feeling was high, Jews were stereotyped as international revolutionaries and sentiment against them reached a peak by the mid-1920s. Some decline apparently was facilitated by the curbing of immigration and by Henry Ford's retraction, in 1927, of his anti-Semitic campaign in the *Dearborn Independent.*[44] But in 1933 Hitler's agents began their worldwide campaign, and during the next seven years there were 121 organizations spreading anti-Semitic propaganda in the United States.[45] Father Charles Coughlin used the radio to spread the message of his Christian Front, and William Pelley's Silver Shirts mailed tons of anti-Semitic literature.[46] The collapse of Nazi Germany and the publicity about the gas chambers brought a sharp decline in, but not the disappearance of, anti-Semitic activity in the United States.[47]

There is no guarantee that a given minority status will stay the same very long, or that it will inevitably improve. Minority-dominant patterns of accommodation are part of the social organization, and they are especially subject to change in complex, mobile societies in which mass communications are numerous and rapid. Interaction between physical and cultural groups involves continuous give and take, and it is influenced by changes in economic, political, and other social conditions. Even long-standing patterns of accommodation between the sexes and among age groups are subject to change.

For all who are concerned about reducing discrimination, it ought to be encouraging that minority statuses are dynamic. Some patterns are much more resistant than others, but changes are very possible and they occur.[48] Organized programs to reduce discrimination may contribute significantly to that end, as we will see in Part IV. Concerted action to increase discrimination may also succeed under the appropriate conditions. Sometimes major efforts are needed to combat downturns in status, especially since the outcomes may be catastrophic.

THEORETICAL ORIENTATIONS

In the theoretical framework outlined in this chapter, minority-dominant relations are depicted as social interaction between groups. This keeps the focus on the responses of members of the groups to each other, rather than exclusively on the minority or the dominant community. Major attention is given to the process of social conflict, to its links with group power, and with patterns of accommodation. Those outcomes of conflict that terminate group contact have been emphasized here, since the rest of the book is concerned with ongoing patterns of interaction. Minority-dominant relations are frequently characterized by change, the understanding of which is facilitated by the interaction approach.

Adequate analysis of minority-dominant relations requires treatment of both the more orderly patterns and of their emergence and change, and of the interrelationships of these twin aspects of the interaction.[49] Whether the emphasis at a given point is on order or change, attention to group power is warranted. A basic assumption in this book is that group power is distributed in widely varying ways in different societies and times. This (power) pluralistic conflict orientation has influenced the selection and interpretation of material, but many different theoretical views are noted. For instance, the power elite variety of conflict analysis is illustrated in the view that the domination of racial groups in noncolonial situations is very similar to colonial control and exploitation.[50]

Some of the attempts to explain emerging and changing patterns of group domination and subordination have resulted in theories of successive stages of interaction. The basic idea is that all racial or cultural contacts result in a uniform sequence of steps, in contrast to the assumption that each situation is unique. From the standpoint that the sequence starts over again when there is contact with another new group, such explanations have been called cycle theories. The most influential of these theories has been Park's race relations sequence, in terms of which relations between two ethnic or racial groups progress through the stages of contact, conflict, accommodation, and assimilation. Except that numerous "accidental" barriers may intervene and retard the sequence for periods of time, according to Park, it is an irreversible, evolutionary process.[51] Despite strong criticism and general rejection of this and other successive stage theories,[52] the heavy emphasis on assimilation continued in sociological thought until well into the 1960s. This bias received support from a recurrent theme in early sociological thought and in later systems theories—the view that loyalty to local and ethnic groups is out of place in complex, urban societies, which suggests that assimilation is inevitable.[53]

Park, following Simmel, made major contributions to understanding the interrelationships between conflict and accommodation.[54] The use of knowledge built on Park's contributions should not be construed as acceptance of his theory of stages. Assimilation occurs only under certain conditions (Part III), and we have seen in this chapter that it is only one possible outcome of minority-dominant interaction. Segregation prevented American blacks from becoming structurally assimilated despite much cultural assimilation, and in time they had to develop their own institutions to meet their needs.[55] Cultural and structural pluralism are forms of accommodation that have received greatly increased attention in recent years as alternatives to assimilation (Chapters 8, 13, and 14).

FOOTNOTES

1 Hunt & Walker, 1974, Ch. 12.
2 Madan, 1972.
3 Hunt & Walker, 1974, pp. 161–63.
4 Hunt & Walker, 1974, Ch. 4.
5 Pettigrew, 1976, p. 465.
6 Park & Burgess, 1970, pp. 281–302; Shibutani & Kwan, 1965, pp. 575–76.

7 Frazier, 1957, Ch. 2.

8 Weber, 1946.

9 Blalock, 1967, Ch. 5.

10 Frisbie & Neidert, 1977, pp. 1021–29.

11 Blalock, 1967, pp. 78–79.

12 Blalock, 1967, p. 139.

13 Staples, 1976, pp. 250–51.

14 Blackwell, 1975, pp. 29–32.

15 Staples, 1976, pp. 266–72.

16 Cook, 1975, pp. 22–24; de Beauvoir, 1952, p. 130; Suter & Miller, 1973.

17 Manners, 1972, Ch. 1.

18 Berry, 1965, pp. 76–79, 162–69.

19 Foreman, 1932, pp. 229–314; Starkey, 1946, pp. 282–301.

20 Ladas, 1932, Ch. 13.

21 Ladas, 1932, pp. 720–24; Bisbee, 1951, pp. 52, 61, 240–41.

22 Miyamoto, 1973.

23 Berry, 1965, pp. 165–69.

24 Kitano, 1974, pp. 215–19.

25 Bloom & Riemer, 1949.

26 Broom & Kitsuse, 1956.

27 Hunt & Walker, 1974, pp. 69–70.

28 Berry, 1965, pp. 156–62.

29 MacCrone, 1937, pp. 89–136.

30 Murdock, 1934, pp. 16–18.

31 MacCrone, 1937, p. 6.

32 Shrieke, 1936, p. 6; Locke & Stern, 1942, pp. 165–70.

33 Brown, 1970; Spencer & Jennings, 1965, pp. 496–506.

34 Kroeber, 1934.

35 Collier, 1947, p. 133.

36 Berry, 1965, pp. 156–57.

37 Hilberg, 1976.

38 Horowitz, 1976.

39 Fein, 1976.

40 Blalock, 1967, p. 79.

41 Turk, 1967, p. 410.

42 Park & Burgess, 1970, pp. 191, 303–5.

43 Park & Burgess, 1970, pp. 360–65.

44 Rose & Rose, 1948, pp. 37–40.

45 Strong, 1941, pp. 146–47.

46 McWilliams, 1943, pp. 38–46.

47 Marden & Meyer, 1973, pp. 453–59.

48 Rose & Rose, 1948, Ch. 2.

49 Newman, 1973, pp. 101–4.

50 Blauner, 1972, Kinloch, 1974.

51 Park, 1950, pp. 15–51, 149–50.

52 Berry, 1965, Ch. 6.

53 Metzger, 1971.

54 Lyman, 1972, pp. 71–72.

55 Blackwell, 1975, pp. 5–12.

REFERENCES

Berry, Brewton
1965   Race and Ethnic Relations, 3rd Edition. Boston: Houghton Mifflin Co.

Bisbee, Eleanor
1951   The New Turks. Philadelphia: University of Pennsylvania Press.

Blackwell, James E.
1975   The Black Community: Diversity and Unity. New York: Dodd, Mead and Co.

Blalock, Hubert M., Jr.
1967   Toward a Theory of Minority-Group Relations. New York: Capricorn Books.

Blauner, Robert
1972   Racial Oppression in America. New York: Harper and Row.

Bloom, Leonard, and Ruth Riemer
1949   Removal and Return: The Socio-Economic Effects of the War on Japanese Americans. Berkeley and Los Angeles: University of California Press.

Broom, Leonard, and John I. Kitsuse
1956   The Managed Casualty: The Japanese-American Family in World War II. Berkeley and Los Angeles: University of California Press.

Brown, Dee
1970   Bury My Heart at Wounded Knee. New York: Holt, Rinehart and Winston, Inc.

Collier, John
1947   Indians of the Americas. New York: Mentor Books, the New American Library of World Literature.

Cook, Alice H.
1975   The Working Mother: A Survey of Problems and Programs in Nine Countries. Ithaca: New York State School of Industrial and Labor Relations, Cornell University.

de Beauvoir, Simone
1952   The Second Sex, Trans. and ed., H. M. Parshley. New York: Alfred A. Knopf, Inc.

Fein, Helen
1976   "A Formula for Genocide: A Grounded Theory Comparing the Turkish Genocide (1915) and Nazi Germany's Holocaust (1939–45)." Paper presented in New York City at the Annual Meetings of the American Sociological Association.

Foreman, Grant
1936   Indians and Pioneers. Norman: Oklahoma University Press.

Frazier, E. Franklin
1957   Race and Culture Contacts in the Modern World. New York: Alfred A. Knopf, Inc.

Frisbie, W. Parker, and Lisa Neidert
1977   "Inequality and the Relative Size of Minority Populations: A Comparative Analysis." American Journal of Sociology 82, 5 (March): 1007–30.

Hilberg, Raul
1976   "The Role of the German Railroads in the Destruction of the Jews." Paper presented in New York City at the Annual Meetings of the American Sociological Association.
Horowitz, Irving Louis
1976   Genocide: State Power and Mass Murder. New Brunswick, New Jersey: Transaction Books.
Hunt, Chester L., and Lewis Walker
1974   Ethnic Dynamics: Patterns of Intergroup Relations in Various Societies. Homewood, Illinois: The Dorsey Press.
Kinloch, Graham C.
1974   The Dynamics of Race Relations: A Sociological Analysis. New York: McGraw-Hill Book Co.
Kitano, Harry H. L.
1974   *Race Relations.* Englewood Cliffs, New Jersey: Prentice-Hall, Inc.
Kroeber, Alfred L.
1934   "Demography of the American Indians." American Anthropologist 36: 1–25.
Ladas, Stephen P.
1932   The Exchange of Minorities: Bulgaria, Greece, and Turkey. New York: The Macmillan Co.
Locke, Alaine, and B. J. Stern
1942   When Peoples Meet. New York: Progressive Education Association.
Lyman, Stanford M.
1972   The Black American in Sociological Thought: A Failure of Perspective. New York: Capricorn Books.
MacCrone, I. D.
1937   Race Attitudes in South Africa. London: Oxford University Press.
Madan, T. N.
1972   "Two Faces of Bengali Ethnicity: Muslim Bengali or Bengali Muslim." Developing Economies 10, 1 (March): 74–85.
Manners, Ande
1972   Poor Cousins. Greenwich, Connecticut: Fawcett Publications, Inc.
Marden, Charles F., and Gladys Meyer
1973   Minorities in American Society. New York: D. Van Nostrand Co.
McWilliams, Carey
1943   A Mask for Privilege: Anti-Semitism in America. Boston: Little, Brown and Co.
Metzger, L. Paul
1971   "American Sociology and Black Assimilation: Conflicting Perspectives." American Journal of Sociology 76 (January): 627–47.
Miyamoto, S. Frank
1973   "The Forced Evacuation of the Japanese Minority During World War II." Journal of Social Issues 29, 2: 11–31.
Murdock, G. P.
1934   Our Primitive Contemporaries. New York: The Macmillan Co.
Newman, William M.
1973   American Pluralism: A Study of Minority Groups and Social Theory. New York: Harper and Row.

Park, Robert E.
1950   Race and Culture. New York: The Free Press.
Park, Robert E., and Ernest W. Burgess
1970   Introduction to the Science of Sociology, Abridged Student Edition. Chicago: The University of Chicago Press.
Pettigrew, Thomas Fraser
1976   "Race and Intergroup Relations," Chapter 10 in Robert K. Merton and Robert Nisbet, Contemporary Social Problems, 4th Edition. New York: Harcourt, Brace, Jovanovich, Inc.
Rose, Arnold, and Caroline Rose
1948   America Divided: Minority Group Relations in the United States. New York: Alfred A. Knopf, Inc.
Shibutani, Tamotsu, and Kian M. Kwan
1965   Ethnic Stratification: A Comparative Approach. New York: The Macmillan Co.
Shrieke, B.
1936   Alien Americans. New York: Viking Press.
Spencer, Robert F., and Jesse D. Jennings
1965   The Native Americans. New York: Harper and Row.
Staples, Robert
1976   Introduction to Black Sociology. New York: McGraw-Hill Book Co.
Starkey, Marion L.
1946   The Cherokee Nation. New York: Alfred A. Knopf, Inc.
Strong, Donald S.
1941   Organized Anti-Semitism in America. Washington, D.C.: American Council on Public Affairs.
Suter, Larry E., and Herman P. Miller
1973   "Income Differences Between Men and Career Women." American Journal of Sociology 78, 4 (January): 962–74.
Turk, Austin F.
1967   "The Futures of South Africa." Social Forces 45, 3 (March): 402–12.
Weber, Max
1946   "Class, Status, Party," in From Max Weber. Translated and edited by Hans Gerth and C. Wright Mills. New York: Oxford University Press.

3

Intergroup Prejudice

It is important to seek understanding of the relationships between attitudes of prejudice and overt acts of discrimination against groups, and the reasons for the lack of high correlation between them. First, however, it is necessary to explore the nature of group prejudice. Attention in this chapter then shifts to theories of the development of prejudice, and to efforts to explain the conditions under which such attitudes change.

PREJUDICE AS ATTITUDE

An *attitude* is a response tendency toward an object or class of objects. Prejudice may be favorable or unfavorable, but when the term is not qualified it is understood to be negative. Thus, *group prejudice may be defined as an attitude unfavorable to a group or its individual members.* The components of attitudes of group prejudice are:

1 cognitive—unfavorable beliefs about the group
2 affective—unfavorable feelings about the group
3 conative—unfavorable behavioral intentions toward the group[1]

Despite a vast amount of research, the relationships among these components are not well understood. The cognitive component is emphasized in this chapter, but attention is given first to behavioral intentions.

SOCIAL DISTANCE

Behavioral intentions toward a group should not be confused with completed acts of discrimination. The conative component has been conceptualized as *social distance*—the degree of closeness with which a person is willing to associate with members of another group.[2] Bogardus operationalized the concept in his Social Distance Scale by asking respondents to make a choice for each of thirty-nine ethnic groups, as follows:[3]

> According to my first feeling reactions I would willingly admit members of each race (as a class, and not the best I have known, nor the worst members) to one or more of the classifications . . .
>
> To close kinship by marriage (1 point)
> To my club as personal chums (2 points)
> To my street as neighbors (3 points)
> To employment in my occupation in my country (4 points)
> To citizenship in my country (5 points)
> As visitors only to my country (6 points)
> Would exclude from my country (7 points).

Variations of this scale have been used for over half a century to study attitudes toward racial and ethnic groups, and sometimes toward occupations, deviant groups, or other social categories.

In national samples taken in the United States, the stability over time of the social distance rank positions of selected racial and ethnic groups is striking. For instance, from 1926 to 1966 the mean social distance scores for blacks, Koreans, and Indians from India remained among the largest, those for Poles and Czechs toward the middle, and those for Canadians and English among the smallest.[4] Allowing for variation in rank positions of some groups with shifts in international relations, and for an overall decline in mean scores for all groups, the continuity in the rankings is impressive. The ranks are also highly consistent from one region of the country to another, and across differences in income, occupation, and education. Even different racial and ethnic groups follow the national pattern in their social distance judgments, except that minority groups move their own group up to the most preferred position, or near the top.[5] This level of national agreement suggests the operation of cultural norms in behavioral intentions toward various racial and ethnic groups.[6] It appears from comparative studies that social distance norms also exist in other countries.[7]

PREJUDICE AND BELIEFS: THE COGNITIVE COMPONENT

The cognitive part of an attitude is an organized set of beliefs. Attitudes of prejudice, therefore, rest at least partly on reasonably coherent systems of belief. From the standpoint of content the beliefs that comprise an attitude are of three types:[8]

1   existential, or fact, beliefs
2   value beliefs
3   prescriptive, or normative, beliefs

The differences among these three types of belief must be kept clearly in mind. It will be helpful to refer back to the latter part of Chapter 1 for the discussion of value and existential beliefs involved in minority-dominant issues.

Existential or fact beliefs, whether correct or demonstrably false, are convictions about what exists in reality. All of the following illustrate existential beliefs: that Chinese are naturally clannish, that racial prejudice is inborn, that discrimination against Jews is now rare, or that a major factor in anti-Semitism is international tensions. Some existential beliefs are descriptive—concerning the existence of a phenomenon, its extent, or trends in its incidence—while others concern statistical and/or causal relationships. The role of existential beliefs in stereotypes will become apparent in the next section.

Value beliefs are convictions about what is desirable or undesirable, and judgments based on them typically include words such as, "should," "worse," "good," or "unhealthy." Although many value beliefs relevant to minority-dominant relations have been cited in Chapter 1, the importance of priorities or rank orders of values must be noted. Many if not most value beliefs require weighing the relative importance of two or more pertinent values. An example is the belief that having equal job opportunities is more important than equality of results among different groups. Another example is the general belief that peaceful relations among groups is more important than either equality or loyalty to one's group.

In a study of Swiss attitudes toward Italian workers in Switzerland, substantial relationships were found between value orientations and behavioral intentions. The latter were measured by three social distance items. Other-centered values (altruism, extended loyalty, and collective responsibility) were moderately associated with acceptance of the Italian workers, while self-centered values (egoism, restricted loyalty, and self-reliance) were associated with rejection.[9] Similar relationships between value systems and social distance had been found in prior studies of American attitudes toward blacks, Mexican Americans, and Jews.[10]

Prescriptive or *normative beliefs* are convictions about which norms (rules for social conduct) are preferable. It is a normative belief to be convinced that the club or lodge is right to have a rule against admitting non-Christians to membership. The conviction that legal norms should prohibit such group exclusion is also a normative belief. So also is belief in affirmative action programs to increase the ratio of women admitted to medical schools, or belief in the unwritten norms of secret agreements to maintain racial housing segregation.

An Hypothesis About Normative Beliefs

The view is taken here that normative beliefs rest on both value and existential beliefs, and thus that a change in either (or both) produces change in the norm-commitments.[11] It is proposed that this operates both on the group level and within the person. Both of these levels are at least implied in the usual sociological emphasis on the connection between values and normative beliefs. There is some evidence that, as attitudes are formed, large numbers of existential beliefs become organized around a small number of beliefs about value priorities.[12] The causal relationships among the three types of beliefs are complex, however, and far from being definitively understood. Value and existential beliefs apparently may influence each other.

Illustration of the above hypothesis will show how it applies to group prejudice. The role of value beliefs is perhaps easier to grasp. If two persons or groups disagree sharply on the importance of equal job opportunities, even if they agree on pertinent existential beliefs, they will likely support different personnel policies and relevant legal norms. Conversely, disagreement on existential beliefs will result in

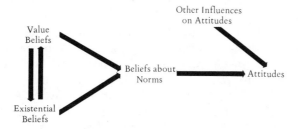

Figure 1   Beliefs and attitudes.

different norm-commitments, even when there is agreement on values. Figure 1 illustrates these postulated relationships.

Suppose three different persons or groups are about equally committed to the value belief in equal opportunity, but hold quite different existential beliefs. Person or group A believes that refugees already admitted from county X are hardworking and capable of succeeding in American society if given a fair chance; B believes that X people are very intelligent, secretive, scheming, and ambitious for money and power; C believes they are genetically lazy and mentally inferior. A will likely believe that the practices and legal norms designed to ensure equal opportunity for all groups should be applied to the X refugees; B may well believe there should be quotas limiting their numbers in professional schools, colleges, social clubs, and executive positions— justifying this norm by saying that equal opportunity does not apply to people who are deviously plotting to seize wealth and power; C is likely to favor legal norms designed to facilitate limited achievements and special protections for the group rather than equal opportunity to succeed.

Stereotypes

Culturally and physically different groups develop conceptions of each other and interact on the basis of them. A conception of a group is a set of existential beliefs about it. In intergroup relations such beliefs are usually stereotyped rather than accurate. *A stereotype is a conception of a group composed of a set of simplified existential beliefs.* Stereotypes usually contain elements of truth, some much more than others, but these are often overgeneralized or distorted.

Overgeneralizations about groups may be made from personal experience, but people may hold images of groups whose members they rarely or never see. The mass media often spread stereotypes rapidly and widely.[13] Stereotypes tend to become shared and transmitted as part of a cultural heritage. Frequently groups even accept cultural stereotypes of themselves, except for extremely negative traits such as stupidity, dirtiness, or treachery.[14]

Learning a stereotype results in selective perception of the group, so that contradictory evidence tends to be unnoticed or not taken into account. As the image is reinforced it becomes more *reified*—i.e., thought of as real. When a stereotype has been strongly reified all negative evidence is ignored or readily explained away. A person who obviously does not fit the stereotype of the group is then considered "one of the good ones," or "the exception that proves the rule." Thus, stereotypes are most resistant to change when they have become rigidly reified.[15]

Although stereotypes tend to be stable they do change, primarily because they are undermined by changes in patterns of intergroup relations.[16] Images of groups reflect the role behavior expected of them in particular social situations.[17] Stereotypes of Chinese and Japanese Americans were extremely negative during the early years when gold miners and labor union members perceived them as dangerous threats in competition for jobs. The stereotypes became less unfavorable when these groups seemed less threatening—after the mass arrival of other immigrant groups and the passage of discriminatory laws against the Chinese and Japanese. World War II revived the more extreme anti-Japanese images, but more recently these two groups have been widely stereotyped as successful, model minorities.[18]

The dominant stereotype of blacks, throughout much of their American experience, has included the beliefs that they are biologically inferior to whites, ignorant, dirty, lazy, pleasure-seeking, and sexually loose. (See Chapter 6 for comment about the Sambo and Jim Crow stereotypes.) This stereotype has been accepted by progressively fewer white Americans in recent decades, as both behavior and attitudes have shifted in favor of racial desegregation. The percentage of whites in a representative national sample who agreed that blacks can learn as much as whites, if given the same opportunity, increased from 42 percent in 1942, to 52 percent in 1952, to 77 percent in 1956, and it has remained high.[19] White attitudes have changed most in the South, and have usually followed the desegregation of schools and other public facilities. Samples of white students at the University of Alabama in 1963, 1966, 1969, and 1972 showed increasing support for desegregation and for norms of political and economic equality. The mean social distance scores (toward blacks) also showed marked declines. Simultaneously there were sharp declines in nine unfavorable beliefs about blacks, including large decreases in the percentages believing that blacks cannot learn as much as whites.[20]

Such evidence suggests that changes in intergroup behavior can change both normative beliefs and the supporting stereotypes (existential beliefs), perhaps also the supporting value beliefs. Other studies

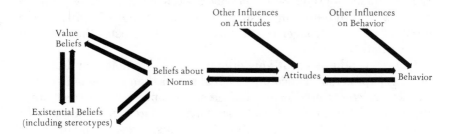

Figure 2   Beliefs, attitudes, and behavior.

have shown that legally induced changes in intergroup practices can produce changes in attitudes,[21] and we have noted that attitudes are organizations of underlying beliefs. This does not contradict the hypothesis advanced in the previous section; instead it suggests that the causal influences may flow in both directions. That is, normative beliefs may operate as cause as well as effect of value and existential beliefs, and we may now add that attitudes and behavior appear to be part of a two-way causal chain (see Figure 2). Attitudes often do not correspond with behavior, however, so the relationships suggested here are apparently part of a highly complex pattern.

Ethnocentrism

People are not neutral about their stereotypes of groups. Perception of a group is based on both value and existential beliefs. What is thought to be the factually correct image of the group is judged to be good or bad, superior or inferior. Out-groups are sometimes admired, but judgments of them are typically ethnocentric. Throughout history the common tendency has been to see out-groups as not just different, but as barbaric, backward and dirty, immoral, as people with false gods and false values. *Ethnocentrism is judging group ways that differ from one's own to be wrong and inferior rather than just different.*[22]

Ethnocentrism involves affective response, not just an intellectual perception that the out-group and its ways are inferior. Adjectives such as, "not nice," "ill-mannered," "disgusting," and "sneaky" convey feelings of disapproval and contempt, often of hatred. There is apparently much variation in the strength of such feelings. They seem especially strong in bigotry and chauvinism, which are aspects or forms of extreme ethnocentrism. *Bigotry* is complete intolerance for the beliefs held by other groups. *Chauvinism* is excessive loyalty to the in-group and belligerent contempt for out-groups.

One effect of ethnocentrism is to promote solidarity (unity) within the group. (We need not assume that group unity requires ethnocentrism, or that ethnocentrism requires high solidarity.) At the same time that it enhances group unity, however, ethnocentrism may promote hostility toward out-groups, especially when feelings of contempt are strong. Thus the stronger the ethnocentrism the greater the potential for conflict.

One hypothesis about how ethnocentrism promotes conflict with other groups is that it encourages tribal rather than universalistic ethics. *Tribal ethics* are norms that prescribe only how to treat other members of the in-group, and that have no force in dealings with outsiders. Be kind to your fellow Christians, Jews, Frenchmen, or whites, but anything goes when you confront non-Christians, gentiles, non-French, or nonwhites. Thou shalt not kill your fellow in-group members, but it is all right—perhaps even right—to slay outsiders on sight. *Universalistic ethics* exist when the in-group extends its ethical norms to all out-groups—"to all races, nations and creeds," "to all peoples, who are all my neighbors." In times of conflict, especially in all-out war, universalistic norms have little force and tribal ethics are dominant.

Minority groups sometimes accept the ethnocentric views of them held by dominant groups, especially when they have occupied a low status for generations and see no prospect of equality. For long centuries many of the outcaste groups in India held the existential belief that it was impossible for them to rise in status, and with Hindu faith they accepted their society's judgment of them as untouchables. Many of the more humanely treated black slaves in the American South, after generations of having been stripped of their African cultures, adopted the stereotyped and ethnocentric perspectives of blacks that were held by their masters.[23] This outlook contrasted with the sharp sense of African tribal identity felt by many of those who were among the later groups to be captured and transported.[24]

However, acquiescing to subordinate status is not necessarily accompanied by acceptance of the view that the minority group and its ways are inferior. Acknowledging the power of a dominant group, and the dependence of one's people on it, is not an admission of its cultural superiority. In fact, the minority often holds ethnocentric views of the dominant group, especially when the minority has a substantial culture of its own.[25] Under colonial domination many people in India, perhaps most, felt culturally superior to the British—a frequent occurrence in colonial areas where the culture remains intact and domination by outsiders is considered temporary. The slave culture that developed from the remnants of African cultures, and from the common American experience on the Southern plantations, provided alternative norms and values to those of the whites.[26] Largely hidden from the masters, this slave culture often included perception of whites as powerful but cruel and unfeeling, immoral, lazy, and easy to outsmart.[27]

Beliefs and Ideologies

An ideology is a system of beliefs used to justify a group's support of desired social arrangements. Status quo ideologies are put forth to justify established social patterns, such as an existing system of racial segregation. *Change ideologies are either reform or revolutionary,* depending on whether the aim is to justify modifications of established social arrangements or their total replacement. Civil rights and women's liberation activities are supported mainly by reform ideologies. Whatever the goals, ideologies enhance in-group solidarity and may also increase group power and influence by persuading others to support the cause. Action can be more realistic if both one's own and opposing ideologies are well understood, as well as deviations from them in practice.

Some ideologies are brief and sketchy while others, such as the justifications of Nazi activities against Jews, become quite systematic. Efforts to defend them add to their complexity. The content of an ideology consists of five kinds of beliefs:[28]

1 *goals,* or desired social arrangements, including appropriate norms of conduct,
2 preferred *means* for reaching the goals,
3 *value beliefs,* including both the values linked with the goals and those involved in the chosen means,
4 *existential beliefs,* including both those concerned with means for achieving the goals and those related to the operation of norms in the desired social pattern, and
5 a general *image of the society.*

Some ideological statements are much more logical and persuasive than others. Most of them include some controversial existential beliefs, including stereotypes. Key value and existential beliefs are frequently left unstated. Much of the content is devoted to rationalizing what outsiders see as logical inconsistencies. The persuasive rhetoric of ideologies often includes propaganda devices—those techniques of suggestion (such as name-calling, plain folks, and card-stacking) that are designed to bypass critical thought.[29]

The ideology long used to justify the traditional wife, mother, and homemaker roles for women emphasizes strongly the value of the stability of individual marriages and families. It includes existential beliefs about deviance from traditional sexual norms, about mothers working outside the home, and about other factors that have been assumed to promote marital and family instability. It emphasizes existential beliefs about the consequences of the breakup of marriages and families, such as the assumed contribution to crime, to mental illness, to alcoholism, and to other forms of deviance.[30] An overall image of society is painted in depictions of the central and essential place occupied by the traditional family in the institution order.

A key set of existential beliefs in this ideology stems from the general conviction that women are biologically suited only for their traditional roles. Thus they are assumed to lack sufficient strength for the physical work traditionally done by men. But biological beliefs have also been advanced for excluding women from the most lucrative and powerful professions—notably law, medicine, and executive-level management. Women have been thought to be naturally lacking in such qualities as the stamina required for demanding professional work, in balanced temperament, in decision-making ability, in driving ambition, and in sustained interest in activities beyond the home.[31]

PERSONALITY THEORIES OF PREJUDICE

Most efforts to explain the causes of prejudice have been in terms of personality processes. This approach is based on the assumption that prejudice serves certain functions for the person. The first three theories discussed below are efforts to show how prejudice reduces exceptionally strong personal anxieties.

Scapegoating

The key concepts in the scapegoat theory of prejudice are frustration, aggression, and displacement. When people are repeatedly frustrated in efforts to meet their needs, according to frustration-aggression theory, a frequent response is to strike out in angry, aggressive actions toward others. Pressures to be loyal to the family and its community often lead to resentment, especially when punishments are used to ensure conformity, and subconscious feelings of hostility develop. Since one cannot consciously admit to such feelings for loved and revered authority figures, aggression is displaced (transferred) to a safer target—a scapegoat. One can more legitimately act out feelings of aggression toward an out-group, especially one regarded ethnocentrically.[32] The out-group concerned need not be a weak one;[33] and members of both dominant and minority groups may engage in scapegoating.

Frustration does not necessarily lead to aggression, and aggression may take various forms. When two groups are in competition, hostility may be a direct response to frustration by the other group rather than displaced aggression. No satisfactory way has been found to measure the mechanism of displacement and thus to test hypotheses about it. It certainly appears as if some groups really "take it out on" others—as the Nazis did with the Jews—but the scapegoat theory provides no clue as to which group will be chosen. Perhaps the theory can help explain the maintenance of prejudice once a target group has been selected, and also why hostility sometimes reaches extremely high levels.[34] In psychoanalytic (Freudian) theory, displacement is a personality mechanism for reducing abnormally high levels of anxiety.

Projection

Another psychoanalytic theory of prejudice is based on the mechanism of projection, which means attributing to others the characteristics one would find it too painful to acknowledge consciously within oneself or one's in-groups. Thus, instead of a conscious admission of sexual interest in black women, the traditional Southern white man has accused black men of coveting white women. Or, not being able to face up to the unscrupulous means they have used to gain and maintain industrial power, corporation executives may accuse Jews of being scheming, unfair competitors. A given group may be stereotyped in a great variety of ways in different times and places, and in contradictory ways within a given context. Jews have been stereotyped as both vulgar and godlike, as both thieves and as too ethical, as both capitalists and Communists, as clannish and as aggressive intruders, as weak and strong, and as impotent and oversexed. This suggests that, as a minority people who have lived in many different social contexts, Jews have had traits projected onto them from a great variety of troubled consciences.[35]

Projection theory has limitations similar to those noted above for the scapegoat theory. It fails to account for the selection of a particular group from among several possible ones as the presumed possessor of certain traits. In stereotyping it frequently looks as if "the pot is calling the kettle black"; but why is it that different out-groups have different negative traits attributed to them? Also, the presumably subconscious mechanism of projection has not successfully been translated into research operations. Both scapegoating and projection seem plausible, but there has been no satisfactory way to test these explanations. Perhaps projection can help to explain how prejudice is maintained, and also why it is sometimes extremely strong. Like scapegoating, projection was designed to help explain how abnormally high levels of anxiety are handled.

The Authoritarian Personality

Many researchers have sought to demonstrate that there is a highly prejudiced personality type. Since midcentury the major effort along this line has been the study of the authoritarian personality.[36] Authoritarian persons are portrayed as submissive toward those with authority and power over them, but aggressive toward minorities and other people with lower status and less power than themselves. They cope with heavy anxieties by projection and by displacing the subconscious aggression they feel toward harsh parents onto people whom they perceive as having no power over them. They are obsessed with adherence to conventional morality, with power, and with violence. Prejudice helps such persons deal with a world they perceive as very uncertain, hostile, and dangerous.

Substantial associations between authoritarianism and prejudice have been reported in a great many studies, but there are some negative findings and some problems of interpretation. For example, in a study of 213 students in introduction to sociology, authoritarianism was found to be related to prejudice less than was concern about social status. Moreover, the moderately high correlation between authoritarianism and anti-Semitism (.53) was reduced to a small one (.12) when the effect of concern about social status was controlled for (held constant statistically). The correlation between status concern and anti-Semitism was reduced only from .66 to .48 when authoritarianism was controlled for.[37] These results must be interpreted carefully because of the fairly large correlation found between the status concern and authoritarianism scales (.71), and the apparent overlap in their content.[38] Very similar findings were reported in a study of 401 adult interviewees, except that the explanatory variable that held up better than authoritarianism was anomia—personal feelings of meaninglessness, powerlessness, and the lack of social norms.[39]

Questions have been raised as to whether the Authoritarianism Scale (also called the F-Scale, meaning Potentiality for Fascism) is a valid measure of the concept defined in the theory. It is apparently multidimensional, composed of nine subscales with wide-ranging content.[40] The meaning of the subscale scores is clearer than that of the total score. Different selections of items for shortened versions of the scale have complicated the comparison of results. One criticism of the scale is that it measures only conforming, right-wing authoritarianism, which is but one variant of dogmatism.[41] The parts of the theory that deal with mechanisms for coping with subconscious feelings and emotions remain immune to research. Finally, most prejudiced people apparently do not have authoritarian personalities, although the number who do have could run into the millions.[42]

Conforming Prejudice

Attitudes of prejudice against groups are learned as part of the cultural heritage. Most people tend to be prejudiced only against those groups they are expected to dislike, so their prejudice is socially conforming. This contrasts with those persons whose anxieties incline them to be hostile toward all out-groups. We have seen some of the ways prejudice may function in persons with a deep-seated need to express repressed feelings. Prejudice also serves a basic personality function for the less anxious majority of prejudiced people—that of social adjustment. Attitudes toward other groups are learned from parents and others in the same ways other attitudes are learned, and they facilitate adjustments to social role expectations.[43]

A study of the effects of textbooks on Canadian children illustrates the learning of conforming prejudice.[44] Those using French-language texts learned the French view of Canadian history, identified strongly with its symbols, and held ethnocentric views of English historical figures and accomplishments. Those using English texts were equally ethnocentric toward the French-Canadians and their history, and for both groups ethnocentric perception increased with age. Such sets of prejudiced perceptions are reinforced throughout the institutional structure. In the United States, for example, the Library of Congress subject matter headings reflect cultural biases toward race groups, nationalities, religions, age groups, deviant groups, men and women, and other social categories.[45] Movements to change terms of address or reference for women, blacks, and other minorities are efforts to intervene in the cultural transmission of ethnocentric attitudes and behavior.

Studies of concern about social status are designed to help explain conforming prejudice.[46] In the study cited above in which status concern held up better than authoritarianism as a correlate of prejudice, status concern was measured by attitude items on such matters as concern about ambition, knowing influential people, and living in the right areas.[47] The greater such concern the more prejudice expected, apparently because of the fear that close contact with lower status groups means loss of status.

In times of rapid social change, continual crises result in a high level of uncertainty about social statuses and attendant role expectations. It has been hypothesized that marked status uncertainty strengthens group prejudices and activates latent ones.[48] Sometimes the concern is for maintaining an existing status, sometimes over being blocked from rising further in the class structure. Groups become concerned about occupational advantages, group prestige, and power.[49] Such concerns become heightened and focused on particular groups when intergroup competition becomes intense. We have seen that highly negative stereotypes of Chinese and other immigrant groups flourished when these groups seemed most threatening as economic competitors.

CHANGING PREJUDICE

Numerous examples of change in attitudes of prejudice have been cited in this chapter. Even rigid stereotypes may change. Conforming prejudice, the most common kind, probably changes more readily than that which is presumably more deeply rooted in the personality. Therapy would seem the logical approach for the latter, although the frequency of its success in reducing prejudice is not known.[50] Educational programs, usually involving some combination of information and exhortation, would seem more suitable for reducing conforming prejudice. The usual conclusion that information and propaganda have little effect on prejudice[51] is oversimplified,[52] as we shall see in Chapter 11.

We have already noted the very important discovery that changes in patterns of discriminatory behavior can produce changes in attitudes of prejudice. According to theories that emphasize the balance of different aspects of the personality, people strive for consistency of attitudes and between attitudes and behavior. Behavioral intentions, group stereotypes, value priorities, and beliefs about the norms of intergroup relations have all been observed to change as a result of changed patterns of behavior. This is illustrated by the study at the University of Alabama cited earlier in the chapter in the discussion of stereotypes. Since much of the behavioral change has been brought about by changes in law and its enforcement, the old adage that law cannot change the hearts and minds of men is evidently false. This means that it is not necessary to change attitudes before laws and behavior can be effectively changed, at least under some circumstances.

Equal-Status Contacts

Allport hypothesized that social contact reduces prejudice when the groups interact as equals in status—especially when they pursue common goals, cooperate rather than compete, or when legal officials and the community oppose prejudice and discrimination.[53] The equal-status contact hypothesis has been supported in many, but not all, studies. White prejudice against blacks was reduced significantly in a number of integrated public housing situations.[54] In similar projects, black prejudice against whites was reportedly reduced in one study,[55] but not in a later one.[56] A training institute for school desegregation reduced prejudice among white teachers but not among black ones, who did not define it as an equal-status contact.[57]

Racially integrated hospital experiences resulted in increased hostility, prompting the researchers to suggest that equal-status contacts cannot reduce prejudice unless the contact is sufficiently long and intimate to challenge stereotypes, and unless the norms in the situation define prejudice as inappropriate.[58] Intimate contacts appeared to reduce prejudice in a study of black anti-Semitism.[59] The racial integration of the American military forces after World War II took place with relatively little tension and conflict, and was largely accomplished by the mid-fifties. It resulted in improved skills and higher ranks for black servicemen—thus an increase in equal-status contact—and in the reduction of prejudice.[60]

In a study of 582 black youths in Washington, D.C., all whites were not perceived as fitting the same stereotype. Instead, behavioral intentions toward whites (willingness to associate in fifteen different situations) were contingent on white attitudes toward blacks. The major criterion in selecting which whites they would associate with—much more important than personality or social class characteristics—was how the whites felt about blacks.[61] This finding was called the Contingency Factor. In studies of international students this has been called the Two-Way Mirror, meaning that favorability of foreign students toward American society depends on how favorable they think Americans are to their country.[62] One implication of the two-way mirror or contingency factor among the black youth is that there was apparently a high level of readiness for interaction with whites on an equal-status basis. It also suggests the hypothesis that one reason equal-status contact may reduce prejudice is that it changes in-group perceptions of out-group attitudes toward the in-group.

Prejudice and Discrimination

Although prejudice and discrimination often reinforce each other, they also occur independently. Possibly Allport was correct a generation ago in suggesting that about four-fifths of the American people had enough prejudice toward minorities to influence their behavior.[63] However, a great many prejudiced people do not discriminate, while many unprejudiced ones do. Prejudice varies in degree, so the matter is oversimplified by reasoning in terms of a dichotomy between the prejudiced and the unprejudiced. Nevertheless it is helpful to look at

Merton's simple cross-tabulation, which produces four attitude-behavior types:[64]

1 the unprejudiced nondiscriminator
2 the unprejudiced discriminator
3 the prejudiced nondiscriminator
4 the prejudiced discriminator

The first type is composed of people whose behavior toward minorities is consistent with their attitudes. Type-2 situations are those in which people go against their attitudes and conform to group expectations to discriminate. For example, in order to stay on good terms with neighbors, relatives, or friends, an unprejudiced person may help keep particular groups from getting housing in the neighborhood. Such persons feel guilty, and they are relieved when the reference group pressures shift into line with their attitudes.

Type 3, prejudiced nondiscriminators, are people who go against their attitudes by conforming to group expectations not to discriminate. The employer who loathes hiring a minority person for a position, but who does so in order to avoid investigation for violating federal hiring guidelines, feels frustrated and would prefer to be free to discriminate. It seems likely that some of the people in Type 3 are authoritarian personalities; they have strong needs to discriminate, but also to accept the dictates of powerful authorities. Probably most persons in Type 3 have conforming prejudice, but now are conforming to strongly opposing constraints. People in both Types 2 and 3 accede to group pressures in their situations rather than their own inclinations. Apparently a substantial proportion of the population falls into these two categories, so it is not surprising that prejudiced attitudes do not predict discriminatory behavior very well.

People in Type 4 have been characterized as hard-core discriminators, meaning that they are the most difficult to change. They consider their actions right and logical; their attitudes and behavior reinforce each other, just as they do for Type 1. However, it must not be assumed that most prejudiced discriminators have authoritarian personalities, or otherwise have deep-seated needs for group prejudice. The majority of people in Type 4 hold attitudes of conforming prejudice of varying strength—attitudes that respond to major changes in patterns of group expectations and behavior. Most of the reduction in anti-black prejudice in the Deep South in recent decades must have involved people who originally were Type 4 conformers.

This consideration of the discrepancies and connections between prejudice and discrimination highlights a theme that has been implicit throughout this chapter, that prejudice is primarily a *social* psychological phenomenon.[65] Shared attitudes emerge from particular patterns of intergroup relations and are transmitted as part of the cultural heritage.

Most prejudice is evidently conforming, the kind that facilitates adjustment to group expectations. The content of prejudiced attitudes betrays their social origins. Social distance judgments, and also the stereotyped and ethnocentric beliefs that make up ideologies, reflect intergroup conflicts and patterns of accommodation. There is often variation in behavior toward minorities and also in related attitudes. Significant shifts in patterns of discrimination tend to produce corresponding changes in prejudice, but for a time discrepancies are often considerable.

FOOTNOTES

1   Ehrlich, 1973, pp. 4, 102–8; Levin, 1975, pp. 13–22.
2   Park, 1924.
3   Bogardus, 1925.
4   Bogardus, 1968.
5   Bogardus, 1959; Brown, 1973.
6   Ehrlich, 1973, pp. 64–80.
7   Bogardus, 1968; Kinloch, 1974.
8   Rokeach, 1968, pp. 112–13.
9   Jeffries, Schweitzer & Morris, 1973.
10   Jeffries, 1971; Jeffries & Morris, 1968.
11   Davis, 1970, pp. 16–34; Davis, 1975, pp. 51–54.
12   Rokeach, 1968, Ch. 7.
13   Levin, 1975, pp. 16–18.
14   Shibutani & Kwan, 1965, pp. 83–89; Maykovich, 1972.
15   Shibutani & Kwan, 1965, pp. 90–91.
16   Ehrlich, 1973, pp. 34–38; Stivers, 1976, Chs. 7, 8.
17   Works, 1972; Pettigrew, 1976, p. 490.
18   Stanley & Kitano, 1973.
19   Hyman & Sheatsley, 1964.
20   Muir, 1974.
21   Pettigrew, 1976, p. 485.
22   Sumner, 1906, pp. 13–15.
23   Blassingame, 1972, pp. 199–200.
24   Haley, 1976.
25   Shibutani & Kwan, 1965, pp. 107–8; 294–96.
26   Blassingame, 1972, pp. 17–103; 206–16.
27   Blassingame, 1972, pp. 201–4.
28   Davis, 1970, pp. 61–68.
29   Lee & Lee, 1939, pp. 23–24; Davis, 1970, pp. 50–53.
30   Davis, 1970, pp. 151–64.
31   Epstein, 1976, pp. 416, 430–32.
32   Dollard et al., 1939.
33   Allport, 1954, pp. 351–52.

34 Blalock, 1967, pp. 42–44; Ehrlich, 1973, pp. 149–51.
35 Ackerman & Jahoda, 1950, pp. 57–59; Bettelheim & Janowitz, 1950, p. 43.
36 Adorno et al., 1950.
37 Kaufman, 1957.
38 Blalock, 1967, p. 54.
39 Srole, 1956.
40 Blalock, 1967, pp. 6–10; Camilleri, 1959.
41 Rokeach, 1960; Ehrlich, 1973, pp. 143–46.
42 Pettigrew, 1976, p. 488.
43 Pettigrew, 1976, p. 487; Ehrlich, 1973, Ch. 5; Levin, 1975, pp. 22–28.
44 Richert, 1974.
45 Berman, 1971.
46 Blalock, 1967, pp. 53–72; Levin, 1975, pp. 46–61.
47 Kaufman, 1957.
48 Tumin, 1971.
49 Levin, 1975, Ch. 3.
50 Allport, 1954, pp. 459–61.
51 Allport, 1954, pp. 452–56.
52 Ehrlich, 1973, pp. 147–49.
53 Allport, 1954, Ch. 16.
54 Deutsch & Collins, 1951; Wilner, Walkley & Cook, 1955; Meer & Freedman, 1966.
55 Works, 1961.
56 Ford, 1973.
57 Robinson & Preston, 1976.
58 Brown & Albee, 1966.
59 Tsukashima & Montero, 1976.
60 Moskos, 1966.
61 McDowell, 1971.
62 Morris, 1960, pp. 7–30; Ibrahim, 1970, p. 40; Davis, 1971, pp. 36–37.
63 Allport, 1954, p. 78.
64 Merton, 1949.
65 Ehrlich, 1973, pp. 160–61.

REFERENCES

Ackerman, Nathan W., and Marie Jahoda
1950   Anti-Semitism and Emotional Disorder. New York: Harper and Row.
Adorno, T. W., Else Frenkel-Brunswik, Daniel J. Levinson, and R. Nevitt Sanford
1950   The Authoritarian Personality. New York: Harper and Row.
Allport, Gordon W.
1954   The Nature of Prejudice. Boston: Beacon Press, Inc.
Berman, Sanford
1971   Prejudices and Antipathies: A Tract on the LC Subject Heads Concerning People. Metuchen, New Jersey: Scarecrow Press, Inc.

Bettelheim, Bruno, and Morris Janowitz
1950   Dynamics of Prejudice. New York: Harper and Row.
Blalock, Hubert M., Jr.
1967   Toward a Theory of Minority-Group Relations. New York: Capricorn Books.
Blassingame, John W.
1972   The Slave Community: Plantation Life in the Antebellum South. New York: Oxford University Press.
Bogardus, Emory S.
1925   "Measuring Social Distances." Journal of Applied Sociology 9: 299–308.
1959   Social Distance. Los Angeles: The Author.
1968   "Comparing Racial Distance in Ethopia, South Africa, and the United States." Sociology and Social Research 52: 149–56.
Brown, Barry S., and George W. Albee
1966   "The Effect of Integrated Hospital Experiences on Racial Attitudes—A Discordant Note." Social Problems 13 (Winter): 324–33.
Brown, Robert Lane
1973   "Social Distance Perception as a Function of Mexican-American and Other Ethnic Identity." Sociology and Social Research 57, 3 (April): 273–87.
Camilleri, Santo F.
1959   "A Factor Analysis of the F-Scale." Social Forces 37 (May): 316–23.
Davis, F. James
1970   Social Problems: Enduring Major Issues and Social Change. New York: The Free Press.
1971   "The Two-Way Mirror and the U-Curve: America as Seen by Turkish Students Returned Home." Sociology and Social Research 56, 1 (October): 29–43.
1975   "Beliefs, Values, Power, and Public Definitions of Deviance," 50–59 in F. James Davis and Richard Stivers (eds.), The Collective Definition of Deviance. New York: The Free Press.
Deutsch, Morton, and Mary Evans Collins
1951   Interracial Housing. Minneapolis: University of Minnesota Press.
Dollard, John, et al.
1939   Frustration and Aggression. New Haven: Yale University Press.
Ehrlich, Howard J.
1973   The Social Psychology of Prejudice. New York: Wiley Interscience.
Epstein, Cynthia Fuchs
1976   "Sex Roles," Ch. 9 in, Robert K. Merton and Robert Nisbet, Contemporary Social Problems. New York: Harcourt, Brace, Jovanovich, Inc.
Ford, W. Scott
1973   "Interracial Public Housing in a Border City: Another Look at the Contact Hypothesis." American Journal of Sociology 78, 6 (May): 1426–47.
Haley, Alex
1976   Roots. Garden City, New York: Doubleday and Co., Inc.
Hyman, H. H., and P. B. Sheatsley
1964   "Attitudes Toward Desegregation." Scientific American 211 (July): 16–23.
Ibrahim, E. M.
1970   "Interaction, Perception, and Attitudes of Arab Students Toward Americans." Sociology and Social Research 55 (October): 29–46.

Jeffries, Vincent
1971 "Cultural Sources of Solidarity and Antagonism Toward Blacks." Social Science Quarterly 51 (March): 860–72.
Jeffries, Vincent, and Richard T. Morris
1968 "Altruism, Egoism and Antagonism Toward Negroes." Social Science Quarterly 49 (December): 697–709.
Jeffries, Vincent, David R. Schweitzer, and Richard T. Morris
1973 "Values, Authoritarianism, and Antagonism Toward Ethnic Minorities." Pacific Sociological Review 16, 3 (July): 357–76.
Kaufman, Walter C.
1957 "Status, Authoritarianism, and Anti-Semitism." American Journal of Sociology 62 (January): 379–82.
Kinloch, Graham C.
1974 "Racial Prejudice in Highly and Less Racist Societies: Social Distance Preferences Among White College Students in South Africa and Hawaii." Sociology and Social Research 59, 1 (October): 1–13.
Lee, Alfred M., and Elizabeth B. Lee
1939 The Fine Art of Propaganda. New York: Harcourt, Brace and Co.
Levin, Jack
1975 The Functions of Prejudice. New York: Harper and Row.
Maykovich, Minako Kurokawa
1972 "Reciprocity in Racial Stereotypes: White, Black and Yellow." American Journal of Sociology 77, 5 (March): 876–97.
McDowell, Sophia
1971 "Patterns of Preference by Negro Youth for White and Negro Associates." Phylon 32, 3 (Fall): 290–301.
Meer, Bernard, and Edward Freedman
1966 "The Impact of Negro Neighbors on White Home Owners." Social Forces 45 (September): 11–19.
Merton, Robert K.
1949 "Discrimination and the American Creed," 99–126 in R. M. MacIver (ed.), Discrimination and National Welfare. New York: Harper and Bros.
Morris, Richard T.
1960 The Two-Way Mirror. Minneapolis: University of Minnesota Press.
Moskos, Charles C., Jr.
1966 "Racial Integration in the Armed Forces," American Journal of Sociology 72 (September): 132–48.
Muir, Donal
1974 "Through the School House Door: Trends in Integration, Attitudes on a Deep-South Campus During the First Decade of Desegregation." Sociology and Social Research 58 (January): 113–21.
Park, Robert E.
1924 "The Concept of Social Distance." Journal of Applied Sociology 8: 339–44.
Pettigrew, Thomas Fraser
1976 "Race and Intergroup Relations," Ch. 10 in Robert K. Merton and Robert Nisbet, Contemporary Social Problems, 4th Edition. New York: Harcourt, Brace, Jovanovich, Inc.

Richert, Jean Pierre
1974 "The Impact of Ethnicity on the Perception of Heroes and Historical Symbols." Canadian Review of Sociology and Anthropology 11, 2 (May): 156–63.

Robinson, Jerry W., Jr., and James D. Preston
1976 "Equal-Status Contact and Modification of Racial Prejudice: A Reexamination of the Contact Hypothesis." Social Forces 54, 4 (June): 900–924.

Rokeach, Milton
1960 The Open and Closed Mind. New York: Basic Books.
1968 Beliefs, Attitudes and Values. San Francisco: Jossey-Bass, Inc., Publishers.

Shibutani, Tamotsu, and Kian M. Kwan
1965 Ethnic Stratification: A Comparative Approach. New York: The Macmillan Co.

Srole, Leo
1956 "Social Integration and Certain Corollaries: An Exploratory Study." American Sociological Review 21 (December): 709–16.

Stanley, Sue, and Harry H. L. Kitano
1973 "Stereotypes as a Measure of Success." Journal of Social Issues 29, 2: 83–98.

Stivers, Richard
1976 A Hair of the Dog: Irish Drinking and American Stereotype. University Park, Pa.: The Pennsylvania State University Press.

Sumner, William G.
1906 Folkways. Boston: Ginn and Co.

Tsukashima, Ronald Tadao, and Darrel Montero
1976 "The Contact Hypothesis: Social and Economic Contact and Generational Changes in the Study of Black Anti-Semitism," Social Forces 55, 1 (September): 149–65.

Tumin, Melvin
1971 "Anti-Semitism and Status Anxiety: A Hypothesis." Jewish Social Studies 33, 4 (October): 307–16.

Williams, Robin M., Jr., et al.
1964 Strangers Next Door. Englewood Cliffs, New Jersey: Prentice-Hall, Inc.

Wilner, Daniel M., Rosabelle Price Walkley, and Stuart W. Cook
1955 Human Relations in Interracial Housing. Minneapolis: University of Minnesota Press.

Works, Ernest
1961 "The Prejudice Interaction Hypothesis from the Point of View of the Negro Minority Group." American Journal of Sociology 67 (July): 47–52.
1972 "Role Violations and Intergroup Prejudice." Pacific Sociological Review 15, 3 (July): 327–44.

TWO

PATTERNS OF ACCOMMODATION

4

Stratified Accommodation and Social Class

Intergroup accommodation exists to the degree that relationships are routinized. In minority-dominant relations groups are accommodated to unequal statuses, so the patterns are those of social stratification. Often many groups are ranked in a status hierarchy or "peck order." To analyze the connections between these vertical arrangements and systems of class and caste is the aim in this chapter.

SOCIAL CLASS

Social classes are broad, self-aware groupings of a society's people, stratified according to differences in economic position, social status, and power.[1] People's awareness of these ranks is reinforced by the subculture shared by members of a class. Social status here refers to prestige, the importance accorded to members of the class by people in general in the society. Economic rank and political power are not perfectly associated with status, but the three dimensions tend to reinforce each other and are fairly highly correlated.

Vertical mobility—movement up or down in the rank structure—is permitted in class systems. *Open-class systems* are those in which vertical mobility is relatively easy and common; *closed-class systems* are those in which vertical mobility is very difficult and rare. Marriage with members of other ranks is permitted in class systems, although people tend to marry within their own class, especially in the more closed-class structures. In *caste systems,* neither vertical mobility nor marriage outside the rank is permitted. The status of persons is ascribed at birth, and castes are strictly endogamous.

Ever since Warner's pioneering studies of social class in American communities, despite the fact that some researchers have reported fewer than six classes, the following scheme has been widely used:[2]

1 the upper-upper class ("old family" aristocrats, in the Social Register or its equivalent)
2 the lower-upper class (the powerful new-rich)
3 the upper-middle class (solid business and professional people, comfortable but not wealthy or "social")
4 the lower-middle class (less-educated and lower-paid white-collar and small business people, and better-paid skilled workers)
5 the upper-lower class (the "working class," semiskilled, and some skilled and some unskilled blue-collar families)
6 the lower-lower class (unskilled and often unemployed manual workers, poor and disreputable).

The dimension stressed in the community studies of class is status, initially measured by Warner and associates by determining who participates with whom in leisure-time activities. They then found their Index of Social Participation to be highly correlated with an Index of Status Characteristics consisting of education, income, and occupation.[3] The approach has been criticized for underemphasizing economic and political power.

Both of the major types of theory about social class—Marxist and functionalist—emphasize competition for scarce values. In Marxism the "haves" are seen as exercising their monopoly of power to exploit the masses of "have-nots," until the latter become sufficiently aware and rebel, and then another round of violent class conflict produces a new elite. In functionalist theories, different social roles in complex societies are seen as being rewarded with different amounts of social status, so that class structures help maintain the social system. Although Parsons has noted that power is involved in authority roles in a complex division of labor,[4] functionalist explanations have been criticized for lack of attention to power and conflict.

GROUP STRATIFICATION, CONFLICT, AND POWER

Group competition, conflict, and power must be stressed in adequate efforts to explain the stratification of groups.[5] In the power elite conflict theories, including the colonial model,[6] all systems of unequal treatment of groups are portrayed as domination of the mass by a powerful elite. In terms of the marginal working class concept, ethnic divisions facilitate the exploitation of low-paid service workers.[7] In Marxist analysis, discrimination against groups is simply an aspect of the economic exploitation of the masses by the powerful few. Pluralistic conflict theorists of group stratification distinguish elite-mass relationships from those in which power is more widely distributed. In one such effort the elite-mass pattern has been attributed to simple, undifferentiated social structure, to ascribed community status, and to the absence of vertical mobility. The minority-dominant pattern in societies such as the United States has been attributed to a complex division of labor, an open-class system, and power pluralism.[8]

The minority-dominant model does not seem apt for relationships between some groups in pluralistic societies. The concept of the dominant community must be used carefully, to refer to groups participating in a pattern of discrimination against a given group or cluster of groups. A group in a stratified pattern has less power than those ranked above it, but more than those ranked below. For instance, urban blacks often have seen Jewish small retailers and teachers as powerful, while the latter are aware of groups with greater control over business and education.[9]

In Noel's theoretical attempt to explain its origins, ethnic stratification is seen as the outcome of the operation of three variables: ethnocentrism, competition, and differential power. Continuing contact is a necessary condition for both equalitarian and stratified accommodation, but without all three of the above variables no stratified pattern would develop. The earliest blacks in the American colonies were indentured servants, and chattel slavery would allegedly not have developed except for the highly ethnocentric perception of the Africans, the crucial need for their labor in competition in the South for landed wealth and prestige, and the extreme powerlessness and lack of identity of the blacks.[10] In an effort to apply this to stratified relations between Mexican Americans and Anglos in Texas, it was concluded that the evidence is clear only for the role of ethnocentrism.[11]

In a landmark theoretical work, by Shibutani and Kwan, ethnic stratification is seen as the result of differential power in group competition and conflict. The arrangements then become legitimized, institutionalized, and justified by ideology. Group isolation limits intergroup communication, thus perpetuating stereotypes, ethnocentrism, and social distance. When challenged, the pattern of accommodation is enforced by political power and justified by reference to ideology. The stratified pattern comes to seem right and natural to the dominant community, and sometimes to the subordinate group(s) as well. When life conditions change significantly, competition and conflict are renewed and the stratified accommodations are sooner or later modified or replaced by a new pattern.[12]

Possibly the stratification of other minorities differs from that of ethnic groups, yet there appear to be similarities, especially in the maintenance of patterns of accommodation. The different age groups compete for jobs and salaries, have different amounts of power, and exhibit stereotyped attitudes toward each other. The handicapped, ex-prisoners, homosexuals, and other deviant groups are negatively stereotyped, relatively powerless, and are often excluded from competition for jobs and other positions in the community. Challenges to the long-standing pattern of stratified male-female accommodation have brought increased awareness of stereotyped beliefs, and of the relative powerlessness of women in competition for scarce rewards.

An important connection between the class system and sex stratification must be noted. In keeping with patriarchal tradition, the class position of the family or other household has been that of the husband and father or other "male head of household." Students of stratification have often defined social classes as rankings of families, and have continued to emphasize the occupation, income, and education of the male head of household. It has now become the exception for the husband and father to be the sole breadwinner, so automatically considering him to be the head of household is more and more problematic. As women make further economic and political gains it seems increasingly essential to consider the person rather than the family to be the basic unit in the class system.[13] Further, study of the processes of sex stratification will help in efforts to understand ethnic stratification and social class.

MINORITIES AND SOCIAL CLASS

The hierarchy of racial and ethnic groups in a community cannot neatly be placed within the class system because of the variation in class that typically exists within a given group. The range in class placement of its members is narrow for some groups and wide for others at a given time, but in any case a reference to the class placement of the group indicates only the central tendency. Other groups' response to a member of a minority group may be influenced by that person's class position, but there is also the tendency toward categoric treatment of all the members of the group. Often there is uncertainty whether to treat a person as a member of a minority or a social class. Shall the unskilled Anglo father treat his child's teacher as a Mexican American or as a middle-class person, and how shall this teacher treat the father? The greater the social distance between the groups, and the more intimate the situation, the more likely it is that group identity will outweigh social class.[14]

One suggestion for conceptualizing the connection between class and ethnicity is to cross-classify them and refer to the resulting combinations by the term "ethclass." Illustrative ethclass positions are: upper-middle-class white Irish Catholic, lower-middle-class black Protestant, or upper-lower-class Jew. This scheme appears to have particular value for understanding social participation in small, informal groups, since such activity is largely with members of the same social class within the ethnic group.[15]

Some Community Patterns of Ethnicity and Class

NEWBURYPORT, MASSACHUSETTS   The length of time an ethnic group has been in a community is a major determinant of its class status. Just over half the population of 17,000 of Warner's "Yankee City" were Yankees (old-line Americans) in the 1930s, but they constituted over four-fifths of the upper-middle class and nearly all of the upper classes.[16] Their average (median and modal) class position was lower-middle, while that of all the ethnic groups was either upper-lower or lower-lower. The earliest ethnic groups had climbed the class ladder somewhat, and the longer a group had been there the higher some of its members had penetrated. The upward movement of the French-Canadians, the earliest group except for the Irish, apparently was slowed by their nearness to their homeland and the consequent retention of their cultural identity. The latest groups (Poles, Russians, and blacks) had started at the bottom of the occupational ladder, as earlier groups had, and were still there.

BURLINGTON, VERMONT   The Yankees were also ranked at the top of the class structure of this city of 25,000 in the 1930s. The small black and Chinese groups were at the bottom of the hierarchy. The Irish had moved upward significantly, but the even earlier and much larger French-Canadian group (40 percent of the community's population) had remained preoccupied with their traditional culture rather than with escaping manual jobs in the mills and factories. Group and class status were associated with residential location in the city. When asked whom they preferred as neighbors, people usually listed their own group first. Blacks and Chinese were usually listed last, except by members of their own group. After themselves, Yankees listed English Canadians, while ethnic groups usually listed Yankees second and Irish third.[17]

MORRIS, ILLINOIS   "Jonesville," also called "Elmtown," had a population of about 6,000 when it was first studied. Having been settled much more recently than New England, Jonesville had no old-line families to constitute an upper-upper class, but most of its upper-middle- and upper-class families were of "American stock."[18] The next settlers were Irish, then Germans, then (after the Civil War) a sizeable number of Norwegians, then Poles and Eastern and Southern European peoples, and finally some blacks, Mexican Americans, and Orientals. The ethnic hierarchy was correlated with the length of group residence in the community, except that the Irish had experienced considerable discrimination and had been held back more than the Germans and Norwegians had. Ethnic stereotypes flourished. There was a fairly definite, but not rigid, pattern of ethnic stratification.[19]

NATCHEZ, MISSISSIPPI   "Old City," with a population of about 10,000 when it was studied before World War II, was considered typical of the dual system of stratification of much of the South. That is, the population was first divided into the black and white castes, and within each caste there was a class system. A child with two white parents was ascribed the status of white; a child with one or both parents known as blacks was ascribed the social status of black, regardless of biological features. Upward class mobility occurred within each caste. In a strict caste arrangement all members of the upper caste are considered superior to those in the lower one. In Old City, however, the whites held black professionals in higher esteem than they did white sharecroppers and other poor whites. Thus the lower-status whites were considered socially inferior to the higher-ranking blacks, so the system actually was castelike or near-caste rather than one of caste.[20] In a later study in Durham, North Carolina ("Crescent City"), there apparently had been still more departure from caste with, "increasing contacts between class equals across color lines."[21]

Upward Social Mobility

The European groups that were attempting to climb the American class ladder earlier in the century have, on the whole, succeeded very well. Some advanced faster than others because of factors favoring their assimilation. Of course, much of the success was accomplished in spite of obstacles, and achievement of a higher average class position does not prove that discrimination against a group has ceased. Ethnic identities have not disappeared, nor has ethnic stratification. Yet large proportions of entire ethnic groups, some very large ones, have moved significantly upward in the class system in a matter of decades. How was this possible? The open-class system provided a necessary general framework, and a number of factors favored assimilation. The answer, however, seems to lie primarily in the following three factors:

1. THE "SUCCESSIVE-WAVE" PATTERN OF IMMIGRATION   A major factor in upward social mobility has been the immigration of new groups to take over the low-status occupations, thus "pushing" the earlier arrivals up the class ladder. Remembering that large numbers of unskilled immigrants came to the United States during the last part of the nineteenth century and the first decades of the twentieth, we may appreciate that this upward "push" was considerable. Despite continuing immigration, the total volume of it has been so curtailed ever since the 1920s that this factor is now much less important in upward mobility than it was for a time. Since World War II the new arrivals in the cities have mostly been rural-to-urban black migrants, with considerable numbers of Puerto Ricans and Mexican Americans.

2. TECHNOLOGICAL AND OCCUPATIONAL CHANGE   The reason the United States could absorb such large numbers of immigrants for many decades after the land was all settled is that the industrial and agricultural revolutions were accelerating so rapidly, creating a great many new jobs, greatly increasing productivity and raising the standard of living. At the same time there were rapid reductions in the proportion of manual workers in the labor force, and increases in the proportions of professionals, proprietors and managers, salespeople, and clerical workers. These changes in the occupational structure propelled large numbers of people up the social class ladder, greatly enlarging the size of the middle class, and thus facilitating the dramatic rise in class position of entire ethnic groups. This shift evidently has facilitated the upward occupational mobility of blacks with a minimum of conflict, because the jobs were not being taken away from whites.[22] The development of sources of power and other aspects of technology in the future is uncertain, but it seems unlikely that shifts in the occupational structure can continue on the scale seen in earlier decades.

3. THE DIFFERENTIAL BIRTH RATE   Still another factor in the favorable balance of upward over downward mobility for many decades was the class differential in birthrates. Lower-class families had the most children, and many of them could rise in status because many middle- and upper-class families were not replacing themselves. In recent decades this differential has become much smaller as birth control has become more universal among the lower classes.[23] There are indications that the differential class birthrate might disappear entirely, or even be reversed.

Intergroup relations would have been different during this century if the above three factors had not been operating to facilitate a considerable excess of upward over downward mobility. Immigration continues, but at a modest level and with a preference for technical and professional people rather than the unskilled. If the occupational structure becomes relatively stable, and the differential class birthrate disappears, it seems inevitable that about as many persons will have to move downward in class status as manage to move up. The prospects for the upward movement of racial and ethnic groups through the mobility of their individual members are not good, especially for the larger groups. Moreover, most of the people at or near the bottom of the urban status hierarchies since the 1950s are members of racial minorities, and these groups cannot shed the handicap of their physical visibility as the earlier ethnics escaped their cultural visibility by assimilation.

Social Class in the Minority Community

Class differences develop within racial and cultural minorities and become important influences on people's values and styles of life. According to one view, the general tendency is for the social class subculture to become more salient to people than that of the ethnic group. That is, people in different social classes in the same ethnic group tend to think and act differently, while those in different ethnic groups but in the same social class tend to think and act alike.[24] However, ethnic identities are apparently stronger than they have often seemed (see Chapter 9).

The longer an ethnic group exists in a society with an open-class system the wider becomes the range of its variation in social class. For example, most of the first generation of Jews from Eastern Europe lived in poverty in urban ghettos, worked in sweatshops, and made sacrifices for their children's education. The second generation tended to emphasize occupational success, often in family businesses, advancement through education, thrift, and respectability. Some in the second generation, but more in the third, began to emphasize the professions, the accumulation of wealth and material possessions, and prestige. The third generation tended to be as critical of the way of life of the second as the second was of the first. The longer the group has been here the more heterogeneous it has become in class and culture.[25] The different generations coexist, and also some persons climb the class ladder while others do not.

STRATIFICATION IN THE BLACK COMMUNITY   Since World War II the class structure of the black community has changed considerably in response to enlarged occupational opportunities. It is complex and still changing, but a brief profile of each class will show that the black community is not monolithic. Some analysts have divided the three major classes into eight subgroupings,[26] as characterized in the following discussion.

The upper-upper-class blacks represent perhaps 3 percent of the nation's black population, and hold such secure occupational positions as judge, lawyer, surgeon, ambassador or other governmental position of high rank, banking or insurance executive, college president, or minister of a prestigious church. The shared values include concern for old family connections, good taste, travel, charity, and affiliation with churches such as Congregational, Presbyterian, Episcopalian, or Catholic. Until World War II this aristocratic class guarded its light color and its heritage of descent from families of freed slaves, but color gradations are apparently less important now.

The lower-upper class, 7 percent or so of the black population, are the new-rich and the newly prominent—people who have "made it big." Typically they have made great advances through education or talent. Occupational examples are: highly successful business executives and professionals, black mayors of major cities, congressmen and women, state officials, top entertainers, and professional athletes. The upper-uppers regard these people as undependable and lacking in taste, in family connections, and in proper morality. The gates are kept with care and it is very difficult for the lower-upper people to become accepted among the top group.

The middle class, perhaps 40 percent of the total, consists of three subgroups: professionals, clerical workers, and skilled blue-collar workers. All three middle-class groups value stable families, religious devotion, occupational achievement, owning property, social status, and political participation. The professionals now generally have college degrees, and they hold such positions as lawyer, administrator, teacher, social worker, proprietor of a business, or accountant. Blacks are underrepresented in these positions, with less than half as many as the proportion of blacks in the American population. The families of this subgroup tend to be stable, and they affiliate with the Presbyterian, Catholic, and Episcopalian churches, and the serene type of Baptist and Methodist ones. They emulate the style of life of the upper classes insofar as possible, and value clubs and Greek-letter organizations. The life-style of the middle-middle group is similar to this, but the clerical and other workers have less financial means and fewer achievements. The blue-collar middle class are the most skilled metal and construction craftsmen, foremen, mechanics, etc. They place heavy emphasis on giving their children a better education than they had. Their families are relatively stable, and they tend to favor the emotionally fulfilling type of Baptist and Methodist churches.

The remaining half of the nation's blacks are in one of the three lower-class groups: the working non-poor, the working poor, and the lower-lower or underclass. The first of these are steadily employed people such as truck drivers, equipment operators, and semiskilled repairmen, craftsmen, and mechanics. They have been largely excluded from unions, and wives usually work to supplement the family income. The family is important, and so also is the church, typically Baptist.

The working poor are in farm labor and such unskilled service jobs as hospital and restaurant work, janitor, and domestic household work. Often they are unemployed. This group best fits the "marginal working class" concept, according to which capitalists profit from having low-paid workers in service jobs, and can control them better when they are divided by racial or ethnic prejudice and discrimination.[27] About one-third of the nation's black families are working poor. These families predominantly have two parents, and they place their hopes for their children in education. Two-parent families also predominate in all the class levels above this one.

Underclass blacks get odd jobs and other low-paying, insecure work when they can, but they are unemployed much of the time. They contribute a good many of the black welfare clients, yet probably the majority of them receive no assistance of any kind. A great many of the black and white underclass are not covered by the payroll insurance plans (unemployment and workmen's compensation, and OASI of the Social Security program). As for public aid for dependent children, the aged, the blind, and the disabled, many of the poorest blacks are discriminated against because of race or perceived immorality. The one-parent (mother-only) family is frequent, possibly predominant among underclass blacks. Many lack knowledge of their rights, and others refuse to cooperate with the welfare bureaucracy and its stigma of dependency. These poorest blacks suffer from poor nutrition, poor health, poor housing, and crime, and many of the families are large. Their style of personal freedom and just "getting by" reflects alienation from society.

CLASS IDENTITY WITHIN THE MINORITY   One theoretical view of the formation of class differences within minority groups is that it facilitates the integration of the group into the dominant community.

The ethnic subculture is weakened as upward mobility occurs and people become loyal to the values and way of life of the class into which they have moved. Then, as more and more people associate across ethnic lines on a class basis, identification with the ethnic group becomes less and less important.[28] By the time it was integrated into the American middle class, the typical European immigrant group evidently was pretty well assimilated. When there are major barriers to assimilation, however, class differences do not promote integration into the dominant community.

In a second view the emphasis is on the tensions created within a minority by class differentiation, and the consequent weakening of its unity in efforts to combat discrimination against the group. Those who have risen in class status are often accused by the classes below them of being "uppity," and also of being "Uncle Toms" for seeming to be more concerned with protecting their own gains than with reducing discrimination against the group. In retaliation the lower-status people may be accused of creating a bad image and holding the whole group back. These conflicts may occur whether a group is well on the way to assimilation or not. Where there are barriers to assimilation, such as racial differences, the intragroup conflicts may hamper other routes to more equal treatment of the group. The increasing white acceptance of blacks as class equals apparently does not portend assimilation or the end of discrimination. If political power is to be the key to more equal treatment the minority must be united, and this is difficult to achieve across class lines.

In pluralistic approaches to class conflicts within a minority, it is assumed that minorities and allied groups can reduce discrimination through existing political processes if they work hard enough at it.[29] In terms of the colonial model, a major rebellion is necessary to get the elites to give up their economic exploitation, and class division within the minority inhibits the raising of political awareness to the necessary point. The dominant community is depicted as deliberately fostering class differences in order to promote tension and conflict within the minority community. The more disunited the group is, in the colonialist view, the more systematically it can be exploited. Classes are set against race groups, yet the elites callously promise assimilation to all minorities. Even the underclass is useful, in terms of the colonial model, providing the elites with a reservoir of cheap labor whenever wanted.[30]

The Culture of Poverty Issue

The concept of poverty as a subculture means that it is a distinctive way of life, transmitted from one generation to another.[31] This conception has been criticized for locating the causes of poverty in the victims

—the poor families with an allegedly defective culture—rather than in the institutional structure that creates the conditions of poverty.[32] The controversial "Moynihan Report," despite its strong stand for economic equality, attributed black poverty to the allegedly deteriorating ghetto family. The central theme was that economic failure produces men who cannot be strong husbands, so that women often must support and rear children with little male assistance. Children then have unstable family lives and drop out of school unprepared for the job market, thus starting the vicious circle over again. In this way the disintegrating family perpetuates school and work failure, crime, illegitimacy, and welfare dependency.[33]

This reasoning provided the chief rationale for the antipoverty programs designed in the 1960s. For example, Head Start, Upward Bound, and other tutoring programs were attempts to intervene in the transmission of the presumed culture of poverty, and to promote learning of dominant American culture in the schools. Those who supported the denial of a significant voice to representatives of the poor in administering antipoverty funds assumed that such people are too disorganized to have good judgment. Despite the controversy over the concept of the culture of poverty, such programs apparently have expanded educational opportunities for many poor children. Culture of poverty reasoning focused on the outlooks and behavior of poor people, resulting in charges that attention was diverted from implementing civil rights laws and from programs designed to create job opportunities and housing for the poor.

In a study in a highly deprived area of Washington, D.C., it was found that poor black men valued the same goals that other Americans do for marriage, family, education, and work. The interpretation made was that failures to achieve these goals derived from independent experience with the same difficulties their fathers had had, not from the transmission of a separate cultural tradition.[34] The culture concept did not even seem to fit the segment of the poor for which it would seem most apt, the "hard-core" or "disreputable" poor—the lower-lower class. In the black underclass, for example, there evidently were "matriarchal" families, but there were other kinds as well. And family stability was valued among the working poor blacks, so care must be used in generalizing about ghetto family life.

MIDDLE MINORITIES

When a need for a special economic role develops in a society, and the dominant community is unable or unwilling to fill it, a minority group with a competitive advantage for the role may move into the status gap.[35] A *middle minority* occupies an intermediate, marginal status position and performs go-between economic functions of value both to the groups above and below it. Economists have called this the "middleman" function, but "middle" will suffice. Very often the activity is commercial, but it may be lending money, contracting for labor, collecting rents or taxes, or other economic liaison tasks. This role has been common in traditional mass-elite social structures, but middle minorities also occur in complex, pluralistic societies. Typically they are immigrant groups, and sometimes—as in Brazil and the Caribbean area—the role has been assumed by racially mixed groups.

Although the middle minority has higher economic status and prestige than groups below it, it is discriminated against by the dominant group. It has little political power and it depends on the goodwill of the dominant community for its protection. Often it mediates between the upper and lower status groups. Its competition with lower-status minorities is resented and the middle group is usually stereotyped as ambitious, greedy, cunning, and clannish. When violent conflicts erupt between groups above and below it, the middle minority is vulnerable and a fairly safe target. At such times it is inadequately protected by the dominant group, at least partly because the latter benefits from having a buffer group. Evidently Jews performed this buffer role century after century in European countries.[36]

In European colonies it was common to import workers for such purposes as construction and plantation labor. Often these workers were indentured until they had paid for their passage. At the turn of the century the British imported indentured servants from India to build the railroads in Kenya, and some of them remained on to seek economic opportunities. The Indians assumed the middle functions of collecting crops for export and distributing European trade goods. Both the British colonists and the Kenyan peoples valued these services, since they were not able or willing to deal with each other. The British discriminated against the Indians in employment and in restrictions on landowning and political participation; they paid them less than half what the British got for the same jobs, but much more than the Africans were paid. When Kenya became independent in 1963, heavy restrictions were placed on the rights of Indians to engage in trade and to gain citizenship, and large numbers of them were dismissed from governmental or private jobs. In 1970 the exodus of Indians from Kenya became considerable, and probably would have been greater if unrestricted entry into either Great Britain or India had been possible. Britons have fared much better than the Indians have under Kenyan rule.[37]

In the Philippines the Chinese began their middle role by collecting crops for export and selling European trade goods under Spanish colonial, and later under American, control. They branched into various kinds of commercial activity, and even into manufacturing and contracting, until "Chinese" and "businessman" became virtual synonyms in the Philippines. Despite some intermarriage and a tendency toward assimilation, the Filipino resentment of the Chinese middle activities continued. The Chinese were stereotyped as selfish and clannish, and their culture was despised. When independence came in 1946 the new government began restricting the business activity of the Chinese severely, including their exclusion from owning land, exploiting natural resources, or running public utilities. In 1954 the Retail Trade Nationalization Law excluded the Chinese from retail trade, and the effect of this was expanded by the courts to cover wholesaling. Their participation in the professions and government service was largely prohibited. The Chinese have survived this severe discrimination, but they obviously had fared better under the colonial regimes. The prospects for assimilation are uncertain, and further conflicts and even expulsion remain possible.[38]

The sojourner theory of middle minorities, formulated by Bonacich, is an attempt to explain the phenomenon primarily in terms of the characteristics of the group. A *sojourner* is an immigrant who plans to return home rather than to settle permanently.[39] Not all sojourning groups become middle minorities, but having the sojourner outlook is held to be a necessary condition.[40] The sojourner concentrates on working hard and saving for the goal of returning home, so the occupations preferred are those that can be liquidated or transported easily, such as trade, the professions, truck farming, and such skilled work as that of jeweler, shoemaker, metalsmith, laundry operator, or restaurant owner. Sojourners rarely had such occupations as these in their homelands, since, like most migrants, they moved to improve their lot. Yet the culture of origin seems to affect adaptability and the inclination toward certain middle occupations. Many middle groups have observed middle minorities in their home countries, such as the Parsis in India or the Armenians in Syria.[41]

Sojourners tend to maintain their own culture and to resist assimilation. They help each other with easy-credit loans for new ventures and with other forms of mutual assistance, according to the theory, often becoming heavily concentrated in certain businesses. Sometimes ethnic guilds and guildlike organizations have even been able to exercise monopoly control over supply, prices, and business locations.[42] This apparently was accomplished by Japanese-Americans in a shoemaker guild early in this century.[43]

Finally, according to the Bonacich sojourner theory, the inherent unity of the middle minority is strengthened by hostile reactions to its activities. Latent conflicts with its buyers, renters, and clients sometimes erupt in violent outbursts against the middle group. There are conflicts with competing businesses, both in the minority and dominant groups. Conflicts may occur with organized labor over the "cheap labor" issue. Charges are heard that the group is unassimilable and even disloyal, that like a parasite it is draining the country of its resources, and that it is gaining undue power.[44] These reactions reinforce the *outlook of the stranger community*—the desire to retain the advantages of remaining free and unassimilated.[45] Thus, even though the sojourner dream of returning home may be abandoned, the group strongly resists assimilation and struggles to maintain the advantages of its stranger status.

Let us examine the sojourner theory. The culture and sense of identity of the middle minority are clearly important, but so are the societal conditions in which they function. Very important among these conditions are the realities of discrimination against the group by the dominant community. For example, before it is assumed that an apparently heavy concentration of a middle group in a particular occupation was entirely a matter of choice, an answer must be given to the question of how many kinds of work they have been systematically excluded from.[46] Perhaps middle minorities are largely absent from major industries, and from kinds of agriculture that tie up capital,[47] because discriminatory practices have excluded them.[48] In interpreting the fact that about half of all Jews in Germany were in "trade, commerce, and peddling" in 1925 as compared with only about 10 percent of the general population[49]—in addition to the need for clarifying what portion of this was peddling—we need to know how much economic activity Jews had been excluded from for some time.

It is very difficult for most first-generation immigrants to get together the small amounts of capital necessary for family enterprises, much less for industrial concerns or large farms or ranches. Perhaps the reason so many businesses of the foreign-born can be liquidated or transported so easily is that they are usually so small. Further, we need to know the extent to which the ready availability of certain businesses was at least originally due to their high risk, or to the stigma attached to them. There is a high risk factor in the clothing business, for instance, and also in small groceries and restaurants. There is high risk, in fact, in small retailing in general. Money-lending had a heavy stigma in the Muslim areas in which Armenians, other Christian groups, and Jews performed that middle task for so long. The small-scale rag and junk business has been both low-status and risky. The entertainment business has often carried a stigma, as it did early in this century when the first shoestring filmmaking activities were associated with burlesque. Alert, adaptive minorities find such marginal economic areas open to them, while safer, larger, and more respectable businesses are controlled by the dominant community.[50]

The sojourner theory has raised significant questions about the culture and solidarity of the middle minority. Unfortunately, the effect of attributing middle experiences almost solely to the group's characteristics is to blame the victim, just as the culture of poverty explanation does. An adequate theory must account for the outlook and sense of identity of the middle minority, but also for the status gap and the pattern of discrimination. The middle minority must be seen in interaction with other groups, and in relation to the institutions of the host society.[51]

CONCLUSION

The major aim in this chapter has been to illuminate the relationships between social class and patterns of ethnic stratification. Comparative perspectives are valuable in analyzing stratification, yet class and caste systems are complex and there is value in concentrating primarily on one society. Except for the discussion of the uneasy patterns of accommodation involving the middle minority, most of the consideration of stratified accommodation has been concerned with the American class system. Upward mobility and other aspects of conflict and change in stratified patterns have been emphasized. Much of the rest of the book is concerned with stratified accommodation and with changes in it, so this chapter adds essential ingredients to the theoretical approach outlined in Part I.

FOOTNOTES

1   Gordon, 1974, pp. 40–42.
2   Warner, 1941.
3   Warner, Meeker & Eells, 1949.
4   Parsons, 1966, pp. 92–128.
5   Newman, 1973, Ch. 4.
6   Kinloch, 1974, pp. 96–97, 154–58, Ch. 15.
7   Tabb, 1971, pp. 437–38.
8   Newman, 1973, pp. 24–30; Van den Berghe, 1967, pp. 25–34.
9   Newman, 1973, pp. 31–33.
10 Noel, 1968. See also, Rose, 1976, Ch. 6; Frazier, 1949, Ch. 2.
11 McLemore, 1973.
12 Shibutani & Kwan, 1965, Ch. 9, Ch. 20.
13 Acker, 1973; Nilson, 1976.
14 Gordon, 1958, pp. 252–53.
15 Gordon, 1964, pp. 47–54; Ransford, 1977, pp. 55–63.
16 Warner & Srole, 1945, pp. 78, 225.

17 Anderson, 1937, Ch. 3.
18 Warner & Associates, 1949, pp. 24–26, 171–85.
19 Hollingshead, 1949.
20 Davis, Gardner & Gardner, 1941.
21 Burgess, 1960, p. 28.
22 Glenn, 1962.
23 Thomlinson, 1976, pp. 214–15.
24 Gordon, 1964, p. 52.
25 Kramer & Leventman, 1961, pp. 3–27, 62–74.
26 Blackwell, 1975, pp. 73–94; Billingsley, 1968, pp. 123–40.
27 Tabb, 1971, p. 438.
28 Shibutani & Kwan, 1965, pp. 491–501; Rose, 1976, pp. 30–32.
29 Blackwell, 1975, pp. 96–98.
30 Staples, 1976, Ch. 7.
31 Lewis, 1966, p. 19; Roach & Gursslin, 1967, pp. 387–89.
32 Rainwater, 1966; Valentine, 1968; Irelan, Moles & O'Shea, 1969; Rainwater, 1974.
33 Moynihan, 1965; Rainwater & Yancey, 1967.
34 Liebow, 1967, pp. 208–31.
35 Blalock, 1967, pp. 79–81.
36 Blalock, 1967, pp. 81–84.
37 Hunt & Walker, 1974, pp. 111–24.
38 Hunt & Walker, 1974, pp. 92–111.
39 Siu, 1952.
40 Bonacich, 1973, p. 585.
41 Bonacich, 1973, pp. 583–89.
42 Stryker, 1959, p. 45; Eitzen, 1971, p. 131.
43 Light, 1972, pp. 68–70.
44 Bonacich, 1973, pp. 589–94.
45 Wolff, 1950, pp. 402–8; Levine, 1977, pp. 17–20.
46 Kephart, 1949.
47 Bonacich, 1973, p. 585.
48 Rose & Rose, 1948, pp. 70–100, 162–66.
49 Bonacich, 1973, pp. 587–88; Stryker, 1959, p. 342.
50 Glazer & Moynihan, 1963, pp. 151–74; McWilliams, 1948, pp. 142–54.
51 Yancey, Ericksen & Juliani, 1976.

REFERENCES

Acker, Joan
1973 "Women and Social Stratification: A Case of Intellectual Sexism." American Journal of Sociology 78, 4 (January): 936–45.
Anderson, E. L.
1937 We Americans: A Study of Cleavage in an American City. Cambridge, Massachusetts: Harvard University Press.

Billingsley, Andrew
1968   Black Families in America. Englewood Cliffs, New Jersey: Prentice-Hall, Inc.
Blackwell, James E.
1975   The Black Community: Diversity and Unity. New York: Dodd, Mead and Co.
Blalock, Hubert M., Jr.
1967   Toward a Theory of Minority-Group Relations. New York: Capricorn Books.
Bonacich, Edna
1973   "A Theory of Middleman Minorities." American Sociological Review 38, 5 (October): 583–94.
Burgess, M. Elaine
1960   Negro Leadership in a Southern City. Chapel Hill: University of North Carolina Press.
Cayton, Horace, and St. Claire Drake
1945   Black Metropolis: A Study of Negro Life in a Northern City. New York: Harper and Row.
Davis, Allison, Burleigh B. Gardner, and Mary R. Gardner
1941   Deep South. Chicago: University of Chicago Press.
Eitzen, D. Stanley
1971   "Two Minorities: The Jews of Poland and the Chinese of the Philippines," pp. 117–38 in Norman R. Yetman and C. Hoy Steele (eds.), Majority and Minority. Boston: Allyn and Bacon.
Frazier, E. Franklin
1949   The Negro in the United States. New York: The Macmillan Co.
Glazer, Nathan, and Daniel P. Moynihan
1963   Beyond the Melting Pot. Cambridge, Massachusetts: The M.I.T. Press and Harvard University Press.
Glenn, Norval D.
1962   "Changes in the American Occupational Structure and Occupational Gains of Negroes During the 1940's." Social Forces 41 (December): 188–95.
Gordon, Milton M.
1958   Social Class in American Sociology. Durham, North Carolina: Duke University Press.
1964   Assimilation in American Life. New York: Oxford University Press.
Hollingshead, A. B.
1949   Elmtown's Youth. New York: John Wiley and Sons.
Hunt, Chester L., and Lewis Walker
1974   Ethnic Dynamics: Patterns of Intergroup, Relations in Various Societies. Homewood, Ill.: The Dorsey Press.
Irelan, Lola M., Oliver C. Moles, and Robert M. O'Shea
1969   "Ethnicity, Poverty, and Selected Attitudes: A Test of the 'Culture of Poverty' Hypothesis." Social Forces 47 (June): 405–13.
Kephart, William M.
1949   "What is the Position of the Jewish Economy in the United States?" Social Forces 28 (December): 153–64.
Kinloch, Graham C.
1974   The Dynamics of Race Relations: A Sociological Analysis. New York: McGraw-Hill Book Co.

Kramer, Judith R., and Seymour Leventman
1961 Children of the Gilded Ghetto. New Haven, Connecticut: Yale University Press.

Levine, Donald N.
1977 "Simmel at a Distance: On the History and Systematics of the Sociology of the Stranger." Sociological Focus, 10, 1 (January): 15–29.

Lewis, Oscar
1966 "The Culture of Poverty." Scientific American (October): 19–25.

Liebow, Elliot
1967 Tally's Corner. Boston: Little, Brown and Co.

Light, Ivan
1972 Ethnic Enterprise in America. Berkeley: University of California Press.

Lipset, Seymour Martin
1976 "Equality and Inequality," Ch. 7 in R. K. Merton and R. Nisbet, Contemporary Social Problems. New York: Harcourt, Brace, Jovanovich, Inc.

McLemore, Dale S.
1973 "The Origins of Mexican American Subordination in Texas." Social Science Quarterly 53: 656–70.

McWilliams, Carey
1948 A Mask for Privilege: Anti-Semitism in America. Boston: Little, Brown and Co.

Moynihan, Daniel P., Paul Barton, et al.
1965 The Negro Family: The Case for National Action. Washington, D.C.: United States Department of Labor.

Newman, William M.
1973 American Pluralism: A Study of Minority Groups and Social Theory. New York: Harper and Row.

Nilson, Linda Burzotta
1976 "The Social Standing of a Married Woman." Social Problems 23, 5 (June): 581–92.

Noel, Donald L.
1968 "A Theory of the Origin of Ethnic Stratification." Social Problems 16, 2 (Fall): 157–72.

Parsons, Talcott
1966 "On the Concept of Political Power," in Reinhard Bendix and S. M. Lipset (eds.), Class, Status, and Power. New York: The Free Press.

Rainwater, Lee
1966 "Crucible of Identity: The Negro Lower-Class Family." Daedalus 95 (Winter): 172–216.
1974 What Money Buys: Inequality and the Social Meanings of Income. New York: Basic Books.

Rainwater, Lee, and William L. Yancey
1967 The Moynihan Report and the Politics of Controversy. Cambridge, Massachusetts: The M.I.T. Press.

Ransford, H. Edward
1977 Race and Class in American Society. Cambridge, Massachusetts: Schenkman Publishing Co., Inc.

Roach, Jack L., and Orville R. Gursslin
1967 "An Evaluation of the Concept 'Culture of Poverty.' " Social Forces 45, 3 (March): 383–92.

Rose, Arnold, and Caroline Rose
1948   America Divided. New York: Alfred A. Knopf, Inc.
Rose, Jerry D.
1976   Peoples: The Ethnic Dimension in Human Relations. Chicago: Rand McNally College Publishing Co.
Shibutani, Tamotsu, and Kian M. Kwan
1965   Ethnic Stratification: A Comparative Approach. New York: The Macmillan Co.
Siu, Paul C. P.
1952   "The Sojourner." American Journal of Sociology 58 (July): 34–44.
Staples, Robert
1976   Introduction to Black Sociology. New York: McGraw-Hill Book Co.
Stryker, Sheldon
1959   "Social Structure and Prejudice." Social Problems 6 (Spring): 340–54.
Tabb, William K.
1971   "Race Relations Models and Social Change." Social Problems 18 (Spring): 431–44.
Thomlinson, Ralph
1976   Population Dynamics: Causes and Consequences of World Demographic Change, 2nd Edition. New York: Random House.
Valentine, Charles A.
1968   Culture and Poverty: Critique and Counter-Proposals. Chicago: The University of Chicago Press.
Van den Berghe, Pierre L.
1967   Race and Racism. New York: Wiley.
Warner, W. Lloyd, and Associates
1949   Democracy in Jonesville. New York: Harper and Row.
Warner, W. Lloyd, and Paul S. Lunt
1941   The Social Life of a Modern Community (Yankee City Series, Vol. 1). New Haven, Connecticut: Yale University Press.
1942   The Status System of a Modern Community (Yankee City Series, Vol. 2). New Haven, Connecticut: Yale University Press.
Warner, W. Lloyd, Marchia Meeker, and Kenneth Eells
1949   Social Class in America. Chicago: Science Research Associates, Inc.
Warner, W. Lloyd, and Leo Srole
1945   The Social System of American Ethnic Groups (Yankee City Series, Vol. 3). New Haven, Connecticut: Yale University Press.
Wolff, Kurt H.
1950   The Sociology of Georg Simmel. Glencoe, Illinois: The Free Press.
Yancey, William L., Eugene P. Ericksen, and Richard N. Juliani
1976   "Emergent Ethnicity: A Review and Reformulation." American Sociological Review 41, 3 (June): 391–403.

5

Race and Racist Ideology

In physical anthropology and biology, *races are classifications of human beings on the basis of average differences in physical traits.* People's beliefs in society about actual or presumed racial groups may bear little if any resemblance to the current scientific knowledge, but their beliefs are the basis on which groups interact with each other. The sociologist's interest is in the role of sets of beliefs about race in intergroup relations. These systems of belief are more readily grasped after a brief consideration of the physical anthropology of race.

RACE IN SCIENCE

Races as Statistical Categories

A great deal of effort has gone into the quest for a satisfactory scheme of racial categories. Until midcentury the implicit goal was to validate a set of fixed racial types—long-standing, genetically stable groupings. For decades it has been apparent that even the best of the typologies provide only rough, overlapping categories, representing average differences. From the standpoint of physical structure races are not discrete categories; they are *subspecies groups.*[1] Identifying groupings below the species level is arbitrary and not very satisfactory.[2] Without the great preoccupation with race in the society this scientific quest might long since have subsided. For some time there has been a strongly articulated view in anthropology that the concept of race is misleading and should not receive so much scientific attention,[3] but this position has not gained widespread support in social science.

THE ANATOMICAL APPROACH   Until midcentury the racial typologists concentrated on measuring anatomical traits, especially the visible ones such as the shape of the head, nose, and body, the length of arms and legs, and the color of skin, hair, and eyes. The assumption was that clear differences would be found in clusters of traits from one race group to another, but such complexes were not demonstrated to exist. Individual traits of human anatomy apparently are transmitted independently, each with its own Mendelian ratio. Further, no single trait provides a dependable criterion for separating mankind into discrete physical groups, although some were found to work better than others.

One of the most reliable traits for anatomical classification is hair form. If a cross-section of a hair strand is round, the hair will be straight (liotrichy); a hair with a fairly flat cross-section will be very curly (ulotrichy); and one with an intermediate, oval cross-section will tend to be wavy (cymotrichy). Another relatively dependable criterion is the nasal index—the ratio of the length of the nose to its width—yielding the narrow, wide, and intermediate types. Another such ratio is the shape of the head (the cephalic index), providing the round-headed, long-headed, and in-between types. The cephalic index helps distinguish the major racial groupings fairly well, but not the subracial ones. The color of skin, hair, and eyes are only somewhat dependable for racial classification, and the same is true for lip form (degree of eversion). Still other anatomical traits, such as stature and breadth of chest, proved to be even less reliable.

Using combinations of anatomical indexes, racial typologists produced classification systems usually composed of three, four, or five races. Some scholars have concentrated on refining the subgroups and have ended up with many races.[4] Kroeber's scheme of three races, each with subgroups, is as follows:[5]

1 Caucasoid
   a Nordic
   b Alpine
   c Mediterranean
   d Hindu (dark skin)
   e Ainu (some noncaucasoid traits)
2 Mongoloid
   a Asiatic
   b Oceanic
   c American Indians
3 Negroid
   a African
   b Oceanic
   c Negrito
   d Bushmen (some nonnegroid traits).

These groupings correspond to those popularly known, respectively, as white, yellow, and black. On the average, caucasoids have the longest heads and mongoloids the roundest; mongoloids the straightest hair and negroids the most tightly curled; caucasoids the narrowest noses and negroids the broadest. Other traits are also used in applying Kroeber's scheme.

There are three groups that Kroeber could not fit into these categories. The Polynesians have traits of two of the major races, and may have resulted from the mixing of caucasoid peoples from Indonesia (or elsewhere) and mongoloid peoples from Southeast Asia. The native Australians and also the Veddoids of Sri Lanka (Ceylon) have both negroid and caucasoid traits, and may be hybrid groups. It should be added that many populations in today's world are racially mixed, as illustrated by the Malay Peninsula, a large proportion of the people of Latin America, and by American blacks. Kroeber's race groups are a better fit for the world geography of the time before European colonial expansion than since, but the types may still be used to describe migrants and mixed populations.

Asiatic mongoloids include the Chinese, Japanese, Koreans and other peoples north of China, and the Vietnamese and other peoples south of China. American Indians are believed to have migrated from Siberia when there was a land bridge to Alaska, then gradually to have spread into North and South America. Oceanic negroid peoples are in the Melanesian (southeast) area of the Pacific. Negritos are pygmy or dwarf peoples found in Zaire and other parts of Africa, in the Andaman Islands, the Malay Peninsula, the Philippines, and in Southern India. The Bushmen of Southern Africa are a short negroid group with relatively light skin color. Before modern times there was so much mixing of the various sub-Saharan groups, along with some amalgamation with Arabs and other caucasoids, that most African groups fit the same subracial type.[6]

"Hindu" is an unfortunate choice for the "dark white" subgroup of caucasoids, since it refers to a religion and Hindi is a language. At any rate, a large portion of the population of India, Pakistan, Bangladesh, and contiguous areas have dark skin, but otherwise they have caucasoid traits. Skin color is poorly correlated with other racial traits. The nordics of Northern Europe (including England and Northern France) have a somewhat higher ratio, but not a preponderance, of blondes and blue-eyed people than other caucasoids have. Alpines are typically the round-headed, stocky caucasoids of Central Europe, including northernmost Italy and part of France. Mediterranean caucasoids include Greeks, Arabs, Jews, Irish (and other Celtic or Gaulic peoples), most Italians, Spanish, and Iranians, and many French. Most Turks are Alpine or Mediterranean, with only a very slight trace of mongoloid ancestry. Race and culture must not be confused. For example, Semites and Aryans are both language categories, not race groups.[7] Jews and Arabs are ethnic groups, not races.

The overlapping statistical nature of anatomical categories like Kroeger's has led to the replacement of the fixed-type assumption with the "breeding population" approach. The view is that geographic and social barriers in the past have isolated populations, thus stabilizing the gene frequencies for particular traits and producing relatively discrete racial groupings. In one such effort nine major races and thirty-two subraces are identified.[8] This gene frequency approach has been used for interpreting anatomical traits, but increasingly for studying physiological and other internal biological characteristics, including blood types.

BLOOD TYPING   Blood types A, B, AB, and O have been found to have different frequencies among the (anatomically identified) caucasoid, mongoloid, and negroid groups. All four types are found in all three of the race groups, however, and the differences are not large. Put another way, the correlation between blood type and external anatomical traits is small. There are other classifications of blood types besides this commonly known one, depending on the variables and the purpose involved. It now seems unlikely that blood typing can contribute significantly to racial classification.

Sickle-cell anemia is a genetic, blood-connected factor that illustrates the dubious relationship of blood type to race. This disease is frequent among American blacks and West African areas from which the slaves came. However, it is also frequent among nonnegroid populations in Greece, southern India, and other areas of the world. In fact, the sickle-cell trait in the past was found in areas of the world that had high rates of malaria, and it appears to have been an adaptive response to that disease. Knowledge of blood-related traits may help to understand human diseases, but caution is in order in suggesting racial interpretations.[9]

RACISM AS IDEOLOGY

Racism is the use of a set of beliefs about race groups to justify institutional discrimination against groups. So defined, racism does not include all institutional discrimination—only that for which justifications are offered in terms of racist beliefs (see Chapter 14). Minorities, as well as dominant groups, may hold racist beliefs. Ideologies of group domination need not involve racist beliefs but they very often do, even when the group differences are cultural rather than racial. Sexist ideology, justifying male domination of females, is similar to racism, and some of the parallels are indicated in the discussion below. Comparisons of racist beliefs and related scientific knowledge are also made.

In Chapter 3 the content of ideologies has been described as consisting of five areas of belief: those concerning group goals, the means preferred for reaching the goals, value priorities related both to goals and means, existential beliefs related both to means and to the operation of norms in the desired state of affairs, and a general image of society. Examples of all five of these will be apparent in the following discussion of five racist beliefs, but the emphasis is on existential beliefs.

Five Beliefs Found in Racism

1. Belief That Some Races Are Physically Superior to Others   Often the form of this belief is that the races can be ranked from the physically strongest to the weakest. Much of the evidence put forth to support this belief consists of racial differences in rates of selected diseases. A complete summary of these differences indicates that a given group appears strong in some respects and weak in others. For instance, among the diseases for which blacks in the United States have traditionally had higher rates than whites are tuberculosis, infant mortality, and sickle-cell anemia; but whites have had higher rates of cancer and several heart diseases. In evaluating such data, differences in group experience must be taken into account—differences in occupation, income, housing, sanitation, nutrition, medical care, education,

and in the development over time of group immunities to diseases. Similar care in controlling for differences in group experience must be used in interpreting racial differences in longevity.[10]

Longevity also poses a problem for those who accept the sexist belief that males are biologically superior to females, since, in our time and place, women have a longer average life expectancy than men. Men have greater muscular strength, yet throughout history women have done a large share of the heavy, physical labor. Men have higher rates of some diseases, and women of others, but these differences apparently decline when occupations and other life experiences are similar. Yet, selective as the "proof" must be, belief in male physical superiority is an important pillar in the ideology supporting traditional sex roles. So is the belief that men and women have biologically different intellectual and temperamental qualities,[11] as noted in Chapter 3.

2.   BELIEF THAT SOME RACES ARE MENTALLY SUPERIOR TO OTHERS
The belief that race groups can be ranked from the most to the least intelligent seemed logical to many Americans after World War I, in the light of differential performance on standardized tests designed to measure intelligence. The average scores of Indians, Mexican Americans, blacks, and immigrants from Southern and Eastern Europe were especially low at that time. Well before World War II, however, the scientific agreement that there was no proof for the above belief had become virtually unanimous. This conclusion rested in large part on the problem of the validity of the tests. Assumed learning capacity (intelligence quotient) cannot be directly measured, thus so-called IQ tests measure an inextricable combination of learning potential and what has been learned. Test scores were found not to be constant; they improved when learning opportunities improved.

Social experiences, including cultural conditioning, were found to be reflected in the test scores. Degree of ability in the language in which a written test is given greatly affects the performance. Other factors shown to be correlated with IQ test scores included the amount and quality of schooling, social class background, health, motivation, attitude toward competition, and attitude toward speed.[12] The most widely used IQ test, the Stanford-Binet, is certainly not "culture-free"; it was standardized on white, middle-class Americans. It has also usually been administered by white, middle-class Americans, and minority children have been found to do better if given the test by a member of their own group.

Also crucial in the scientific rejection of the belief in the mental superiority and inferiority of race groups was evidence that groups dramatically improve their IQ test scores after gaining experience with the matters included in the tests. After living for some time in the North, black migrants from the South had higher average scores than blacks who had remained in the South. Black migrants also had higher average scores than the whites in some Southern states. The longer a sample of the blacks lived in New York City, the more their scores increased.[13] In Philadelphia, migrant black schoolchildren's scores increased steadily each year; and, by the time those who had migrated as first-graders were in the ninth grade, their IQ scores were less than one point below those of children born in the city.[14] For some time the scores of Indian groups averaged no higher than in the 80s, well below the median average of 100 for the test. After oil was discovered on the land of the Osage Indians, and their education and living standards had greatly improved, their average score was 104 on a nonlanguage IQ test and 100 on a language-dependent test.[15] Generalizing from these and other observations, Pettigrew suggests that average IQ test scores improve, "when any racial group moves from a restrictive to a comparatively stimulating environment."[16]

The race and IQ issue became a scientific controversy again in the 1960s, perhaps in part due to the publication of a report showing large racial and ethnic differences in the test scores of 605,000 pupils from some four thousand schools across the country. The scores were from students in the first, third, sixth, ninth, and twelfth grades. Blacks had the lowest average score of the racial and ethnic groups focused on; next lowest were Puerto Ricans, next Mexican Americans, and then Indians.[17] Jensen, an educational psychologist on whose writings much of the controversy has centered, has maintained that a 15-point gap in the average IQ scores of American blacks and whites demonstrates a racial difference in the capacity for problem solving and abstract reasoning. He asserts that 80 percent of what is measured by IQ tests is hereditary and only 20 percent environmental, so that compensatory educational programs can never make blacks the equal of whites in "conceptual learning."[18]

The critiques of Jensen's interpretations began at once,[19] and have continued, many of them concerned with his oversimplifications of complex problems of method and theory. His motives, and the role of science in perpetuating racism, have also been questioned.[20] His assumption of the largely genetic determination of IQ scores, and the presumed connection of the heritability of intelligence with that of race, have been challenged.[21] Jensen has repeated the errors of interpretation of the meaning of IQ scores, and of assuming that racial traits are inherited in clusters. He has confused the genetics of physical traits with that of problem solving.[22] And, despite the thin deductive ground on which his conclusions rest, he has made broad policy suggestions.

3.   BELIEF THAT RACE CAUSES CULTURE   One form of this belief is that each of the major race groups has a distinct "racial culture" that is inherited along with its physical traits. Thus it is just "in" all whites

to think and act in certain ways, and all blacks in other ways. This stereotyped belief is easy to refute, for those wishing to consider all the evidence, by noting the wide cultural variation within each major race. The Japanese, Chinese, Thai, American Indians, and other mongoloid groups have had very different cultures, just as Norwegians, Poles, Greeks, Arabs, and other caucasoid groups have. The many traditional cultures of blacks in Africa are different from each other, and all of them differ greatly from those of blacks in Latin America and the United States.

The more common form of the belief that race causes culture attributes national or other ethnic traits to common biological ancestry. It is assumed that a group that shares a common cultural tradition has been an inbreeding population for a long time, and that the shared physical and cultural traits are genetically transmitted together. People in the ethnic group are presumed to act as they do because it is "in their blood." The Germans, it has often been believed, are just naturally industrious and oriented toward authority. The Germans and most other European national groups actually reflect a great mixture of biological stocks, due to the many waves of conquest. During the period of European colonial expansion it became common to refer to any culturally distinctive group, whatever its physical features, as a race. The strange ways of the natives appeared to be "born into" them.

A particular application of the belief that race causes culture is the notion of racial morality. A race, or an ethnic group called a race, may be thought to be naturally prone to criminality, or sexual looseness, or drug use, or dishonest business practices. Their alleged moral depravity is attributed to racial heredity. Adequate comparisons across cultural and social class lines readily show this type of belief to be an overgeneralized and distorted view, but we have seen that group stereotypes may be reified so that negative evidence is ignored or explained away. A minority group may have a high rate of crime or drug use at least partly because it is subjected to disproportionate surveillance, prosecution, and conviction.[23] In this way law-enforcement officials reinforce the stereotype. The fact that members of the group with higher social class status do not have high rates of deviance is ignored by those determined to maintain a genetic interpretation.[24] Also, white-collar crime, other deviant behavior in the dominant community, and discrimination against minorities are overlooked by those who believe immorality is natural for the other race, but not for one's own.

The belief that culture is caused by race, along with some other racist beliefs, involves a profound confusion of race and culture.[25] Racial traits are physical, and they are transmitted from generation to generation through the genes. Cultural traits are learned; they are transmitted in the process of socialization by communication. People have the biological capacity to learn a culture, but it must be learned.

Parental values and habits cannot be transmitted genetically. A Korean baby who is adopted by a (non-Korean) family in St. Louis will internalize American culture, and will probably learn little of Korean ways. The medium (carrier) of culture is communication; the medium of race is the genes.[26]

4. BELIEF THAT RACE DETERMINES TEMPERAMENT   Images of other races or supposed races include stereotyped views of their temperamental dispositions, and very often the belief that they are inherited with racial traits. Examples are the belief that Italians are "by nature" emotional and gregarious, or that blacks are naturally rhythmic, or that the Chinese or the English have an "inborn reserve." Such stereotypes overgeneralize and distort observed conduct, and ignore wide individual variations, yet there are average group differences in personal disposition. Students of culture and personality attribute such differences to cultural conditioning. A person's temperament is assumed to be developed in the process of socialization, or largely so, rather than genetically determined.

A good way to separate the genetic from the processes of cultural transmission involved in temperament is to note major changes in culture and personality in groups that have had a relatively high degree of biological continuity. In the Bronze Age the Scandinavians were bold, raiding, risk-taking seafarers; later they became a much more sedentary, peaceful, industrious people. And, despite the risk that we are dealing in stereotypes, the typically reserved, prudish Englishmen in the Victorian era were descendants of the loud, lusty people of Elizabethan times.[27] Even if temperament is at least partially a function of genetic factors, there is no scientific reason to think it is part of a supposed complex of racial traits.

5. BELIEF THAT RACIAL MIXING LOWERS BIOLOGICAL QUALITY
It is is not surprising that people who believe that physical, mental, and behavioral traits are tied to racial heredity would consider racial amalgamation to be dangerous. All these beliefs are connected with ethnocentric value judgments, so that racial amalgamation is a biological fusing of presumably superior stocks with inferior and detested ones. It allegedly leads to blood poisoning and other physical deterioration, to mental inferiority, to immorality and cultural degeneracy.[28]

In an essay in the first century A.D., the Roman writer Tacitus attributed the advanced culture of the Teutonic Germans to their racial superiority and racial purity. This view was resurrected in France in the mid-nineteenth century by de Gobineau, who held that the cultural superiority of the Aryan (or Nordic) race was due to its racial superiority, and that racial mixture causes a superior race to degenerate.[29] From his views stemmed the claims of Teutonism, Celticism, and Anglo-Saxonism. Thomas Carlyle was among the prominent promoters of

Anglo-Saxon superiority, but Kipling's chauvinism about the British Empire and his slogan of the "white man's burden" became more powerfully appealing.[30]

Richard Wagner, the German composer, cited de Gobineau in support of his views about the heroic superiority of the Aryans and the extreme cultural inferiority of the Jews. Wagner's English son-in-law and biographer—Chamberlain—became a major proponent of Teutonism.[31] Adolph Hitler's views of the Aryans as cultural builders and maintainers and the Jews as destroyers were heavily influenced by Wagner and Chamberlain. Hitler and his chief racial ideologist, Rosenberg, inspired a vast literature on "racial purity" that provided the justification for the Nazi actions against the Jews.[32]

In the United States the American Nordic movement replaced the Anglo-Saxon emphasis by the beginning of the twentieth century. This helped crystallize ideological opposition to immigration, and also to the "mongrelization" of the races, as the Southern system of racial segregation reached its peak. Among the most influential promoters of these views were two lawyers. In 1916 Grant maintained that racial mixture would cause the deterioration of the noble Nordic race. He asserted that blacks cannot be civilized by schools and churches, and that they should be put into totally segregated colonies of manual laborers. He wrote of the unscrupulousness of the Polish Jew, the inferiority of Italians and other Southern and Eastern European immigrants, and he looked with horror on the New York "melting pot."[33] Stoddard called for the sharp restriction of immigration, contending that the one-time largely Nordic population of the country was being drastically lowered by being mixed with Alpines, Mediterraneans, Jews, Asiatics, and other inferior races.[34] It is clear that the fear of amalgamation has been central in racist ideologies.

The genetic mixing of human groups has been going on a very long time, and certainly it is a myth that European national and subracial groups were genetically pure types not so many generations ago. There is no scientific proof that racial mixing leads to lower or higher biological quality. Racially mixed persons are often socially marginal, not a full member of either parent group. Whatever the disadvantages or advantages faced by racially mixed persons in particular situations, they result from social reactions to their physical features. "High" civilizations have sprung up in parts of the world where many peoples have come into contact and become amalgamated, as in the Middle East and Central America. This does not prove the thesis of heterosis (hybrid vigor), but it apparently demonstrates the stimulating effects of cultural contact and communication. Racial mixing may have major social consequences, then, but this is not to be confused with genetics.[35]

The five racist beliefs discussed above are found both in the more organized efforts to express an ideology and in the everyday slogans and explanations people give as they rationalize their actions. Sometimes one belief is prominent, sometimes another, and all of them are at least implied in strong expressions of anxiety about racial mixing. These beliefs also become crystallized in the ways particular groups are defined in society.

The Social Definition of Race

Immigration control is but one example of the consequences of the way a race, or a presumed race, is defined in society. The Gypsies, whose name derives from the fact that they were mistakenly thought to have come from Egypt, have been defined as a race in many European countries. Originally a religious sect in the Punjab region of northwest India (now partly in Pakistan), the Gypsies are caucasoids of the relatively dark, Hindu type. Their language, Romany, is Indo-Aryan, and they have remained largely nomadic, illiterate, and unassimilated wherever they have wandered. In Nazi ideology both the Gypsies and the Jews were defined as degenerate, extremely inferior races who threaten the racial and cultural purity of the Nordics, and both of them were ultimately sent to the gas chambers to be exterminated.

The social and legal definition of American blacks as a whole incorporates the racist beliefs that were used to justify the Southern castelike system. After three and a half centuries of amalgamation, three-fourths or more of all people defined as black Americans have some white ancestry, and many have American Indian ancestry as well. Probably one-fourth of the genes in the black Americans' genetic pool are caucasoid.[36] Most of the amalgamation resulted from access to slave women by white men, but considerable exploitation of black women continued after emancipation.[37]

The social definition of blacks that developed in the South became the nation's social and legal definition, ratified by the courts. The Bureau of the Census follows this definition when it enumerates "negroes," since nations count those things they consider significant. The various instructions to the census takers have been designed to count as blacks all people who are considered as such by their communities.[38] Thus a person who is predominantly (even almost totally) white but who has some known black ancestry is counted as black, obviously a social rather than a biologically meaningful classification. This socio-legal definition has usually been ignored in interpretations of American studies of race and IQ or other matters assumed to be genetic.

If our census takers followed the definition typical of Latin American nations they would count far fewer blacks, because they would include only persons who are pure or nearly pure negroids. In Latin

America the relationship of racial traits to social class status has been quite different from ours, so the social definition of race is different. There is a correlation between lightness of skin and class status, so "white" suggests the middle or upper class. However, color may be outweighed by occupation, wealth, and education, so a great many mulattoes (persons of mixed negroid and caucasoid ancestry) are classed socially as whites.[39]

It is well to remember that students of minorities use the social definition when referring to American blacks, and that this differs from the negroid race as defined in physical anthropology and biology. It has been argued that sociologists should define race groups as they are socially defined,[40] but this would make it very difficult to refer to discrepancies between the societal and biological definitions. All manner of ethnic groups have been perceived as race groups, as we have seen, and the associated beliefs involve genetic assumptions. We need to understand these beliefs, and to be able to relate them to the taxonomy and genetics of human races. It would be awkward to keep repeating "perceived race group," but that is what a socially defined race is.

THE SOCIAL ROLE OF RACISM

Ideologies help groups to justify their actions, both to themselves and others. Most racist ideology has been developed by dominant groups, either to rationalize existing intergroup relations or emergent ones. Often the belief systems emerge to rationalize desired or actual changes in stratified arrangements, such as colonial domination, slavery, or enforced segregation. Then, as these patterns become institutionalized, essentially the same beliefs are used to justify the status quo.[41] Minority people sometimes accept such beliefs as true. Minorities may also develop racist beliefs about their oppressors, or other out-groups, and this plays a role in some of the efforts to resist discrimination.

The views on Aryan superiority were advanced by de Gobineau (who was a French count) to provide justification for the suppression of the masses by the French elite.[42] His ideas clearly played political roles in Germany, France, and England when they were extended to Teutonism, Celticism, and Anglo-Saxonism. These ideas loomed large in the justifications of colonialism, the slave trade, and later in immigration control. Aryan racism was embodied in law in the Nuremberg Laws of 1935, which denied citizenship to all who were not of "German or kindred blood," and anyone with one (full) Jewish grandparent was defined as a Jew. Jews were forbidden to marry Christians, and were legally denied participation in German institutional life. This apparently enhanced German pride and unity, had economic benefits, helped the Nazis to gain and hold power, and to justify aggressive and extended warfare.[43]

Modern and Western societies hold no monopoly on the concept of race or on racist beliefs. Aristotle praised slavery as a valuable institution, saying that peoples lacking in reasoning power cannot be happy with freedom, and that their menial labor frees those with superior minds to concentrate on higher pursuits. His ideas were used to justify slavery in the American South.[44] The Incas of Peru thought the Sun God had chosen them to raise other groups up from their subhuman ways, and they systematically destroyed the historical records of all the peoples with whom they came into contact. The old Japanese term for the Ainu (of the Island of Hokkaido) and for whites in general was "keto," meaning hairy barbarian.[45] The traditional Japanese view that they were divinely chosen to be courageous and intellectually superior was used to justify their policies of military expansion before and during World War II. Chauvinistic ethnocentrism has often become racism.

In Chapter 3 some evidence was noted that the acceptance of racist beliefs has declined in the United States in recent decades. At the same time the culture of poverty concept (see Chapter 4) has had wide currency, and in public discussion it has been applied chiefly to the racial minorities. Even when racist beliefs decline (or at least cease to be publicly respectable), a group may still be blamed for its own poverty by pointing to its defective culture. Such concepts as the culture of poverty may be less virile, however, than racist beliefs. Racism seems to have the potential for justifying the most bestial extremes in group domination. Therefore, knowledge of how racist beliefs become less acceptable to people is of great importance.

FOOTNOTES

1 Osborne, 1971, p. 163.
2 Howells, 1971, pp. 4–5.
3 Montagu, 1964, Ch. 1.
4 Hooton, 1948, Part V; Coon, 1962; 1965.
5 Kroeber, 1948, p. 140.
6 Reuter, 1970, pp. 23–24.
7 Coon, 1958, Chs. 4, 5, 10; Snyder, 1962, Chs. 4, 8.

8 Garn, 1965.

9 Goldsby, 1971, pp. 97–101; Newman, 1973, pp. 266–67; Damon, 1971, pp. 65–72.

10 Reuter, 1970, Ch. 10.

11 Montagu, 1964, Ch. 9.

12 Pettigrew, 1971, pp. 95–106; Loehlin, Lindsey & Spuhler, 1975, pp. 62–71.

13 Klineberg, 1935.

14 Lee, 1951.

15 Rohrer, 1942.

16 Pettigrew, 1971, pp. 106–13.

17 Coleman, Campbell, et al., 1966.

18 Jensen, 1969.

19 Deutsch, 1969.

20 Newman, 1973, pp. 266–74.

21 Lewontin, 1975; Layzer, 1975; Loehlin, Lindsey & Spuhler, 1975, Ch. 4.

22 Montagu, 1975, pp. 1–16.

23 Piliavin & Briar, 1964; Ferdinand & Luchterhand, 1970.

24 Wolfgang, 1964, p. 16.

25 Montagu, 1964, Ch. 12.

26 Montagu, 1964, p. 228.

27 Montagu, 1964, p. 249.

28 Snyder, 1962, pp. 23–24.

29 de Gobineau, 1853–55; Newman, 1973, pp. 255–57.

30 Snyder, 1962, Chs. 4, 5, 6.

31 Chamberlain, 1899.

32 Hitler, 1943; Rosenberg, 1934; Snyder, 1962, Ch. 9.

33 Grant, 1916.

34 Stoddard, 1920.

35 Berry, 1965, pp. 280–87.

36 Pettigrew, 1975, p. xiii.

37 Rose, 1956, pp. 44–51; Frazier, 1957, pp. 67–68, 185–87, 310–11.

38 Thomlinson, 1965, pp. 440–44.

39 Wagley, 1952, p. 14; Edwards, 1968, Ch. 6; Pitt-Rivers, 1972.

40 Kinloch, 1974, pp. 51–53.

41 Shibutani & Kwan, 1965, pp. 241–49.

42 Newman, 1973, p. 255.

43 Snyder, 1962, p. 85.

44 Campbell, 1974.

45 Shibutani & Kwan, 1965, pp. 245–48.

REFERENCES

Campbell, Mavis
1974 "Aristotle and Black Slavery: A Study in Race Prejudice." Race 15, 3 (January): 283–301.

Chamberlain, Houston Stewart
1899   Foundations of the Nineteenth Century, trans. John Lees, 2 vols. London: Bodley Head Ltd.
Coleman, James S., Ernest Q. Campbell, et al.
1966   Equality of Educational Opportunity. Washington, D.C.: U.S. Government Printing Office.
Coon, Carleton S.
1958   Caravan, Rev. Edition. New York: Henry Holt and Co.
1962   The Origin of Races. New York: Alfred A. Knopf, Inc.
Coon, Carleton, Stanley M. Garn, and J. B. Birdsell
1950   Races. Springfield, Illinois: Charles C Thomas.
Damon, Albert
1971   "Race, Ethnic Group and Disease," pp. 57–74 in Richard H. Osborne, The Biological and Social Meaning of Race. San Francisco: W. H. Freeman and Co.
de Gobineau, Arthur
1853–55   Essai sur inégalité des races humaines, trans. Adrian Collins. London: Heinemann.
Deutsch, Martin
1969   "Happenings on the Way Back to the Forum: Social Science, IQ, and Race Differences Revisited." Harvard Educational Review 39: 1–35.
Edwards, G. Franklin (ed.)
1968   E. Franklin Frazier on Race Relations. Chicago: University of Chicago Press.
Ferdinand, Theodore N., and Elmer G. Luchterhand
1970   "Inner-City Youth, The Police, The Juvenile Court, and Justice." Social Problems 17 (Spring): 510–27.
Frazier, E. Franklin
1957   The Negro in the United States, Rev. Edition. New York: The Macmillan Co.
Garn, Stanley M.
1965   Human Races, 2nd Edition. Springfield, Illinois: Charles C Thomas.
Grant, Madison
1916   The Passing of a Great Race. New York: Scribner.
Hitler, Adolph
1943   Mein Kampf, 805th–809th printing. Munich.
Hooton, Ernest A.
1948   Up From the Ape. New York: The Macmillan Co.
Howells, William W.
1971   "The Meaning of Race," pp. 4–10 in Richard H. Osborne, The Biological and Social Meaning of Race. San Francisco: W. H. Freeman and Co.
Jensen, Arthur R.
1969   "How Much Can We Boost IQ and Scholastic Achievement?" Harvard Educational Review 39: 1–123.
Kinloch, Graham C.
1974   The Dynamics of Race Relations. New York: McGraw-Hill Book Co.
Klineberg, Otto
1935   Negro Intelligence and Selective Migration. New York: Columbia University Press.

Kroeber, A. L.
1948   Anthropology. New York: Harcourt, Brace and Co.
Layzer, David
1975   "Heritability Analyses of IQ Scores: Science or Numerology?" pp. 192–219 in Ashley Montagu (ed.), Race and IQ. New York: Oxford University Press.
Lee, Everett S.
1951   "Negro Intelligence and Selective Migration: A Philadelphia Test of the Klineberg Hypothesis." American Sociological Review 16 (April): 227–33.
Lewontin, Richard C.
1975   "Race and Intelligence," pp. 174–91 in Ashley Montagu (ed.), Race and IQ. New York: Oxford University Press.
Loehlin, John C., Gardner Lindsey, and J. N. Spuhler
1975   Race Differences in Intelligence. San Francisco: W. H. Freeman and Co.
Montagu, Ashley
1964   Man's Most Dangerous Myth: The Fallacy of Race, Rev. Edition. New York: Harcourt, Brace, Jovanovich, Inc.
1975   Race and IQ (ed.). New York: Oxford University Press.
Newman, William M.
1973   American Pluralism: A Study of Minority Groups and Social Theory. New York: Harper and Row.
Osborne, Richard H.
1971   "The History and Nature of Racial Classification," pp. 159–70 in Richard H. Osborne (ed.), The Biological and Social Meaning of Race. San Francisco: W. H. Freeman and Co.
Pettigrew, Thomas F.
1971   "Race, Mental Illness and Intelligence: A Social Psychological View," pp. 87–124 in Richard H. Osborne (ed.), The Biological and Social Meaning of Race. San Francisco: W. H. Freeman and Co.
1975   Racial Discrimination in the United States (ed.). New York: Harper and Row.
Piliavin, Irving, and Scott Briar
1969   "Police Encounters with Juveniles." American Journal of Sociology 70 (September): 206–14.
Pitt-Rivers, Julian
1972   "Race, Color, and Class in Central America and the Andes." Daedalus 92, 2: 253–75.
Reuter, Edward Byron
1970   The American Race Problem, 3rd Edition (prepared by Jitsuichi Masuoka). New York: Thomas Y. Crowell Co.
Rohrer, John H.
1942   "The Test Intelligence of Osage Indians." Journal of Social Psychology 16: 99–105.
Rose, Arnold
1956   The Negro in America. Boston: The Beacon Press.
Rosenberg, Alfred
1934   The Myth of the Twentieth Century, 39th–40th Editions. Munich.

Shibutani, Tamotsu, and Kian M. Kwan
1965   Ethnic Stratification: A Comparative Approach. New York: The Macmillan Co.
Snyder, Louis L.
1962   The Idea of Racialism. New York: Van Nostrand Reinhold Co.
Stoddard, Theodore Lothrop
1920   The Rising Tide of Color Against White World-Supremacy. New York: Scribner.
Thomlinson, Ralph
1965   Population Dynamics. New York: Random House.
Wagley, Charles (ed.)
1952   Race and Class in Rural Brazil. Paris: UNESCO.
Wolfgang, Marvin E.
1964   Crime and Race: Conceptions and Misconceptions. New York: Institute of Human Relations Press.

6

Involuntary Segregation

Stratified accommodation usually, if not always, involves some form and degree of involuntary segregation of groups. The more rigid and total such systems are, the more the activities of minorities are circumscribed by role expectations imposed on them. The dominant community uses its power to enforce these discriminatory norms both by custom and by law.[1] The patterns of involuntary segregation discussed in this chapter are Jim Crow, *de facto* racial segregation in the North, "social" segregation, Indian reservations, and *apartheid* in South Africa.

THE JIM CROW PATTERN

Reconstruction

The pattern of racial segregation that developed in the last decades of the nineteenth century in the American South reflected the power struggles over the freeing of the slaves. The Thirteenth Amendment to the Constitution, the Emancipation Proclamation, freed the slaves in 1865. During the next decade—the Reconstruction period—the North attempted to oversee the rebuilding of the South along the lines of racial equality. The economic development programs largely failed, including efforts to get blacks and landless whites settled on their own land. Eight Southern states adopted Black Codes providing for economic discrimination against blacks with respect to labor contracts, apprenticeship, debts, and vagrancy. The federal response was to pass the Fourteenth and Fifteenth Amendments to the Constitution.[2] The Fourteenth, ratified in 1868, provided that all citizens were entitled to the equal protection and due process of law. The Fifteenth, ratified in 1870, ensured equal voting rights to all citizens, regardless of "race, color, or previous condition of servitude." All citizens except women, that is; the attempt to get the word "sex" added to this amendment failed. The purpose of these three Reconstruction Amendments was clearly to ensure the freed slaves equal rights under the law. In 1867 the federal Congress had also passed a number of reconstruction acts providing for temporary military rule of the South. During the next years many blacks served in state legislatures and twenty served in the Congress.

The Heritage of Slavery

After emancipation blacks could no longer be owned as property objects, but the demand for cheap labor was great in the South. The drive was strong to consign blacks to jobs with the lowest pay and status, comparable to the "nigger work" of slave days, and to restrict them to separate and inferior public facilities that seemed good enough for people used to slave quarters.[3] Even the name that came to symbolize the new system of segregation, Jim Crow, had been a widespread stereotype of blacks during the last decades before emancipation. Derived from a blackface singer-dancer-comedian routine, this image portrayed blacks as childlike and irresponsible, inefficient, lazy, ridiculous in speech, pleasure seeking, and happy.[4] This image became dominant over the Nat (the rebellious, cunning, treacherous runaway) and Jack (sullen, resentful, and shrewd) stereotypes. Eventually the Jim Crow image became part of the clowning Sambo stereotype, which also incorporated the loyal, devoted, story-loving Uncle Remus and Uncle Tom.[5] These images were to help Southern whites to justify Jim Crow segregation, just as they had helped to justify slavery.

Another heritage from slave days was the discrimination that had been experienced by the half million or so "free negroes," about half of them in the North. The Southern states, fearing that the freedmen would lead slave revolts, had denied them the vote, public assembly, equality in the courts, freedom of movement, and education. Many of these restrictions were extended to the newly emancipated blacks in 1865. In many Northern states before the Civil War the freedmen had experienced anti-black violence, separate schools, and the denial or restriction of the right to vote. Two Northern states had prohibited intermarriage; one had prevented blacks from owning real estate or signing contracts; and five had not allowed blacks to testify in court. The nation thus had some precedents well before 1865 for handling "free" blacks.[6]

The Restoration

In the Civil Rights Bill of 1875 Congress provided that states must not impede equal access to public facilities for all citizens, regardless of race or prior slave status. Also in 1875 the military occupation of the South ended, and Southern efforts were redoubled to restore blacks to a low status. In 1883 the United States Supreme Court held the Civil Rights Bill of 1875 to be unconstitutional with respect to "personal acts of social discrimination." This meant that state laws requiring segregated facilities were constitutional, since they regulated "only" close interpersonal contacts. This opened the gates for a flood of Jim Crow (segregation) statutes to be passed by the Southern legislatures—laws requiring separate schools, buses, trains, restaurants, rest rooms, drinking fountains, parks, swimming pools, and other public facilities, and prohibiting racial intermarriage. The federal courts upheld these state laws, building on the 1883 decision.

Louisiana passed a statute in 1890 requiring separate seating of the races on trains. In the case of *Plessy* v. *Ferguson,* in 1896, the United States Supreme Court accepted this statute as constitutional. This became the key precedent for the long-standing constitutional doctrine of "separate but equal" public facilities. The doctrine legitimized segregation, but facilities did not become equal. The court had little difficulty with the lawyer's argument that Mr. Plessy was seven-eighths white, could easily pass as white, and was therefore entitled to ride in a white train coach. Such a person is legally a negro under constitutional law, as are those with much less than one-eighth black ancestry, even as little as one sixty-fourth. The federal courts, like the census takers, thus follow the nation's racist social definition of what a "negro" is. It is anyone with any known black ancestry.

By 1910 the castelike Jim Crow system was firmly entrenched, so the restoration of Southern blacks to an inferior status was complete.

The pattern was most rigid in the Deep South states (Louisiana, Mississippi, Alabama, Georgia, South Carolina, and Florida), but with some variations it prevailed throughout the South. The system of involuntary segregation was enforced both by law and by force and threats of force outside the law. The ultimate threat was death by lynching, a threat that evidently was carried out more often in the years when the norms of Jim Crow were being established than later on when accommodation was more thoroughgoing. Figures kept by the Tuskegee Institute and the *Chicago Tribune* show 1,111 blacks lynched during the last decade of the nineteenth century, and the following figures for the first five decades of the twentieth: 791, 563, 281, 120, and 32. Sometimes the only accusation against the person lynched was insulting white people, not knowing a black's place, or attempting to vote; and these probably were often the real offenses when the much more usual accusations of homicide, rape or attempted rape, robbery or other theft were made.[7] The Ku Klux Klan became a major force in the extralegal support of the norms of the Jim Crow system.

Most blacks became sharecroppers for white landowners after emancipation, and by 1900 most of them were limited to that role or to other humble labor. Their schools were separate and inferior, so that good field hands would not be spoiled by too much education. Opening and closing dates of rural black schools, school hours, curricula, and tolerance of absenteeism and dropping out all became governed by the demands of the sharecropping system. Very early in the twentieth century, when Southern blacks were being pushed to their lowest post-slavery status, Booker T. Washington promoted vocational schools as a means of economic improvement for blacks. Large industries were rapidly expanding, and Washington's schools were both industrial and agricultural. These schools apparently had little effect except to channel some blacks into cooking and other menial service jobs. Some began to move to the cities, often in the North,[8] but most blacks continued as sharecroppers under the system of segregation. Half a century was to pass before federal courts began declaring Jim Crow laws unconstitutional.

The Rank Order of Discriminations

Until the beginning of World War II, when Myrdal and associates made their study, Jim Crow segregation was little changed from the classic pattern it had become at the turn of the century. Myrdal reported that Southern white attitudes supported segregation in some areas of life more strongly than in others. The more intimate the contact, the stronger the attitude of whites that discrimination must be maintained. Myrdal indicated the following rank order of discriminations:[9]

1 intermarriage and sexual contacts with white women
2 personal relations (greeting, talking, eating, dancing, swimming, and other matters governed by the interracial "etiquette")
3 public facilities (segregated schools, churches, trains, parks, etc.)
4 political participation (voting and holding public office)
5 legal treatment (in courts, and by the police)
6 economic activities (jobs, credit, housing, getting land, public assistance, etc.)

Evidence for such a rank order has been found in studies in the North as well as others in the South.[10] The economic area was found to rank third in a more recent study of students at the Universities of Texas, North Carolina, and Washington, with the rest of the rank order the same as Myrdal's.[11] Two interpretations seem plausible: that the degree of direct competition affects attitudes toward the economic area, and that the rank order may vary from one region or community to another. After the first two of Myrdal's ranks it is difficult to arrange them in terms of the degree of intimacy; and the inclusion of housing in the economic area must be noted because residential location affects personal contacts.

Myrdal also found that Southern blacks had a rank order of attitudes of *resistance* to discriminations that was just the reverse of the whites' rank order of discriminations. In other words, blacks resisted segregation and discrimination most in the economic area, next in legal treatment, etc., and what they wanted least was intermarriage and sexual contacts with white women. Support for this finding was found in another study in the South,[12] and in one in Ohio.[13] Myrdal optimistically suggested that orderly changes ought to be possible, because blacks wanted change most in those areas of life that whites were least anxious about. This did not prove to be a successful prophecy, and not because of some possible shifting in the rank orders. Changes have been resisted in all aspects of life, particularly in the Deep South, not just in the most intimate areas. For instance, the desegregation of schools and other public facilities met strong resistance in the 1950s and 1960s, as did also the moves toward political, legal, and economic equality.

Yet "white womanhood" (rank #1) has been guarded zealously in the Jim Crow system. Why is it tragic, and therefore unthinkable, for a white woman to have a racially mixed child, but not for a black woman to have one? Racial amalgamation takes place in both cases, yet in practice the taboo against racial mixing has been applied only to white women. The strong community expectation is that the child stays with the mother, and if a black woman has a mixed child it is defined as a black by social custom, law, and by the census taker. The racist ideology says the "mongrel" child is inferior, but the white group's dominance is not threatened if the child becomes part of the black community. The supposed degeneracy of the mixed children poses no threat so long as the dominant community remains "pure." For a white girl or woman to keep a mixed child would threaten her family and the whole system of white superiority, so they would have to move away, give the child to a black family, or join the black community.

The Jim Crow norms require marked segregation in the second-ranked area, personal relationships, and a strict pattern of interracial etiquette when tolerated contacts occur. In all interaction the white must be clearly in charge, and the black must indicate that he "knows his place." The black must be deferential in tone and body language, and never contradict the white or broach a delicate subject. The black must become clownish if any suggestion of lack of deference arises. The courtesies expected of blacks are not reciprocated. The white goes to the black's front door and need not knock; the black goes to the white's back door. The white man must be called "Mr.," but he calls the black man "boy," or "Uncle," or uses his first name. In short, the etiquette calls for blacks to act out their acceptance of their inferior status, in much the same ways that the slaves had to.

Stereotypes of blacks are constantly reinforced by the restricted form, content, and contexts of interracial conversations. Thus whites may feel they know "their" blacks, but much of what they observe under the norms of Jim Crow etiquette is only stereotyped role playing. A "good nigger" (Sambo) is one who carefully observes the racial etiquette, and thus stays out of trouble. When among themselves, like India's untouchables, the blacks drop the mask and stop clowning.[14] The fact that this etiquette was so strongly demanded and so widely observed indicates a large measure of accommodation to the Jim Crow system by both blacks and whites. However, outward conformity to the etiquette by blacks covered up widespread resentment of the role-playing performances and of the entire system of involuntary segregation.

Economic changes are apparently not heavily threatening when competition is not direct or keen, and changes in law enforcement cause less anxiety among whites than intermarriage and close personal relations do. Yet threats to any of the four lower ranks in the whites' rank order of discriminations have often elicited charges that blacks are seeking to attack white womanhood. Moves to desegregate the schools and other public facilities, as well as jobs, have often prompted the question, "Would you want your daughter to marry one?" Violence and threats of it have been correlated with Southern black attempts to vote, to testify in court or serve on juries, and with direct racial competition for jobs and welfare benefits. White threats and actions in such situations have typically been justified by talk about protecting white womanhood, indicating the connectedness of the different areas of the Jim Crow system of institutionalized discrimination. Thus the racial etiquette serves not only to protect ranks #1 and 2, but as a crucial means of maintaining the whole system of segregation.[15]

The Mississippi Chinese

Loewen's study of the Chinese in Mississippi throws further light on the Jim Crow system, and on the delicate accommodations required of an upwardly mobile, middle minority. The study is based on historical and governmental records, participant observation, and interviews with the Chinese, blacks, and whites.[16] The area involved is the Yazoo-Mississippi Delta, the northwest part of Mississippi, constituting one-sixth of the land and one-fifth of the population of the state. It is a flat, rich plain sixty miles wide and about 180 miles long, stretching from near Vicksburg almost to Memphis, Tennessee. It was cleared after the Civil War and most of the sharecroppers brought in were blacks.

Most of the Chinese in the delta in 1970 were descendants of those who originally came in 1869 and 1870, when planters were recruiting agricultural labor. Most of them came in as sharecroppers, and whites at that time perceived the Chinese as essentially blacks. The blacks were feared as a political threat because they were voting then, and voting Republican. The Chinese were deliberately sought, partly because they had demonstrated their capacity for hard labor at railroad building in the West, and partly because they were sojourners and were not expected to become interested in citizenship and voting. When the Jim Crow laws were passed they were applied to the Mississippi Chinese, who were thus excluded from white schools and other public facilities, and they were expected to conform to the racial etiquette.

Before long the Chinese began to leave the cotton fields to become grocers in the small crossroads trading centers, and their economic status began to rise. Over several decades their economic position improved considerably, and their overall status as a group also went up. For some time they were marginal, considered neither black nor white. During the 1930s and 1940s there were triply segregated schools in Cleveland, Greenville, and several other delta towns, with separate buildings for Chinese pupils. These buildings were abandoned by the 1950s and the Chinese were admitted to white schools, as well as to other public facilities. Despite a marginal identity and some discrimination against them, they achieved a status closer to whites than to blacks. So, once viewed as essentially black, the delta Chinese crossed the castelike color line. The Mexican Americans in the delta remained in sharecropping, and in 1970 were still below the color line—considered to be essentially blacks. School desegregation had been ordered and was beginning in the delta in 1970, but blacks and Mexican Americans were still heavily segregated and Jim Crow was far from dead.

Why did the delta Chinese concentrate in the grocery business? They desired to improve their economic position, of course, and perceived that they could not do so as sharecroppers. Hard work in commercial enterprise was valued in traditional Chinese culture, and so was the sharing of capital within the extended family. But, without the niche that opened up in the structure of involuntary segregation in the sharecropping system, the Chinese could not have assumed the role of middle minority. The whites did not want to sell groceries to blacks, or do the manual labor of unloading wagons and stocking shelves. The ex-slaves identified with agriculture, and had no experience in small business. Many of the small groups of Lebanese, Syrians, Jews, and some of the Italians in the delta became merchants also, but in the larger communities. The delta Chinese were on the land when the gap opened up for the rural grocery business; they seized the opportunity and developed a near-monopoly.

How did the Chinese manage to take advantage of their improved economic status to pull the entire group above the color bar? Their numbers were small and they remained nonpolitical, motivated to prosper under the system rather than to try to change it. Being cultural outsiders, they could appear ignorant of the racial etiquette and be allowed some leeway. They remained marginal, flexible, and alert to opportunities. There was tension and much white opposition to their advances in group status, yet they avoided overt conflicts. They kept a good deal of their own culture, establishing a style of life different from that of the blacks. They made an effort to "act white" in speech, walking, dancing, and in establishing residences away from the store. They made contacts with white ministers, wholesalers, and bankers, and gradually persuaded the white power structure to admit them to hospitals, schools, and other white facilities.

Most of the original delta Chinese were single men, and many of them married blacks. At one time perhaps one-fourth of the Chinese were in mixed marriages. Then the Chinese deliberately rejected amalgamation with the blacks, since that held the entire group down. They "left behind" in the black community those Chinese who married blacks, or compelled them to leave their black families. These mixed black-Chinese families remained marginal, not fully accepted by the blacks, and by 1970 all but a dozen of them had left the delta.

In 1970 the Chinese as a whole had begun to leave the delta, mainly for Western cities, and only twelve hundred of them remained, 90 percent of them still in the grocery stores. Mechanization began pushing blacks off delta land from 1950 on, so the whole sharecropping system has been dying and the country grocery stores have been losing their customers. Segregation is slowly retreating, as court-ordered integration of black and white schools continues. Some violence has attended these developments, and some of it has been directed at the delta Chinese, the group in the middle. The Chinese have been resentful of continuing discrimination, including the white resistance to hiring them as teachers. The status gap they have filled is vanishing, along with the demise of the Jim Crow sharecropping system in which the gap appeared.

RACIAL SEGREGATION IN THE NORTH

Urban Concentration

In 1910 most American blacks lived in the rural South, but by 1970 the majority lived outside the South, with four-fifths in urban areas. By 1973 over three-fourths of the nation's blacks lived in metropolitan areas and three-fifths were in central cities; for whites the comparable proportions were approximately two-thirds and one-fourth.[17] In Chapter 1 we noted that the Spanish-speaking minorities are even more urban than blacks, and they, too, are heavily concentrated in the central cities. In 1950 only about 11 percent of the people in the nation's central cities were blacks; by 1970 it was 21 percent. Blacks were in the majority in the city of Washington, D.C., and in Newark and Atlanta, and constituted at least 40 percent in a dozen major cities.[18]

De Facto Segregation

While Jim Crow held sway in the South there was institutionalized racial segregation in the North as well, but it was less uniform and rigid. Most Northern segregation has resulted from discriminatory practices rather than from laws explicitly requiring racial separation, so it is *de facto* (in fact) rather than *de jure* (by law) segregation. Blacks and other nonwhite city migrants occupied increasing proportions of the crowded, low-rent slums, as the Southern and Eastern European immigrants moved out of them. These European ethnics were only partly replaced by new arrivals from their countries because immigration was sharply curtailed in the early 1920s. The nonwhite, new "urban ethnics" could not readily move out of the slums when their economic status improved because of their racial visibility. Residential separation produced segregation in schools and other facilities. Thus the term *ghetto* came to be applied to the nonwhite areas of the inner cities.

Housing Segregation

Segregated housing is the key to overall racial separation in the North, and in the newer urban areas in the South,[19] although discrimination in employment and in the use of restaurants and other public facilities also has had segregating effects. Racial separation in housing has remained at high levels in recent decades.[20] Blacks have become more widely dispersed, but this has not reduced segregation because it has reflected the expansion of predominantly nonwhite areas or large-scale black movement into older suburbs.[21] From 1960 to 1970 urban racial segregation remained about the same nationally,[22] despite legal, educational, and some economic gains for blacks.[23]

Economic status can account for only a small part of this marked pattern of racial segregation in urban housing. Evidently the main reason for remaining in the ghetto is actual or expected racial discrimination.[24] Another reason for remaining is to be near a job, relatives, friends, church, settlement house, transportation, or other facilities.[25] Still another reason, increasingly important since the latter 1960s, is to build group unity and thereby a strong base of political power from which to demand more equal treatment of the group.[26] However, according to national polls, a substantial majority of blacks continue to prefer racially integrated housing.[27] A major reason is the low quality of so much of the ghetto housing.

Racially segregated urban housing has been produced and maintained by a number of related practices and policies.[28] Laws directly requiring residential segregation of the races were tried, but declared unconstitutional in 1917 by the United States Supreme Court, so other means were developed. One is the restrictive housing covenant, which is a buyer's promise in the purchase contract that the real estate will not be sold to people in certain named minority groups. This was declared illegal by the Supreme Court in 1948 in the case of *Shelly* v. *Kraemer.* Individual owners are often pressured to conform to informal understandings ("gentlemen's agreements"), however, and they may legally refuse to rent or sell to whomever they please.

Zoning laws have been used a good deal to control racial occupancy of municipal land. One device is to restrict housing lots in an area to a minimum size of one, two, or more acres, making them very expensive. Another is to apply zoning regulations, such as footage requirements for buildings, very strictly when nonwhites apply but not when whites do. To keep nonwhites from occupying certain areas, the land may be condemned for public use, zoned for industrial or commercial use, or requests may be denied for the construction of public housing, or apartments, or other multifamily dwellings.

Government housing policies have contributed heavily to racial segregation in the cities. The Federal Housing Administration (begun in 1934) has favored individual family dwellings and middle-income families. Further, the FHA officially discouraged from the beginning the insuring of mortgages for houses in racially integrated neighborhoods, basing this policy on the belief that racial "invasion" lowers property values, a belief research has shown to be false.[29] The FHA gave massive help to whites moving to the suburbs, especially after World War II.

Public housing (since the Housing Act of 1937) has given substantial help to needy whites, but buildings occupied by nonwhites have received inadequate funds for maintenance and security. The nonwhites, very often on welfare, have usually been unable to manage the repairs and other maintenance themselves. They have then been blamed by whites for not appreciating the subsidized housing, especially when rebellious vandalizing has occurred, thus reinforcing traditional stereotypes of nonwhite groups. Public housing projects for nonwhites have in general been such a failure that in many cities they were eventually included in massive programs of slum clearance under the federal Urban Renewal Authority. In 1973, for example, the decision was made to destroy the massive Pruitt-Igoe development in St. Louis. The legislative objective of replacing the residences destroyed by Urban Renewal projects with new, low-cost housing has rarely been realized.[30] This has still further reduced the tight supply of housing for low-income groups, a supply that developers prefer to ignore because middle- and upper-income housing is more profitable.

The selling and financing of urban real estate has involved a great deal of racial discrimination. Before World War II there were very few black realtors, and they were not members of the National Association of Real Estate Boards, which controlled the housing market. Black realtors formed their own group, in 1947, the National Association of Real Estate Brokers. White realtors continued such practices as quoting inflated prices to nonwhite buyers, claiming that the house had just been bought, showing only very poor houses, arousing fears about potential reactions of white neighbors, and "blockbusting." This last device consists of creating panic by telling white owners that a nonwhite family has entered the neighborhood and that the whole area is going black, enabling the realtors to buy entire blocks at low cost and sell them to nonwhites at inflated prices. Banks and other lending institutions frequently have discriminated by distorting the appraisals of property, or by finding nonwhites ineligible for loans.

Internal Colonialism in the Ghetto

The application of the colonial model of race relations to the urban ghetto is based on the view that the residents have had no more control over their living areas and resources than blacks had under sharecropping. The land, buildings, jobs, and financial power of the ghetto are mainly in outside hands. There is evidence that white owners have the larger ghetto businesses, and that they tend to hire whites and outsiders.[31] Ghetto residents are depicted in the colonial model as exploited consumers of goods, as a source of cheap labor, and of high profits from rents for overcrowded, deteriorating housing. The land involved is in transition from residential to commercial and industrial use, and its value is rising, so the owners are motivated to make short-run profits rather than to keep buildings in repair. Housing practices that keep nonwhites from leaving the ghetto ensure the continuation of their economic exploitation. The only way to break this pattern, in terms of the colonial model, is for the colonized group to unite and gain enough political power to break the grip of their oppressors. This sense of unity can be built on the shared experiences of exploitation in the ghetto.[32]

National polls show the majority of whites to be in favor of racially integrated housing, and the percentage has increased in recent decades, especially among the younger, college-educated people. Yet strong opposition remains, particularly among the more homogeneous Northern ethnic groups, Southern whites, and among the aged and the least educated.[33] In terms of the colonial model, even if most whites favor integrated housing, that outcome is prevented by the relatively small but powerful group of economic exploiters of the ghetto. Their power is enhanced by the holdout groups who are highly vocal in their opposition.

A study of the effects on racial housing segregation of a freeway clearance in St. Paul, Minnesota, will serve to raise some questions about the colonialist interpretation. The demolition (1959–61) went through the racially mixed Selby-Dale area, the city's most nonwhite section. Seventy-two percent of the 433 displaced households were nonwhite, but whites were also involved, so differences in relocation experiences could be tested.[34] Over nine-tenths of the displaced whites (who could be accounted for) succeeded in moving out of the Selby-Dale area, but only 15.5 percent of the nonwhites did, and these had mostly moved into some small, middle-class, black pockets in the city. However, interviews with a sample of the families indicated that this large racial difference in relocation overstates the amount of discrimination actually experienced by blacks in the housing market. Only about one-third of the nonwhites attempted to leave the area, and just two-fifths of these reported discriminatory experiences, mainly in getting to see the house they wanted or in the preloan stages of completing a purchase. Some of the nonwhites who said they had met with no discrimination reported helpful acts by white friends, lawyers, realtors, or potential neighbors. Some who met no difficulty said they discontinued their efforts because they feared discrimination if they went ahead.

Finally, the interviewees who said they tried to move out of the nonwhite area were asked if they had moved. All the whites who tried had succeeded, but only about one-third of the nonwhites who tried had moved out. Thus, the nonwhite chances of getting out of the area were actually one in three, considerably better than the relocation figure of 15.5 percent would suggest; and less than half of those who made some effort to leave said they were discriminated against in the process. Discrimination was found, of course, and many did not try to leave the area for fear of it. Yet discrimination in the housing market was imperfectly institutionalized, not a tight, monolithic structure.

The number and proportion of blacks in the city's population was relatively small compared to those in cities such as Chicago, Milwaukee, Indianapolis, or Dallas, so perhaps housing integration was less of a threat in St. Paul. Even so, the view that the dominant community is divided on the race and housing issue suggests that considerable strides toward equal treatment in the housing market may be possible. Perhaps it is not necessary to wait for what is implied in the colonial model —a decisive takeover of power—at least not in cities with relatively small nonwhite populations.

"SOCIAL" SEGREGATION

Social Discrimination and Power

In the popular meaning of the term, social segregation refers only to close personal interaction (Myrdal's second rank)—to parties, dating, friendships, neighboring, and to membership in voluntary organizations. We have seen how the only interaction of this type allowed in the Jim Crow system has been closely regulated by the norms of the racial etiquette, and that this has been crucial in maintaining the whole system of segregation. Social segregation under Jim Crow thus has not been trivial, or just a matter of preferring to be with one's "own kind"; it has been a major means of group domination. An "uppity" black is seen as getting out of his place and acting as if he thought he were as good as whites, thus perhaps trying to take over their jobs and political offices. This suggests a close connection between the master-servant kind of intergroup etiquette and economic (and overall) dominance and submission.

But is this not, perhaps, a special case? What about other forms of social discrimination, against other groups? What about the social segregation practiced by the dominant community's friendship cliques, neighborhoods, fraternities and sororities, lodges, churches, and business and professional groups? Even when such practices are admittedly designed to prevent informal contacts with Jews, Catholics, or other groups, isn't this just a matter of exercising the right to choose compatible friends? The answer must be no. Social discrimination against an entire group requires consensus and organization; it is systematic, not a private matter of choosing personal friends. In fact, when these norms are strong, individuals are not free to choose friends in the other group. The imposition of involuntary social segregation on a minority means that the group as a whole is *excluded* from the primary group activities of the dominant community. This exclusion plays a major role in the maintenance of group power and domination.[35]

In closed-class societies, landed nobility and hereditary titles help the upper classes maintain their status and power. In an open-class society with democratic ideals, the upper classes rely heavily on social segregation to defend their wealth, status, and power against free, open competition. "The club" helps smooth the way to higher status for those who are included, and it shuts the gate on those who are not.[36] Ethnic groups participate almost exclusively in their own informal activities, as we saw in Chapter 4, but much of this is probably a defense reaction. When ethnic groups are pointedly excluded, they tend not only to retain their traditional social activities, but also to invent social forms that parallel those from which the dominant community has excluded them. Excluded groups have established their own resorts, residential hotels, fraternities and sororities, lodges, recreation centers, and clubs of all kinds.[37] The typical reaction of the dominant community to this is that the groups concerned are too clannish.

Social Segregation of Jews

Social discrimination is practiced against minorities in general, but the forms used against middle minorities are especially systematic and illuminating. Social discriminating against Jews in the United States has been marked since early in the twentieth century, reaching peaks in the 1920s and 1930s. Anti-Semitism evidently developed strongly in the upper and upper-middle classes, and the stereotypes, jokes, and anxieties filtered downward in the status structure. Names became a great preoccupation as a means of identifying Jews, since their supposedly distinctive physical appearance was not dependable.

Stoddard and Grant, cited in Chapter 5 for their racist views early in the century, considered Jews a danger to "Nordic cultural superiority." During that era Burton J. Hendrick wrote extensively of the danger of Jews in America. These three men were upper-class Americans, two born in New England and one in New York, and were educated at Yale, Harvard and Columbia Universities. All belonged to the same white, Anglo-Saxon, Protestant social clubs at one time or another.[38] They shared and spread anxieties about the more upwardly mobile new immigrant groups, including the long-standing European prejudices against the Jews as a cunning, ruthless, middle group. The Jews were portrayed as aggressively seeking economic success in order to seize political control, and many clubs that had previously had Jewish members began excluding them.[39] The political fear has largely subsided since World War II, but the stereotype of Jews as clannish and unethical in business has not declined as much.[40]

Occupational discrimination against American Jews was very heavy during the first half of this century, especially in the 1930s.[41] The result was their almost total exclusion from significant positions in heavy industry, public utilities, banking, finance, insurance, transportation, oil, mining, lumber, farming, and food processing. Jews still do not figure prominently in all these lines, although in recent decades they have gotten into such areas as construction, light industry, and real estate to some extent. Finding large segments of the economy closed to them, many Jews have sought opportunities in the professions, but despite some success have found many barriers there too. Self-employment in retailing or wholesaling has remained the most frequent employment of Jews, with clerical occupations second, and the professions third.[42] Jewish concentration in the clothing business is a result of their exclusion from the dominant businesses and industries of the economy. Typical Jewish businesses are characterized by a large risk factor, and many of them by social stigma, marginality to the economy, or having been regarded when new as unimportant.[43]

Social segregation has been a key means of restricting the economic opportunities of Jewish Americans. Being excluded from the club, the fraternity, or the coffee group has meant exclusion from managerial and other significant opportunities in the major businesses and industries. A study in the latter 1960s revealed that about four-fifths of the downtown men's clubs in the United States had no Jewish members.[44] Explicit or informal admissions quotas for Jews flourished in medical or other professional schools from the early 1920s on. Many private schools and colleges, especially the "old" schools that provide access to top opportunities, have had quotas also.[45] Since World War II there apparently has been a major decline in such quotas and in the exclusion of Jews by fraternities and sororities.[46] However, various means of social segregation continue to restrict the life chances of Jews and other minorities.

Social Segregation of Women

American males and females have remained socially segregated to a considerable degree, although there are class differences, and there have been many changes since World War I. The movement for equality for women has included challenges to such surviving areas of social segregation as all-male clubs and bars, men-only areas and activities at mixed clubs, sex-segregated competitive sports from the Little League on up, and segregated classes and other school activities. The usual rationale for these challenges, and also for related social research,[47] has been to bring about change in the process of socialization into male and female roles. Challenges to male occupational domination, and research related to these challenges,[48] have tended to focus on higher education and on legal, political, and other possibilities for direct action. The ways in which social segregation operates to exclude women and to sponsor men for the more lucrative and powerful economic roles are complex, and much in need of study. The general proposition advanced here is that the social segregation of the sexes has played a key role in maintaining economic and overall domination of women.

The more subtle aspect of the social segregation of the sexes parallels the Southern racial etiquette. Traditionally much of the interaction between males and females, even apparently between a great many husbands and wives, has followed a ritual pattern that restricts conversations to certain subjects and reinforces male control. Thus men and women to a remarkable degree remain a mystery to each other, and stereotypes of man and woman flourish in spite of what may appear on the surface to be close communication. Beliefs about biological differences in endurance, interests, temperament, and intelligence remain prominent in ideological responses to feminist challenges, including those to the different facets of social segregation of the sexes.

A comparative example of the effects of social segregation is the filmmaking experiences of women and Jews, both of whom were very prominent in the pioneering years when it was a new, risky, low-status business early in the century. Women were involved in all phases, and costs were low for people able and willing to invest their time; so minority peoples were welcome to it. When the industry prospered, male managers assumed control of both making and distributing films, and the numbers and influence of women declined sharply, even on the screen. The omission of women from significant informal contacts apparently facilitated this process, and the unions also played an important role.[49] Many Jews succeeded in both production and distribution, and Jewish actors became acceptable to the public by adopting English names. By the 1940s the motion picture industry had become respectable and recognized as a "good thing" by the dominant community and, aided by social segregation, Jewish influence began to decline.[50] Only since the late 1960s have women become more involved in filmmaking again, but not in the lucrative motion picture industry. Women able and willing to risk their time and small amounts of capital have found a fairly open field in experimental, art, educational, and certain new types of commercial films.

INDIAN RESERVATIONS

Very strong force is required to institute a system of involuntary confinement of a minority to designated areas of land, under the absolute control of the dominant group. As we noted in Chapter 2, only when the Indians had been heavily decimated and rendered completely powerless was an effective policy of genocide replaced by the reservation system. Sociologically a reservation is a "total institution," analogous to a military "boot camp," a mental hospital, or a prison. The inmates are powerless, and not expected to participate in significant decisions about their needs or to take important initiatives. Congress withdrew recognition of the tribes as independent political entities with which treaties could be signed, and made Indians wards of the federal government. The camps to which the Japanese Americans were confined during World War II were clearly temporary; the Indian reservations were established as a permanent means of controlling the rebellious tribes.

As we shall see in some detail in Chapter 10, the reservation policy for the first several decades was to try to force the Indians to assimilate American culture. The chief effect of the first quarter-century of the reservation system, however, was genocidal. (Genocide is defined in Chapter 2.) There was so much death from disease and starvation, especially after the government's punitive slaughter of the buffalo from 1872 to 1874 (in response to the rebellion of the Plains Indians against the reservation system), that the population of the reservations was reduced by one-half by the end of the century. Whites were allowed to settle on much of the original reservation land, eventually (by 1915) reducing the total area by about two-thirds.[51]

The reservation system is not unique to the United States. There are many similarities between ours and the one operated by the Indian Affairs Branch of the Canadian government, including the barring of the Indians from selling "their" land, and the use of tribal law and courts on the reservations rather than the Constitution and federal courts. In Australia there is a system of "reserves" and "missions" for the aborigines, who object when mining, oil, and iron interests are granted rights on land they consider rightfully theirs.[52] Reservations have been proposed for the Muslims in the Philippines, in answer to their Independence Movement. A reservation system has also been a key part of *apartheid.*

APARTHEID

The South African government's policy has been to promote racial segregation (apartness) as fully as possible since 1948, when the Nationalist Party gained control. When it became a republic in 1961, South Africa broke its last ties with the British Commonwealth over the issue of white supremacy. The whites (about three-fifths of them of Dutch descent, most of the rest British) make up less than one-fifth of the population. The blacks (mostly Bantu-speaking tribes) constitute over two-thirds of the population; about 3 percent of the total are Asians, mostly from India; and the remaining one-tenth are "coloureds"—meaning persons of mixed ancestry involving Europeans and either blacks or Indians (or Malayans). The coloureds vary widely in racial characteristics, and are partially assimilated. They have long had a marginal position, with better jobs and a higher status than that of the blacks, but much discriminated against by the whites. The Indians and other Asians have been a middle minority and have often been the target of the anger of the Africans, as they were in 1949 when over 1,000 were injured and about 150 killed in Zulu outbursts.

To facilitate the *apartheid* policies, race classification boards were established to issue pass cards that identify persons as white, coloured, Indian, or African. The "pass" laws restrict the areas in which Africans and coloureds can live, and require Africans to be in their own places by curfew time. Intermarriage and sexual relations across the racial lines were defined as serious crimes under the Immorality Act, for whites as well as for the other categories. There have been frequent requests for reclassification, to enable couples to marry or avoid prosecution. The blacks lost all political rights, and in 1972 the coloureds lost their remaining one—the right to vote for parliamentary representatives. The parliament, by law, is all white. Blacks are a source of cheap labor, and have been paid as little as one-tenth the amount whites receive for the same work. The Africans and coloureds have been considered essential for industrial development, but integrated urban life has been sharply rejected.[53]

The national policies have been implemented by three different forms of segregation, designed for different situations. Van den Berghe has called these micro-, meso-, and macro-segregation.[54] *Micro-segregation* means separation in washrooms, waiting rooms, trains, post office counters, and other public facilities. This aspect of *apartheid* corresponds to the Jim Crow laws, and is designed to segregate the racial groups as much as possible in areas where all of them work or make other frequent contacts. The ban on intermarriage and interracial sexual relations is the ultimate barrier of this kind.

Meso-segregation means legally imposed urban residential ghettos for the three racial categories. Africans, coloureds, and whites are required by law to live in different parts of the urban areas where the nonwhites are needed for industrial work. Hundreds of thousands of nonwhites were compelled to move when this was put into effect, and migration has been carefully policed. One of the curfew laws has prohibited nonwhite domestic servants from remaining overnight in white households. The nonwhites have experienced crowded, substandard living conditions and many—especially the Africans—have had to travel long distances to work. Apparently it was resentment over such restrictions and living conditions that precipitated the urban outbursts of the coloureds and Africans during the latter half of 1976. Hundreds were killed, mostly Africans and coloureds.

Macro-segregation means geographical separation of the Africans on reservations, with tribal cultural development and a considerable degree of self-government, subject to national control. The government claimed that these nine semiautonomous reserves, called Bantustans, would facilitate both economic development and political self-determination of the African tribes. Totally separate development of the racial groups under this arrangement was considered the ultimate goal of *apartheid.* However, the Bantustans comprise less than 14 percent of the nation's land and the Africans are nearly seven-tenths of the population. There are no major cities, industries, or seaports in the reserves, few mineral resources; and the Bantustans are made up of a large number of scattered tribal areas rather than contiguous zones. The reserves do not appear to be at all economically feasible. In less than two decades after 1948, when the system was established, over one million Africans moved from the reservations to the cities for work.

Transkei, the most developed of the Bantustans, was granted so-called self-government in 1963. The Transkei legislature was empowered to pass laws, but they had to be approved by the president of the republic. Subject to this crucial restriction, the Transkei government had the power to levy taxes, maintain law and order, and to influence policies on such matters as education and agriculture. It was allowed no control over such matters as the mass media, firearms or explosives, mass transportation, or the constitution. A relatively small proportion of the Transkeians have found employment on the reserve; far more have had to find it outside, mostly in the mines or on white farms.[55]

In October 1976, the republic announced that Transkei had been granted independence, and that other Bantustans would be gaining the same status. This was during a period of racial disorders, and a time when South Africa joined in the pressure on Rhodesia to negotiate for blacks to take over control of that government. Portuguese control of nearby Angola and Mozambique had also recently been terminated under the pressure of native military actions. Apparently the Transkei government will have more autonomy than before, but it clearly is not independent, being subject to the power of the central government. Africans living in urban areas continue to be regarded as urban sojourners who are citizens of their Bantustans, with no political rights in the republic. The conflict in the dominant community between carrying out the Bantustan policy and alternatives to it has become sharper, and the future of South Africa is very uncertain. Perhaps the only reasonable prediction is that—like settlers in general as opposed to colonials—the whites will retain their power as fully and as long as possible, and salvage all the advantages they can if they are forced to relinquish their dominance.[56] At any rate, in 1977 the protests were met with strongly repressive measures.

CONCLUSION

Involuntary segregation appears in a variety of forms, all designed to establish and maintain the domination of physical or cultural groups. Segregation symbolizes the stratified pattern of accommodation and aids in the unequal distribution of opportunities and rewards. Such forms of involuntary segregation as reservations, legally required urban residential separation, and legally segregated public facilities, are deliberate and obvious ways of maintaining group dominance. *De facto* segregation is less intentional and less obvious, yet its discriminatory effects may become marked and strongly institutionalized.

"Social" segregation, far from being just a matter of choosing personal friends, is a major means of maintaining group dominance. The occupational opportunities of Jews and women, for example, have been greatly influenced by social exclusion. Probably a great many people who participate in social segregation are unaware of its effects on the life chances of members of excluded groups. Social segregation is sometimes supplemented by a special etiquette—norms that prescribe the form and content of unavoidable personal interaction across group lines. These norms prevent effective communication, enhance group stereotypes, and require persons to act out the superior and inferior status positions of their groups. A master-servant racial etiquette was an important part of the Jim Crow system.

The *apartheid* system in the Republic of South Africa involves three forms of segregation, all of which have at least partial parallels in the United States. The South African laws requiring segregated public facilities and prohibiting intermarriage are similar to the retreating Jim Crow system of the American South. One significant difference is that South Africa forbids sexual relations as well as intermarriage across racial lines, and criminally punishes white violators as well as members of the other racial categories. Under Jim Crow (and earlier under slavery) the white violator was not treated as deviant. The *apartheid* laws requiring racially segregated urban housing areas are more drastic attempts to accomplish by law essentially what *de facto* racial separation has done in the United States. There are other important differences: the South Africans must carry racial classification cards, and the nonwhite groups must observe curfews and other restrictions on their movement and conduct. The Bantustans are somewhat parallel to the American Indian reservations, except that the former must accommodate a far higher proportion of the country's population. Also, the South African policy for the reserves has been to promote separate racial development, a strongly anti-integrationist stance. High unemployment and poverty have characterized both of these reservation systems. And, in both nations, the several patterns of segregation have come under heavy pressure to change.

FOOTNOTES

1   Hunt & Walker, 1974, pp. 6–7.
2   Marden & Meyer, 1973, pp. 162–65.
3   Woodward, 1957.
4   Dormon, 1969–70.
5   Blassingame, 1972, Ch. 5.
6   Litwach, 1961.
7   Vander Zanden, 1972, pp. 162–63.
8   Henri, 1975.
9   Myrdal et al., 1944, pp. 60–61; Rose, 1956, pp. 24–26.
10   Killian & Grigg, 1961; Edmunds, 1954.
11   Williams & Wienir, 1967.
12   Killian & Grigg, 1961.
13   Banks, 1950.
14   Shibutani & Kwan, 1965, pp. 304–5.
15   Rose & Rose, 1948, pp. 154–65.
16   Loewen, 1971.
17   U.S. Bureau of Census, 1974, p. 11.
18   Van Valey, Roof & Wilcox, 1977.
19   Schnore & Evenson, 1966; Roof, 1972.
20   Mayer & Hoult, 1962, p. 7; Grier & Grier, 1960, p. 11; Taeuber & Taeuber, 1965.
21   Connolly, 1973.
22   Van Valey, Roof & Wilcox, 1977.
23   U.S. Bureau of Census, 1974, p. 54.
24   McEntire, 1960, p. 5; Taeuber & Taeuber, 1964; Bahr & Gibbs, 1967.
25   Davis, 1965.
26   Blackwell, 1975, pp. 158–59.
27   Pettigrew, 1975, pp. 105–23.
28   Blackwell, 1975, pp. 150–59.
29   Laurenti, 1960.
30   Blackwell, 1975, pp. 145–46, 152.
31   Aldrich, 1973.
32   Blackwell, 1975, pp. 139–50.
33   Pettigrew, 1975, pp. 92–105.
34   Davis, 1965.
35   Rose & Rose, 1948, Ch. 6; McWilliams, 1948, pp. 115–26.
36   McWilliams, 1948, pp. 118–20.

37 McWilliams, 1948, pp. 114–115, 127–32.
38 McWilliams, 1948, pp. 56–67.
39 McWilliams, 1948, pp. 122–24.
40 Selznick & Steinberg, 1969, p. 8.
41 Epstein & Forster, 1962.
42 Glazer & Moynihan, 1963, pp. 73, 151.
43 Rose & Rose, 1948, pp. 164, 176; McWilliams, 1948, pp. 142–54.
44 Carlson, 1969.
45 Rose & Rose, 1948, pp. 163–64; McWilliams, 1948, pp. 132–41.
46 Vander Zanden, 1972, p. 219.
47 Tresemer, 1975.
48 Daniels, 1975.
49 Smith, 1975.
50 McWilliams, 1948, p. 150.
51 Shepard, 1942, p. 11.
52 Thomlinson, 1974.
53 Hunt & Walker, Ch. 6.
54 Van den Berghe, 1971, p. 37.
55 Hunt & Walker, 1974, pp. 171–75.
56 Hunt & Walker, 1974, pp. 161–63, 198–203.

REFERENCES

Aldrich, Howard E.
1973 "Employment Opportunities for Blacks in the Black Ghetto: The Role of White-Owned Businesses." American Journal of Sociology 78, 6 (May): 1403–25.
Bahr, Howard M., and Jack P. Gibbs
1967 "Racial Differentiation in American Metropolitan Areas." Social Forces 46 (June): 521–32.
Banks, W. S. M., II
1950 "The Rank Order of Sensitivity to Discriminations of Negroes in Columbus, Ohio." American Sociological Review 15 (August):529–34.
Blackwell, James E.
1975 The Black Community: Diversity and Unity. New York: Dodd, Mead and Co.
Blassingame, John W.
1972 The Slave Community: Plantation Life in the Antebellum South. New York: Oxford University Press.
Carlson, Elliot
1969 "Negroes, Jews Press Efforts to Join Groups That Now Refuse Them." Wall Street Journal, September 10.
Connolly, Harold X.
1973 "Black Movement into the Suburbs: Suburbs Doubling Their Black Population During the 1960s." Urban Affairs Quarterly 9, 1 (September): 91–111.

Daniels, Arlene Kaplan
1975   "Feminist Perspectives in Sociological Research," Ch. 12 in, Another Voice: Feminist Perspectives on Social Life and Social Science. New York: Anchor Books.
Davis, F. James
1965   "The Effects of a Freeway Displacement on Racial Housing in a Northern City." Phylon 26 (Fall): 209–15.
Dormon, James H.
1969–70   "The Strange Career of Jim Crow Rice (with Apologies to Professor Woodward)." Journal of Social History 3, 2 (Winter): 109–22.
Edmunds, Edwin R.
1954   "The Myrdalian Thesis: Rank Order of Discriminations." Phylon 15: 297–303.
Epstein, Benjamin R., and Arnold Forster
1962   "Some of My Best Friends ... " New York: Farrar, Straus and Giroux.
Glazer, Nathan, and Daniel Patrick Moynihan
1963   Beyond the Melting Pot. Cambridge, Massachusetts: The M.I.T. Press and Harvard University Press.
Grier, Eunice, and George Grier
1960   Discrimination in Housing. New York: Anti-Defamation League of B'nai B'rith.
Henri, Florette
1975   Black Migration: Movement North, 1900–1920. New York: Anchor Books.
Hunt, Chester L., and Lewis Walker
1974   Ethnic Dynamics: Patterns of Intergroup Relations in Various Societies. Homewood, Illinois: The Dorsey Press.
Killiam, Lewis, and Charles M. Grigg
1961   "Rank Orders of Discrimination of Negroes and Whites in a Southern City." Social Forces 40 (March): 235–39.
Laurenti, Luigi
1960   Property Values and Race. Berkeley: University of California Press.
Litwach, Leon F.
1961   North of Slavery. Chicago: University of Chicago Press.
Loewen, James W.
1971   The Mississippi Chinese: Between Black and White. Cambridge, Massachusetts: Harvard University Press.
Marden, Charles F., and Gladys Meyer
1973   Minorities in American Society, 4th Edition. New York: D. Van Nostrand Co.
Mayer, Albert J., and Thomas F. Hoult
1962   Race and Residence in Detroit. Detroit: Detroit Institute for Urban Studies, Wayne State University.
McEntire, Davis
1960   Residence and Race. Berkeley and Los Angeles: University of California Press.
McWilliams, Carey
1948   A Mask for Privilege: Anti-Semitism in America. Boston: Little, Brown and Co.

Myrdal, Gunnar, assisted by Richard Sterner and Arnold M. Rose
1944   An American Dilemma: The Negro Problem and Modern Democracy. New York: Harper and Bros.

Pettigrew, Thomas F.
1975   "Black and White Attitudes Toward Race and Housing," pp. 92–126 in Thomas F. Pettigrew (ed.), Racial Discrimination in the United States. New York: Harper and Row.

Roof, W. Clark
1972   "Residential Segregation of Blacks and Racial Inequality in Southern Cities: Toward a Causal Model." Social Problems 19 (Winter): 393–407.

Rose, Arnold
1956   The Negro in America. Boston: The Beacon Press.

Rose, Arnold, and Caroline Rose
1948   America Divided: Minority Group Relations in the United States. New York: Alfred A. Knopf, Inc.

Schnore, Leo F., and Philip C. Evenson
1966   "Segregation in Southern Cities." American Journal of Sociology 72 (July): 58–67.

Selznick, Gertrude J., and Stephen Steinberg
1969   The Tenacity of Prejudice. New York: Harper and Row.

Shepard, Ward
1942   "Land Problems of an Expanding Indian Population," in Oliver LaFarge (ed.), The Changing Indian. Norman: University of Oklahoma Press.

Shibutani, Tamotsu, and Kian M. Kwan
1965   Ethnic Stratification: A Comparative Approach. New York: The Macmillan Co.

Smith, Sharon
1975   Women Who Make Movies. New York: Hopkinson and Blake.

Taeuber, Karl E., and Alma F. Taeuber
1964   "The Negro as an Immigrant Group: Recent Trends in Racial and Ethnic Segregation in Chicago." American Journal of Sociology 69 (January): 374–82.
1965   Negroes in Cities: Residential Segregation and Neighborhood Change. Chicago: Aldine Publishing Co.

Thomlinson, John R.
1974   "Land Rights or Death." Australian Journal of Social Issues 9, 1 (February): 45–55.

Tresemer, David
1975   "Assumptions Made About Gender Roles," Ch. 11 in Another Voice: Feminist Perspectives on Social Life and Social Science. New York: Anchor Books.

United States Bureau of the Census
1974   The Social and Economic Status of the Black Population in the United States, 1973. Washington, D.C.: U.S. Government Printing Office.

Van den Berghe, Pierre L.
1971   "Racial Separation in South Africa: Degrees and Kinds," in Herbert Adam (ed.), South Africa: Sociological Perspectives. London: Oxford University Press.

Vander Zanden, James W.
1972   American Minority Relations, 3rd Edition. New York: The Ronald Press
       Co.
Van Valey, Thomas L., Wade Clark Roof, and Jerome E. Wilcox
1977   "Trends in Residential Segregation: 1960–1970." American Journal of So-
       ciology 82, 4 (January): 826–44.
Williams, J. Allen, Jr., and Paul L. Wienir
1967   "A Reexamination of Myrdal's Rank Order of Discriminations." Social
       Problems 14 (Spring): 443–54.
Woodward, C. Vann
1957   The Strange Career of Jim Crow. Fair Lawn, New Jersey: Oxford Univer-
       sity Press.

7

Minority Responses

Minority responses to systematic group domination vary all the way from complete acceptance to either total rebellion or separation. Minorities also vary in the extent to which they attempt partial escape from discrimination by avoiding contacts, and in whether they are assimilationist or pluralistic. Some modes of compliance are less onerous than others, and minorities find that some matters are negotiable or otherwise subject to their influence. Some of the inconvenience and degradation of patterns of discrimination can be avoided, and there are ways to act out aggressive feelings without directly challenging the dominant community. Separatist movements represent hope for the most complete escape from systems of group inequality, but they often fall short of the goal. Active resistance takes both covert and overt forms, with variable effects on patterns of accommodation.

RESIGNATION AND ACCEPTANCE

Some of the reasons given by minority persons for complying with systems of discrimination[1] indicate resignation while others reflect acceptance. *Resignation* means outward compliance but inner dislike and rejection of the system; *acceptance* is internal as well as outward assent.[2] In either case there is accommodation, although acceptance is the more complete form, since any compliance means conforming to norms that define role behavior for group members.

Resignation

As defined above, resignation evidently rests on the existential belief that the group is powerless to change its status. Black conformity to the Jim Crow racial etiquette has indicated compliance with the system, not necessarily acceptance. The Japanese Americans largely resigned themselves to, but did not accept, the relocation camps during World War II. Many women who have believed male domination to be wrong have nevertheless resigned themselves to it. As women or other minorities come to believe they have the power to change their status, they become less resigned to unequal treatment.

Sometimes resignation to systematic discrimination is seen as a temporary condition.[3] Sojourners tolerate unequal treatment in order to achieve their goal of returning home. Immigrants who expect to stay and move up the status ladder make the best of discriminatory treatment while they must. Colonized people often consider their situation temporary, and resign themselves to domination by people they are likely to consider inferior to themselves. They may even emphasize certain perceived advantages, such as economic gains, help in combating diseases, or other technological assistance.[4]

Complete powerlessness tends to promote complete resignation, or acceptance. When there seems no possibility of change in a resented system of discrimination, or of upward mobility for individual members of a group, many minority persons become fatalistically resigned.

People who believe there is no hope for improvement in this life may embrace an otherworldly religion, one that promises equal treatment in the next life. Resignation may become so deep that, despite resentment of the system, alternative thoughts and daily habits become virtually impossible. The ex-slaves in the South who stayed with their ex-masters were not necessarily those who had accepted the slave status; many simply did not know what else to do.[5]

Acceptance

Acceptance of the inferior status of one's group means coming to feel that compliance is right, and even agreeing with ideological doctrines such as male or white superiority. There is a sense of the separate identity of one's group, but not much pride in it, because the dominant group's stereotypes and ethnocentric evaluations have been adopted. Apparently the least educated members of the group are most prone to acceptance.[6] When individual upward mobility is readily possible, as it has been for European ethnics in America, lack of pride in the group facilitates assimilation. Some minority persons express feelings of hatred of their own group, especially when there are difficult barriers to upward mobility.[7]

Socialization of minority children to acceptance occurs in stable patterns of stratified accommodation. Much of the learning is through observing their elders perform their roles unquestioningly as they comply with the system, but some of it results from explicit teaching of an ideology of acceptance. The child is taught that a good person knows his or her limitations and does not have unrealistic aspirations, that self-respect comes through personal integrity, that self-restraint is extremely important, and that security comes from doing what is expected and staying out of trouble.[8] Unless there are major challenges to the system or strongly opposing learning experiences, such as upwardly mobile ethnic groups have at school, socialization to acceptance is likely to be highly effective.

Accommodation Leadership

VESTED INTERESTS IN THE MINORITY COMMUNITY   When a pattern of stratified accommodation becomes highly segregated, a separate set of institutions develops to serve the minority group. This may include retail businesses, insurance companies, newspapers, professional practices and associations, separate schools, churches, fraternal societies, libraries, hospitals, welfare organizations, labor unions, restaurants, funeral parlors, barbershops, and other personal services. All of these, and more, developed under Jim Crow in the South as well as in Northern cities, staffed largely by middle- and upper-class blacks.[9] Minority persons who make their living in these separate institutions, and thereby attain respected positions in their communities, have vested interests in the minority-dominant pattern. Because the businesses are typically small, the prices are often higher than those in the dominant community, but separation protects them from competing with the latter. Minority professionals also profit from having a guaranteed clientele, and from a double standard of performance.[10]

TYPES OF MINORITY LEADERSHIP   Minority leaders in stable patterns of accommodation occupy the key liaison roles between the minority and dominant communities, representing each to the other. In his study of black leadership in New Orleans, Thompson identified three types, the first two of which are accommodation leaders. His *Uncle Tom* type accepts the subordinate status and begs for favors rather than making demands, and expresses appreciation. The *Racial Diplomat*—while not accepting the rightness of the system of unequal treatment—interprets black needs, and appeals to whites in terms of human welfare in the total community rather than making strong demands. The *Race Man* makes militant demands for change toward more equal treatment, and criticizes accommodating leaders for protecting their vested interests.[11] This typology might be applied to any minority by adopting more general terms, such as Accepting Leader, Diplomat, and Militant Leader.

During the peak years of the Jim Crow system there apparently were many Uncle Tom leaders, especially at the local community level, and many white representatives refused to deal with any other type. For many decades, except for a very few militant leaders such as W. E. B. DuBois, the Race Diplomat was the only black voice for the ideal of equal opportunity. Booker T. Washington's program of economic improvement through vocational education illustrates the turn-of-the-century Race Diplomat's gradualistic approach to achieving equality.[12] In his "Atlanta Compromise" speech in 1895, Washington accepted segregation in "purely social" areas, but called for racial cooperation in "all things essential to mutual progress."[13] Although this indicated resignation to the system of segregated public facilities, this was the time when the status of blacks was being pushed to its lowest since slavery, and equal opportunity seemed a far-off goal. Accommodating leadership predominated until after midcentury, and began to be displaced by Race Man types in the latter 1950s, after the success of the Montgomery and Tallahassee bus boycotts.[14] We will return to this period and later developments, including the emergence of more militant leaders of blacks and other minorities, in Part IV.

PARTIAL ESCAPE

Avoidance

Without either openly challenging a discriminatory system or attempting to become totally separated from it, minority persons often find ways to limit direct contact to the necessary minimum. Avoidance may be motivated by the fear of conflict, or by hostile feelings toward the dominant community, or by the possibility of being embarrassed by acts of discrimination. When facing changing, ambiguous situations, minority persons frequently avoid contacts rather than risk painful rebuffs. In Chapter 6 we noted a situation in which many blacks who had to move avoided seeking integrated housing in a city in which responses in the housing market were uncertain. In the early 1960s, many Southern blacks were reluctant at first to utilize desegregated lunch counters and other public facilities.[15]

Being self-employed facilitates control of the nature and timing of contacts. Patronizing establishments that are polite and appreciative of minority customers is a way of avoiding those that are not. Among other means of avoidance are paying bills by mail, shopping by telephone, not attending public gatherings where conspicuous discrimination may occur, and not using segregated buses or other separate public facilities. The automobile has greatly facilitated avoidance by enhancing the freedom of movement of minorities.[16] Living in a voluntarily segregated community automatically facilitates a large measure of avoidance of the dominant community.

Voluntary Segregation

One way for a group to cope with discriminatory treatment is *voluntary segregation*—withdrawal into its own community life to a considerable extent, but not totally. The attempt to withdraw completely is separatism, although the result may be more like voluntary segregation. Voluntarily segregated groups have attempted to determine which areas of life they will keep separate, while in involuntary segregation these decisions have been made by the dominant community. Groups that feel alien tend to prefer at least some degree of closed community life, in which they can communicate with and help each other. Sometimes voluntary segregation is a retreat from severe discrimination to the security of a relatively closed community. This has been called "voluntary segregation with involuntary factors"; often, too, there is "involuntary segregation with voluntary factors."[17] The cultivation of women's social activities has not been wholly voluntary.

Outside of work contacts, American blacks have a largely separate community life, but much of it has been the involuntary result of *de facto* housing segregation. Black subcultures, which vary from one class level to another (see Chapter 4), are collective adaptations to a variety of experiences with systematic discrimination over hundreds of years. The emphasis on group unity and pride in the past decade has caused many blacks to support voluntary segregation (with involuntary factors) rather than integration.

Many members of voluntarily segregated groups work outside but return at night, or as often as possible, to the community where they feel at home. Here they can see relatives and friends, use their own language, eat preferred foods, and share in holidays or other special occasions. Leisure-time activities are engaged in largely within the ethnic community, especially where there is exclusion from outside ones. The subculture is typically a selective mixture of the group's traditional pattern and that of the dominant culture.[18]

IMMIGRANT COMMUNITIES   Communities of immigrants are more than networks of family, friends, and leisure-time activities. The better-educated members of immigrant communities usually establish organizations to help new arrivals make the initial adjustments—to get located, to get work, and to begin to learn the strange, new ways. The immigrant ethnic community typically has included boarding houses, community centers, language schools, aid to travelers, organizations for defense against discrimination, and mutual aid societies for the crises of sickness and death.[19] Other common ethnic institutions are banks, real estate agencies, labor unions, special newspapers, churches or temples, schools, and theaters. The larger rural-urban migrant communities—notably those of blacks and Mexican Americans—tend to develop much the same range of institutions. Such facilities, and networks of family and friends, cushion the shocks for newcomers—but they also isolate continuing residents from outside contacts. Movement to residence outside the ethnic community is associated with assimilation, as we will see in Chapter 9.

CHINATOWNS   Chinese Americans experienced sharp economic conflicts in the Western states in the latter part of the nineteenth century. They experienced harassment, and riots in which Chinese Americans were the victims of stone throwing, beatings, burnings or other violence, and even killings. Many dispersed eastward; some returned to China; and many retreated to the deteriorating areas that became the Chinatowns of San Francisco, New York, Los Angeles, and other large cities.[20] They established their own police systems, courts, welfare institutions, protective and fraternal associations, and civic improvement programs. City authorities generally cooperated with this pattern of voluntary (with involuntary factors) segregation, which provided relative safety, although property destruction and police raids continued in some Chinatowns.

The ghetto Chinese were apparently cautious about entering new occupations, staying in low-paying work rather than risking direct economic competition and conflict with the dominant community. For many decades they concentrated in a few areas that seemed safe, such as work in restaurants, laundries, sewing, domestic service, curio shops, and small grocery stores. The sojourner outlook continued among many, and the traditional culture was maintained in China-towns to a considerable extent, until after the Communist government took power in China in 1949. The exodus of the younger generations from the Chinatowns began before World War II and accelerated after-wards, accompanied by entry into many new occupations.[21] This left the older, poorer, less educated people in the Chinatowns during a time of clearances for freeways, urban renewal, and of heavy migration of new racial minorities into the ghettos. The poverty and the substan-dard housing and health conditions in the Chinatowns became aggra-vated.[22] Considerable new immigration from Taiwan and Hong Kong since the abolition of the quota system in the mid-1960s (see Chapter 10) has placed a greater strain on the already crowded housing in the Chinatowns.[23]

The Chinatowns undoubtedly reduced overt conflict by sharply restricting contacts with the dominant community, and by success-fully controlling their internal problems. At the same time the isola-tion permitted stereotypes to flourish, and for a long time Chinese were portrayed in cartoons and films as mysterious, sinister villains. Many Chinese Americans clung to the security of voluntary segregation so tenaciously that they had no outside contacts at all. The leaders of the Chinatowns were generally race diplomats who worked to maintain peaceful accommodation with the dominant community, and there were internal conflicts among the various vested interests. Many peo-ple hung onto the security of voluntary segregation after antipathy against Chinese Americans began to decline. Finally, when dispersal from the Chinatowns became widespread, Chinese Americans contin-ued to maintain family customs and ethnic contacts, and to minimize economic rivalry with the dominant community.

ASSIMILATIONIST VERSUS PLURALISTIC ORIENTATION

Many of the factors involved in assimilation (see Chapters 9 and 10) are primarily under the control of the dominant community, but the minority orientation also influences the process. It is difficult to assimi-late a group with a pluralistic preference—one that strongly prefers to retain its own culture and primary group associations while remaining in the society. Conversely, assimilation is forwarded when a group hides its own language and other distinctive cultural traits as much as possible and seeks to lose its separate identity. Many second-generation immigrants at school have tried to minimize their group identity and be as American as possible.

A minority with an assimilationist orientation, especially the members of its older generations, may resign itself to discrimination (or even accept it) as a temporary burden. Another assimilationist minority, particularly one that espouses equalitarian ideals strongly, may resist discriminatory treatment.[24] A group with a pluralistic outlook, if it expects equal treatment, will tend to oppose discrimination. Jewish supporters of the Anti-Defamation League of B'nai B'rith illustrate this stance. Another pluralisticly inclined group, particularly if it feels quite powerless, may resign itself to a subordinate status that promises security and a large measure of cultural and institutional autonomy. This last situation is illustrated by the millet system, discussed in Chapter 8. As for the question of partial escape through avoidance, an assimilationist group may seek to avoid painful contacts in the short run, and may later be less avoiding. Minorities that desire pluralism vary in the extent to which they seek to avoid contacts with the dominant community.

ACTIVE MODES OF RESISTANCE

Covert Aggression

Aggression against the dominant community indicates lack of acceptance or of resignation. Acts of aggression are *covert* from the standpoint of the dominant community if they are hidden, or if their meanings are not understood. Such acts reflect fear of retaliation against more overt aggression. Much covert aggression is expressive. Many spirituals sung by blacks under American slavery had secret protest meanings, including " underground railroad" themes. The folk art of minorities is full of the moods and thoughts of oppressive treatment, and much of this art remains unknown to the dominant community. Stereotypes of the cruelty, arrogance, and absurdity of the dominant group are communicated in songs, stories, jokes, and cartoons. Derogatory names for the dominant group are common—such as Yankees, palefaces, gringos, pinks, devils, or honkies. Minority people also laugh at the stereotypes of themselves held in the dominant community. Concealment of information about the minority's "dirty linen" or other matters is common, along with stories about how easily the dominant group can be outwitted.[25]

Minority persons fight back against discrimination with a wide variety of covertly aggressive acts, such as spreading rumors about members of the dominant community, loafing or doing shoddy work on the job, malingering, quitting a job at a bad time for the employer, wrecking tools or work materials, injuring one's self (even committing suicide), causing accidents, poisoning members of the dominant group or their animals, driving recklessly, stealing, or burning property.[26] Some of the crimes or other actions against members of the minority group, or against another minority, may be aggression displaced from the dominant community.[27]

Rebellion

A dominative system may be challenged by open force in order to try to end it or to escape from it. Minority rebellion rests on two existential beliefs: (1) that lesser protest and political action are either impossible or ineffective, or at least that rebellion is necessary to get them started; and (2) that the minority group is not totally powerless to influence its own fate. A related belief that lends support to the second one is that help is available. Those who believe the objectives can be reached by other means will not favor the extreme risks and costs of rebellion, and those who believe there is absolutely no hope will see no point to rebelling. Minority rebellion also rests on two value beliefs: (1) that it is morally wrong for a group to accept or become resigned to unequal treatment, and (2) that violence is justifiable to achieve worthy ends.

A highly oppressive and rigid system of group domination is evidently necessary to the occurrence of minority rebellion. Significant minority influence on change through negotiation or political processes is perceived as unavailable. Yet many groups in this situation, even those whose values permit or require aggressive action, have remained accommodated to stratified systems for long periods of time. A group that is small in numbers in comparison with the dominant community is likely to believe that rebellion would be futile. Even relatively large subordinate groups will not see much hope in rebelling if the dominant community is perceived as monopolizing the means of violent force. One way to change this perception is to smuggle in arms, as has happened in Rhodesia and other colonial areas. Major disagreement on minority issues in the dominant community or in outside societies encourages the belief that help is available, and that the group is therefore not totally powerless.

Evidently many American slaves neither became resigned to the system nor accepted it. Slavery remained a national issue, and some help was available to runaways and freedpersons. Large numbers of slaves tried to escape, usually as individuals but sometimes in groups, and some succeeded. Some joined free ("maroon") communities in the swamps and mountains, and others escaped to the North. Court records show that many slaves fought back against whippings or other harsh treatment, and there were at least nine planned revolts. Rebellion was small in scale and unsuccessful as compared with Latin America, where black slaves were much more numerous.[28] Toussaint L'Ouverture's revolt of 100,000 slaves in 1791 led to the abolition of slavery on the French-controlled island of Haiti.[29] Grapevine communications about such events kept hope alive in many Southern blacks, and the news kept white owners uneasy.

Nat Turner's revolt in Virginia in 1831 killed fifty-five or so whites in one day before state and federal troops subdued the slaves, killing over one hundred of them; thirteen other slaves and three free blacks were then hanged, and Turner was captured and executed. Denmark Vesey, a freedman, organized a force of several thousand for an attack on Charleston, South Carolina, in 1822, but the plot was divulged by a slave and put down. Gabriel Prosser led one thousand blacks in an attempted attack against the city of Richmond, Virginia.[30] Turner, Vesey, and Prosser were three of the slave preachers at camp meetings who apparently used biblical teachings to inspire revolts from 1800 to 1831, a practice that led to restraints on slave assembly and worship.[31] So Christianity played a role in black resistance to slavery, as well as in resignation and acceptance.

Protest and Action Toward Change

Public protest and political action against a pattern of discrimination are based on the belief that the minority has sufficient power within the established institutional structure to bring about significant change. In many instances such action reflects a belief that the dominant community is divided on minority questions, or that it is potentially so because of conflicting values and interests. Protest implies the belief not only that certain channels of expression are open to the minority, but also that the dominant community will listen and respond. Political action suggests the belief not only that the group has access to meaningful power, but also that its actions can accomplish shifts in the balance of power and influence major decisions about intergroup relations.

Overt protest varies from songs, poems, and other artistic expressions to various forms of public demonstration. Such activities communicate the feelings and thoughts of protesters, dramatize the seriousness of the problems, and suggest some alternatives. Programs designed to effect change are based on a number of different strategies, which are discussed in Part IV, each resting on particular existential and value beliefs.

SEPARATISM

We have seen that partial escape from a pattern of discrimination may be achieved by avoidance techniques or through voluntary segregation. *Separatism* refers to attempts to withdraw from all contacts with the dominant community, thus escaping its discriminatory system completely. Usually this involves either voluntary emigration or migration to an isolated area within the society, so that group contacts are terminated by territorial separation. Separatist groups typically have sought the open, rural spaces, but the Hasidic Jews in the United States illustrate the attempt of a religious sect to be isolated within a self-imposed urban ghetto.

Separatist Sects

Many religious sects have been separatist, reflecting the clash between their beliefs and norms and those of the surrounding community, and their unwillingness to make the compromises that lead to denominational status. Some refuse to pay taxes, give military service, attend public schools, heed marriage laws, or give allegiance to the national government. Many, including groups of religious dissenters from Europe, have made international migrations. In the United States the more usual attempt of religious separatists has been to find an isolated place within the country. The Mormons, for example, migrated by stages to Utah in order to be free to create their ideal society. They became less and less isolated, and then made the necessary concessions to the federal government rather than to try to move again. Many separatist groups have had essentially the same experience, ending up as voluntarily and partially segregated groups, accommodated to neighbors and governments. Other illustrations of this are the Quakers, the Mennonites, the Amananites, the Oneida Community, New Harmony, and hippie communes. Among the most successful groups at maintaining a high degree of isolation, despite great difficulties, have been the Amish and the Hutterites.

Nomadism

One way for a group to try to maintain social separation is through perpetual mobility, so that it has minimal contacts with settled peoples and established institutions. In modern nation-states, nomadic groups must heed geographical boundaries and come to terms with the countries in which they wander. Sometimes there are sharp conflicts, even warfare. Despite pressure on them to settle down, considerable numbers of tribal people in Asia and the Middle East still cling to the relative freedom of life on the road. The Gypsies (see Chapter 5) remain as nomadic as they can in European and American countries, avoiding a large measure of governmental control and running their own affairs as much as possible. Migratory workers, whose mobility is sometimes as much involuntary as it is voluntary, are not totally separated, but they are effectively segregated.[32]

The Garvey Movement

At the end of World War I a black separatist movement, led by Marcus Garvey, received widespread support among disillusioned Southern black migrants to Northern cities. Garvey had come to New York from the West Indies to get assistance for Jamaican blacks. Convinced that whites in the United States would never allow assimilation, he attacked integrationist leaders. He praised racial purity and blackness, contending that Christ was black and that blacks were highly cultured rulers of the world when whites were still naked savages living in caves.[33] He opposed further racial mixture vehemently, and threatened to dismiss from his universal Negro Improvement Association anyone who married a white. The Ku Klux Klan and other white racist groups were delighted with this stance. He ridiculed the light-skinned leaders of blacks, even the militant W. E. B. DuBois, for allegedly being subservient to whites.

Garvey aspired to establish a black empire in Africa, and he assumed that the New World blacks who did not go to Africa would benefit from having a strong, protective nation there.[34] He made use of parades, ceremonies, rituals, and rewards. He organized cooperative businesses and published a newspaper to advance the cause. In 1923 Garvey became involved in lawsuits, and in 1925 was imprisoned for allegedly fraudulent use of the mails to sell stock in a steamship company. In 1927 he was deported and the movement lost support, but apparently it had helped large numbers of newly arrived urban blacks to develop a sense of identity and pride.[35]

The Lost Nation of Islam

Another black separatist group is the racial-religious sect known as the Black Muslims, started in Detroit in 1930 by the teachings of a visiting peddler (probably an Arab) whose name was Wali Farrad, or something similar. (There are numerous variations of his name.) When Farrad disappeared in 1934, Elijah Muhammad assumed the title of "the Messenger of Allah" and the leadership of the "Lost Nation of Islam." When factions developed, Muhammad moved the headquarters to Chicago.[36] There now are eighty or more Temples of Islam in larger cities around the country, but membership is secret and may be as low as a few thousand or as high as a quarter of a million.

The Black Muslims have insisted on strict separation of whites and blacks. They have rejected the racial integration of public facilities as a false hope, just another trap set by the "blue-eyed devils."[37] They have also opposed intermarriage, believing that blacks are racially superior to whites and that amalgamation weakens the Black Nation.[38] They believe the other races developed from the blacks, the original humans. Whites are seen as temporarily dominant, and as keeping the blacks ignorant of their long history of cultural superiority and rule over the barbaric whites. Black Muslims replace their slave names with Arabic ones and insist on being called blacks rather than "so-called negroes."[39]

Many of their historical and religious teachings conflict with those of the world Islamic movement, and the Black Muslims are not considered legitimate by the Federation of Islamic Associations in Canada and the United States.[40] Much of their moral code, however, follows the Islamic spirit of the puritanical pursuit of the righteous life by prohibiting a great many acts, among which are drinking, smoking, using narcotics, gambling, adultery, dancing, seeing movies, lying, stealing, eating pork, eating typically Southern black food, and straightening or dyeing the hair. There is also heavy stress on courtesy, cleanliness, good taste, and other middle-class values.[41] Members are commanded to work hard as employees of whites, obey white laws and keep out of trouble, and not to show aggression unless attacked.[42]

The political program of the Black Muslims has been much less specific than their economic activities have. No political machinery has been developed to implement the demand that four or five states be turned over for blacks to develop in complete separation from whites.[43] Some progress would appear to have been made toward the ultimate goal of a totally separate black economy.[44] Capital derived from the religious practice of tithing has been invested in a variety of business enterprises in nearly every city in which there is a Temple of Islam. The Black Muslims own large farms in Michigan and several Southern states, and they operate parochial schools in several cities.

Bitter factional conflict developed in 1964 when Malcolm X, the highly articulate Black Muslim leader in New York and the Eastern states, broke off to form the Organization of African-American Unity. He departed from total separatism, contending that limited cooperation with whites is both possible and necessary, so long as blacks control their own organizations. This conviction was at least partly due to his having been treated as an equal by whites (Arabs, mainly) during a visit to North African countries. Malcolm X stressed black pride and black control of their own communities, and called for a more concrete and aggressive program of black participation in politics.[45] He was shot and killed on February 21, 1965, probably by followers of Muhammad. He has remained one of the outstanding symbols of the black-power movement (see Chapter 13).

The emphasis has shifted in the past decade or more from anti-white to pro-black sentiments, and the Black Muslims may be less separatist than they were. It has been contended that separatism may be helping blacks to gain more economic and political power within the society. According to one analysis, separatism can lead to this result through these five stages:[46]

1 separatism—the identity-defining stage
2 nationalism—the ideological, unity-building stage
3 capitalism—the stage of building an ethnic base for businesses and job opportunities
4 pluralism—the stage of building a political power bloc on the economic base
5 egalitarianism—the democratic stage of using political power to secure equal treatment for the group

Perhaps the Black Muslims have contributed to this pluralistic sequence, although their goals—at least originally—were quite separatist. If, instead of separate states or cities, the Black Muslims settle for control of the institutions within black communities, they will have abandoned separatism for an acceptable form and degree of voluntary segregation. They will have accommodated to a pattern that is seen as a significant improvement over the one they originally felt impelled to withdraw from completely.

The membership of the Black Muslims, like the support for Garveyism, has come chiefly from the less-educated, poorer, urban migrants from the rural South. To many in the black ghettos who feel confused and powerless it offers discipline and a meaningful identity in which they can take pride.[47] Most American blacks, however, reject the goal of separate states or their own nation. In both a nationwide poll in 1963[48] and a fifteen-city survey in 1968[49] only about 4 percent of blacks favored a separate nation in the South or in Africa. In a national poll in 1969, 21 percent of the blacks favored separate states within the United States.[50] In still another national survey in 1968, 5 percent of the blacks sampled and 25 percent of the whites supported separate states for blacks. In this last study only 8 percent of the blacks accepted either separate states or a separate nation (or both), as compared with 41 percent of the whites.[51] Whites over fifty, Southerners, and those with less education and occupational status were most likely to be separatist.[52] Thus it would appear that in recent years racial separatism has been supported much more by whites than by blacks in the United States. It was whites who first proposed separatist solutions in the eighteenth century, and such proposals have received substantial white support in every century since.[53]

CONCLUSION

The range of minority response to systematic discrimination is wide indeed, all the way from acceptance and resignation to violent rebellion and separatism, and from assimilationism to pluralism. Even within highly stable patterns of accommodation there are ways to avoid some of the impact of discrimination, by voluntary segregation and other means. Minority aggression can often be expressed covertly, yet latent tensions may result in overt aggression and conflict with the dominant community. The more powerless a minority group feels, the more its aggression will be covert. Open challenges to the system will take the form of protest and political action toward change if the group believes it has some chance of achieving its goals within the system, but rebellion will occur if it does not. Separatism reflects the belief that the only possible and acceptable route open to the group is total withdrawal from the dominant community. More often than not, separatism results in partial segregation, requiring some compromises but yielding some perceived benefits; so that the outcome is a somewhat more satisfactory accommodation rather than the utopia originally envisioned. Perhaps the separatist Black Muslim movement is accommodating to the prospect of greater black economic and political power within American society.

FOOTNOTES

1 Johnson, 1943, pp. 244–66; Berry, 1965, pp. 384–85.
2 Vander Zanden, 1972, pp. 308–15.
3 Shibutani & Kwan, 1965, pp. 292–94.
4 Gluckman, 1955, pp. 140–51.
5 Frazier, 1949, pp. 109–22.
6 Frazier, 1940, pp. 42–43.
7 Rose & Rose, 1948, pp. 210–17.
8 Shibutani & Kwan, 1965, p. 99.

9 Edwards, 1968, Chs. 18 and 19.

10 Edwards, 1968, pp. 285–89; Back & Simpson, 1964; Howard, 1966.

11 Thompson, 1963, Ch. 5.

12 Rose, 1956, Ch. 15.

13 Woodward, 1951, p. 356.

14 Thompson, 1963, pp. 116, 164–71; Killian & Smith, 1960; Burgess, 1960, Ch. 7.

15 Pettigrew, 1964, pp. 162–64.

16 Berry, 1965, p. 387.

17 Yuan, 1973.

18 Shibutani & Kwan, 1965, pp. 284–88.

19 *cf.* Mohl & Betten, 1972. From 1919 to 1940 the International Institutes of the Young Women's Christian Association provided such services to immigrant groups in over sixty American cities.

20 Lee, 1960, Chs. 3 and 4.

21 Yuan, 1969.

22 Yuan, 1966.

23 Light & Wong, 1975.

24 Noel, 1969.

25 Shibutani & Kwan, 1965, pp. 302–7.

26 Johnson, 1943, pp. 294–315.

27 Dollard, 1939, pp. 267–86.

28 Blassingame, 1972, Ch. 4.

29 Berry, 1965, pp. 395–98.

30 Blassingame, 1972, pp. 125–31; Hunt & Walker, 1974, pp. 333–34.

31 Staples, 1976, pp. 154–55.

32 Newman, 1973, p. 172.

33 Cronon, 1955, pp. 172–76.

34 Cronon, 1955, pp. 184–93.

35 Cronon, 1955, p. 222; Martin, 1976.

36 Lincoln, 1961, pp. 10–16.

37 Lincoln, 1961, pp. 123–24.

38 Lincoln, 1961, pp. 88–90.

39 Lincoln, 1961, pp. 68–70.

40 Lincoln, 1961, pp. 71–73, 218–19.

41 Essien-Udom, 1964, p. 28.

42 Lincoln, 1961, pp. 248–53.

43 Staples, 1976, p. 302.

44 Lincoln, 1961, pp. 40–42.

45 Malcolm X, 1965; Bracey et al., 1970, Part 5.

46 Sizemore, 1973, pp. 321–24.

47 Essien-Udom, 1964, pp. 201–203, 354–55.

48 Brink & Harris, 1964, p. 119.

49 Campbell & Schuman, 1970, p. 367.

50 Kosner, 1969, p. 20.

51 Feagin, 1971, pp. 170–71.

52 Feagin, 1971, pp. 172–75, 179.

53 Feagin, 1971, pp. 168–69.

REFERENCES

Back, Kurt W., and Ida H. Simpson
1964 "The Dilemma of the Negro Professional." The Journal of Social Issues 20 (April): 60–71.
Berry, Brewton
1965 Race and Ethnic Relations. Boston: Houghton Mifflin Co.
Blassingame, John W.
1972 The Slave Community: Plantation Life in the Antebellum South. New York: Oxford University Press.
Bracey, John H., Jr., et al.
1970 Black Nationalism in America. New York: Bobbs-Merrill.
Brink, William, and Louis Harris
1964 The Negro Revolution in America. New York: Simon and Schuster.
Burgess, M. Elaine
1960 Negro Leadership in a Southern City. Chapel Hill: University of North Carolina Press.
Campbell, A., and H. Schuman
1970 "Black Views of Racial Issues," pp. 346–65 in Marcel L. Goldschmid (ed.), Black Americans and White Racism: Theory and Research. New York: Holt, Rinehart and Winston, Inc.
Cronon, Edmund David
1955 Black Moses. Madison: University of Wisconsin Press.
Dollard, John, et al.
1939 Frustration and Aggression. New Haven: Yale University Press.
Edwards, G. Franklin
1968 E. Franklin Frazier on Race Relations. Chicago: The University of Chicago Press.
Essien-Udom, E. U.
1964 Black Nationalism. New York: Dell Publishing Co., Inc.
Feagin, Joe R.
1971 "White Separatists and Black Separatists: A Comparative Analysis." Social Problems 19, 2 (Fall): 167–80.
Frazier, E. Franklin
1940 Negro Youth at the Crossways. Washington, D.C.: American Council on Education
1949 The Negro in the United States. Glencoe, Illinois: The Free Press.
Gluckman, Max
1955 Custom and Conflict in Africa. Glencoe, Illinois: The Free Press.
Howard, David H.
1966 "An Exploratory Study of Attitudes of Negro Professionals Toward Competition with Whites." Social Forces 45 (September): 20–27.
Hunt, Chester L., and Lewis Walker
1974 Ethnic Dynamics: Patterns of Intergroup Relations in Various Societies. Homewood, Illinois: The Dorsey Press.
Johnson, Charles S.
1943 Patterns of Segregation. New York: Harper and Row.

Killian, Lewis M., and Charles U. Smith
1960   "Negro Protest Leaders in a Southern Community." Social Forces 38 (March): 253–57.
Kosner, Edward, et al.
1969   "Angry—but they still have a dream." Newsweek 73 (June 30): 19–32.
Lee, Rose Hum
1960   The Chinese in the United States of America. Hong Kong: Hong Kong University Press.
Light, Ivan, and Charles Choy Wong
1975   "Protest or Work: Dilemmas of the Tourist Industry in American Chinatowns." American Journal of Sociology 80, 6 (May): 1342–68.
Lincoln, C. Eric
1961   The Black Muslims in America. Boston: Beacon Press, Inc.
Malcolm X
1965   The Autobiography of Malcolm X. With an introduction by M. S. Handler. New York: Grove Press.
Martin, Tony
1976   Race First: The Ideological and Organizational Struggles of Marcus Garvey and the Universal Negro Improvement Association. Westport, Connecticut: Greenwood Press.
Mohl, Raymond A., and Neil Betten
1972   Ethnic Adjustment in the Industrial City: The International Institute of Gary, 1919–1940. International Migration Review 6, 4 (Winter): 361–76.
Newman, William M.
1973   American Pluralism: A Study of Minority Groups and Social Theory. New York: Harper and Row.
Noel, Donald L.
1969   "Minority Responses to Intergroup Situations." Phylon 30, 4 (Winter): 367–74.
Pettigrew, Thomas F.
1964   A Profile of the Negro American. Princeton, New Jersey: D. Van Nostrand Co., Inc.
Rose, Arnold, and Caroline Rose
1948   America Divided: Minority Group Relations in the United States. New York: Alfred A. Knopf, Inc.
1956   The Negro in America. Boston: The Beacon Press.
Shibutani, Tamotsu, and Kian M. Kwan
1965   Ethnic Stratification: A Comparative Approach. New York: The Macmillan Co.
Sizemore, Barbara
1973   "Separatism: A Reality Approach to Inclusion?" pp. 305–31 in Edgar G. Epps (ed.), Race Relations: Current Perspectives. Cambridge, Massachusetts: Winthrop Publishers, Inc.
Staples, Robert
1976   Introduction to Black Sociology. New York: McGraw Hill Book Co.
Thompson, Daniel C.
1963   The Negro Leadership Class. Englewood Cliffs, New Jersey: Prentice-Hall, Inc.

Vander Zanden, James W.

1972   American Minority Relations, 3rd Edition. New York: The Ronald Press Co.

Woodward, C. Vann

1951   Origins of the New South, 1877–1913. Baton Rouge: Louisiana State University Press.

Yuan, D. Y

1966   "Chinatown and Beyond: The Chinese Population of Metropolitan New York." Phylon 27 (Winter): 321–32.

1969   "Division of Labor Between Native-Born and Foreign-Born Chinese in the United States." Phylon 30 (Summer): 160–69.

1973   "Voluntary Segregation: A Study of New York Chinatown," pp. 151–62 in Edgar G. Epps (ed.), Race Relations: Current Perspectives. Cambridge, Massachusetts: Winthrop Publishers, Inc.

8

Pluralistic Accommodation

We have seen that ethnocentric responses to other groups are typical in relatively stable systems of stratified accommodation. Also, the dominant community usually has little tolerance for perpetuating the identity of a minority group during the process of assimilation. Respect for the identity and the ways of other groups is even less apparent in patterns of uneasy accommodation and frequent conflict, as illustrated by the Protestants and the Catholic minority in Northern Ireland, or the volatile relationship in Belgium between the Walloons (French-speaking and Catholic) and the Flemish (Dutch dialect–speaking and Catholic).[1] It is uncommon for a plurality of culturally or physically different groups to maintain mutual tolerance for each other's ways, but such a pattern has sometimes been envisioned and occasionally realized.

THREE DIMENSIONS OF PLURALISM

Three of the four uses of the term pluralism in social science[2] may be conceived of as different dimensions of a type of intergroup accommodation. These three empirical aspects are discussed below. The original usage of the term is ideological. In this sense, pluralism is a system of beliefs justifying the value of preserving the ways and the identities of different groups. References in the previous chapter to "pluralistic minorities" were to those whose orientation is to maintain their identities, and who seek tolerance for their differences.[3]

The philosophy of the positive contribution of immigrant groups was advanced during and after World War I by Jane Addams[4] and also by Horace Kallen, who used the term "cultural pluralism" in 1924.[5] Louis Adamic later used this concept in his ideological writings, along with Walt Whitman's slogan, "a nation of nations."[6] This usage of the concept has been called "normative pluralism,"[7] but perhaps "pluralistic ideology" is clearer. The ideological view that pluralistic policy ought to be promoted must be distinguished from the three dimensions of the concept of pluralism as a social reality.

Cultural Pluralism

All three empirical aspects of pluralism have often been included, by implication at least, in conceptions of *cultural pluralism,* which means the mutual toleration, or peaceful coexistence, of groups with different cultures. Each group is free to maintain and develop its own culture, not totally separated, but voluntarily segregated to a considerable degree. It means nonpersecution of groups with different ways, and the absence of pressure for them to become assimilated. A governmental guarantee of religious freedom, for example, is a promise of religious pluralism.

Cultural pluralism does not necessarily mean mutual love and admiration, although this ideal is often expressed in pluralistic ideologies. Groups that fear physical violence or other discrimination often seek reasonable control over their own lives, as illustrated by the Chinese American retreat to the Chinatowns (see Chapter 7). Groups that become disillusioned over the prospects of integration may shift to the development of pluralism, as illustrated by the rise of black pride. Cultural pluralism often reflects about as much mutual ethnocentrism as separatism does. The dominant community's culture may be disdained by the minority, and assimilation considered traitorous. To most orthodox Jews, for instance, assimilation is a crime.[8] Even when ethnocentrism is prominent, however, cultural pluralism differs from other forms of intergroup accommodation in the noninterference with the ways of the other group(s).

Political equality does not necessarily accompany cultural plural-ism,[9] although in some cases this ideal is realized. French-Canadians have a large degree of both cultural and political autonomy in Quebec, and equal political participation nationally. They consider themselves an underprivileged minority, however, victims of prejudice and dis-crimination on the part of the English-speaking Canadians.[10] The Republic of South Africa has presented its Bantustan system (Chapter 6) as a means of implementing cultural pluralism, although the racist beliefs and the native opposition to the restrictions hardly represent mutual toleration of cultural differences and peaceful coexistence. Different degrees of political equality are apparent in the discussions below of the millet system, Switzerland, and Yugoslavia.

Structural Pluralism

Social structure consists of patterns of social participation in social institutions and informal social arrangements. *Structural pluralism* is participation by different groups in different institutions and informal arrangements rather than in the same ones. The degree of group enclo-sure of units or areas of social structure varies widely. *Minimal struc-tural pluralism* exists when a group maintains only one or two separate units of interaction, such as kinship or church, and participates in all other community institutions with other groups. *Maximal structural pluralism* exists when different groups participate in common in only one institution, usually government or the economy, and otherwise have separate institutions and informal social arrangements.[11] The lat-ter is but one step removed from separatism.

In his widely cited analysis of assimilation, Gordon limits his definition of the structural separation of ethnic groups to situations in which only the more personal (primary group) contacts are separate, and groups have an abundance of secondary group contacts (at work and in public) with each other.[12] It is apparent that this usage limits the meaning of structural pluralism to a particular degree of it, toward the minimum end of the scale. It is more useful to be able to refer to different degrees of pluralism, which requires specification of the areas that are structurally separated and those that are integrated.

Social structural and cultural pluralism are often highly corre-lated, but they are not identical.[13] Cultural patterns are shared norms and ways of behaving that include institutional structures, and cul-tures are transmitted generationally by participants in common social units. These two dimensions of pluralism are correlated to the extent that groups that are structurally separated also have quite different cultural patterns. When the same cultural patterns are reflected in separate institutions, as when an excluded group invents fraternal organizations that parallel those of the dominant group, cultural assimilation accompanies structural pluralism.

Political or Power Pluralism

In earlier chapters (1, 2, and 4) the distribution of political power among various interest groups and organizations has been contrasted with the monopoly of power by elites. The more political power is distributed among different political parties, business interests, labor, agriculture, reform organizations, and other interest groups, the less likely it is that one group of any type can gain total domination over another.[14] Political pluralism does not require the various groups to have equal amounts of power, but to have an equal right to organize, to join coalitions, and to try to influence political decisions. Through such efforts a group can often improve its power position and reduce discrimination, although success varies with existing social conditions. Political pluralism is not a guarantee of equality to minority groups; but the more widely power is distributed the less unequal intergroup relations tend to be.

Often the concept of cultural pluralism has been used to include power pluralism, and even to suggest equality of power among groups.[15] When the term "pluralism" is used without qualification, the cultural, structural, and political dimensions are all three usually implied. If the dimension(s) being referred to is (are) specified, an otherwise knotty problem—such as whether relations with a middle minority are pluralistic or not[16]—becomes simpler. The middle minority has little political power, especially when it is clearly a sojourning group; it retains its culture, and its social participation is limited largely to the economic area. Thus, typical middle minority situations are markedly pluralistic in the social structural and cultural senses, but not the political.

THE MILLET SYSTEM: A CASE OF NONEQUALITARIAN PLURALISM

A *millet* is a religious community. In the traditional Islamic world, minority groups were non-Islamic religious groups rather than racial or national groups. Religious identity remains important in Islamic countries today, but the concern here is with the millet system in its classical form. Started under two earlier Arab empires, this system reached its classical form under the Turkish Empire—a huge, somewhat crescent-shaped domain centered in Anatolia (Asia Minor) and stretching from North Africa to the Balkans. Despite discrimination and occasional conflict, this form of pluralistic accommodation provided considerable autonomy and security for religious minorities under Turkish rule for nearly seven centuries.[17]

The empire was a political community of Muslims, subject to the sacred law, and under the protection of the sultan.[18] Jews and Christians living in the empire were considered deserving of special protection as nonpagan, one-God, People of the Book (the Bible), even though they were infidels because they rejected Mohammed as the supreme prophet. The Jewish and Christian communities had to acknowledge the absolute political power of the sultan, and they paid higher taxes than Muslims did. Jews and Christians could be converted to Islam, but they could not proselytize and Muslims could not convert. It is clear that the millet system was not equalitarian.

By giving their political allegiance, the religious minorities indicated that they were not a threat to Islam. In exchange the millets were given protection, exempted from military service, and allowed to worship and govern their community affairs according to their own religious laws. They had their own family systems, courts, and schools, but they participated in the economic institutions of the empire. Often they held middle minority positions—in commerce, money-lending, or the professions, even in government. Movement of the religious minorities within the empire was not restricted, and their communities were not sharply delineated geographically.[19] Thus the millet system involved marked cultural and social structural, but not political, pluralism.

While the empire was vigorous, the millet system generally provided autonomy and security for the minorities, but during the long period of decline the minority communities came under increasing strain. They were often suspected of subversive activity in collusion with members of their religious groups in other countries. Concessions were made to allow the emerging nation-states of Europe to offer special protections to the Christian millets, which the Europeans perceived as national groups with political rights, and in the nineteenth century this led to the independence of Greece, Serbia, Bulgaria, and Roumania. In the final, desperate attempts to save the empire some extremely violent actions were taken against the religious minorities, especially the Armenians (see "Expulsion" in Chapter 2). As the empire crumbled, the Arabs, Kurds, and other largely Islamic groups also became nationalistic and sought independence.

Non-Muslims are citizens of the modern nation-state of Turkey, and have no special protections. Their numbers are very small because of the population exchanges of 1924 (see Chapter 2), and Turkey is very aware of its much larger Kurdish national minority, which is Islamic.

In other Islamic countries today there is also awareness of both national and religious minorities. Although nationalism, secular social structure, and centralized economic planning have outmoded the millet system, it was a long-standing demonstration that cultural and structural pluralism can work.[20]

RELATIVELY EQUALITARIAN PLURALISM

Switzerland

The Swiss have provided an example of all three dimensions of pluralism, toward the equalitarian end of the political scale. The ethnic diversity is considerable and complex. German is spoken by the majority; but there is no official language, and French, Italian, and German enjoy equal status. A fourth language, ancient Romansch, is spoken by a small group. There are both Protestants and Roman Catholics among those of German and French background; most Italian-speaking Swiss are Catholics. A policy of religious toleration is followed, and state support is given to both Catholic and Protestant churches.[21] A firm policy of neutrality minimizes international tensions.

The federal government of Switzerland has considerable strength, but a large degree of authority has been left to the local units of government. There are twenty-two cantons, each divided into communes (municipalities). Three cantons are mainly French, one is Italian, three are mixed French and German, and fifteen are mainly German. The communes are ethnically homogeneous, and the cantons largely so, which means there is a large degree of ethnic self-rule in Switzerland. When adjacent communes differ in language they often have a common religious affiliation, and vice versa. When they differ in both they usually have either common agricultural or industrial interests. This crosscutting nature of the economic, religious, and language interests seems to promote unity.

An important historical factor in Switzerland's pluralism is that the various regions joined together voluntarily for mutual defense. However, the northern part of the Jura region of the canton of Berne was annexed to Switzerland in 1815 by action of the foreign powers that defeated Napoleon and took this territory from France. German-speaking people predominate in the canton, but the Jura region is largely French. The long-standing resentment resulted in a separatist movement in this area in 1947, and in the late 1960s and early 1970s there were some militant protests and violence against property. The separatists have not been satisfied with proposed concessions, such as greater use of the French language in the canton, or more autonomy for the region. Yet the population of the Jura region as a whole will not agree to separation from the canton or from Switzerland. The northern communes are agricultural and relatively poor, French-speaking, and Catholic. So the usual crosscutting of interests is lacking within the northern part, but the southern part of the Jura region is industrial, more prosperous, and mainly Protestant.[22]

In 1960 about 60 percent of the Swiss lived in the canton in which they were born, but urbanization is bringing greater mobility and making the more homogeneous communes less important. Foreign workers have been brought in for the industries, and in 1970 one in six persons in Switzerland was an alien, presumably sojourning. Perhaps these industrial-urban changes are undermining the long-standing federal mosaic of homogeneous local units, so the pattern of pluralistic accommodation may well undergo some modification.

Yugoslavia

The government of the Socialist Federal Republic of Yugoslavia is based on the cultural identities of its peoples. It is a pluralistic political arrangement designed to guarantee cultural autonomy and, by implication, a large measure of social structural pluralism. In adopting the blueprint from the Soviet Union when the republic replaced the kingdom in 1946, the desire was to establish a structure that would prevent the sharp ethnic conflicts of the past.

The dominant nationality, the Serbs, make up about 40 percent of the population. The other major nationalities are the Croats, Slovenes, Macedonians, and Montenegrins. The next nine largest groups (Albanians, Hungarians, Bulgarians, Slovaks, Czechs, Ruthenians, Italians, and Turks) constitute about one-eighth of the country's population, and there are many smaller groups. Roman Catholicism vies with Eastern Orthodoxy and a good-sized minority of Muslims. Five of the six republics are populated primarily by one of the five major nationalities; the sixth (Bosnia-Hercegovina) is composed mostly of Serbs, Croats, and Muslims who are chiefly Slavic.

The twin Yugoslavian goals have been cultural self-determination and economic equalization of its different groups.[23] From 1950 on (following the break with the Soviet Union in 1948), economic planning and administration were decentralized, and the republics were given considerable authority over their own development. This accentuated the uneven economic conditions among the republics and brought the ethnic groups into conflict. The most serious and persistent tension is between the Serbs and the Croatians. A mixed Serbo-Croatian language has been attempted to defuse one of the issues; but the Croats have complained that the combined language is mainly Serbian, and have demanded that Croatian be officially recognized.

A number of the other cultural groups have experienced tensions and conflict, and the federal government continues to try to resolve the issues. For instance, the protest demonstrations in 1968 by the Albanians in the province of Kossovo resulted in additional economic investment and improvements in university education there. Rather than try to protect individuals from ethnic discrimination, the Yugoslavian strategy has been to try to guarantee to entire cultural groups both their continued identity and economic parity.[24] The policy of largely autonomous economic development in the republics, although seemingly consistent with a high degree of cultural and structural pluralism, continues to place strains on the pluralistic political federation of cultural groups.

Temporary Accommodation

People who leave their own societies for limited periods of time become involved in patterns of temporary accommodation in the host country.[25] Sojourning migrants seek work in the host society and often remain indefinitely, and we have seen that the accommodations are tenuous and heavily subject to unilateral actions by the dominant community. There are many categories of more clearly temporary sojourners, including representatives abroad of businesses or governments, military personnel, missionaries and other religious representatives, visiting teachers and researchers, foreign students, Peace Corps and similar representatives of governmental or private programs of international development, and travelers. People in such positions are usually very aware of their minority status, although some view the host society with disdainful ethnocentrism. The relevant international agreements and understandings provide minimum guarantees of toleration of the ways of foreign guests. The existence of such guarantees implies political pluralism, and the norms call for a good measure of cultural and social structural pluralism. The patterns of temporary accommodation can disintegrate rapidly when relations between the two nations worsen, and sojourners sometimes become the targets of aggressive actions on the part of the host people.

International trade, peace among nations, and the advancement of knowledge are three of the chief economic, political, and educational benefits desired from the international movement of sojourning groups. In various exchange programs it is commonly assumed that these aims are forwarded by knowledge of other peoples and their cultures. Underlying especially the educational exchanges, and other "people-to-people" programs, is the pluralistic assumption that equal-status contacts promote mutual understanding and goodwill. There seems to be some support for this latter assumption in studies of international students.[26]

The "Two-Way Mirror" has been found in a number of the studies of foreign students in American colleges and universities. This means that the student's favorability toward the host country reflects the degree to which he (she) believes its people are favorable to his (her) nation.[27] Underlying this hypothesis is the assumption that the student's sense of self is closely identified with the home country. A further hypothesis about the two-way mirror has been suggested in Chapter 3—that equal-status contacts often change foreign student perceptions of host attitudes toward the home country, thus increasing favorability toward the host people.

Another finding in some of the studies is a U-curved relationship between length of stay and favorability toward the host country. That is, attitudes toward the United States are quite favorable among new arrivals, least favorable among those here for several months (from Europe)[28] or two years or so (from non-Western nations),[29] and very favorable again among longer sojourners. Disillusionment with the pattern of hospitality or other features of host-country life may account for the decline in favorability, but other factors may be important. One factor may be cultural fatigue, which refers to exhaustion from the strain of efforts to adjust to another culture. The later rise of favorability may be due to acculturation, supportive personal relationships, or the achievement of educational objectives. The U-curve needs more longitudinal testing, and more investigation to determine its meaning.

Temporary minorities are inclined to spend much of their time in enclaves, such as military bases, diplomatic quarters, mission compounds, or special housing areas for business or governmental employees. Such enclaves cushion culture shock, facilitate many adjustments, and reduce the strains that lead to cultural fatigue. Enclaves also limit contacts, although they cannot be totally isolated, and accentuate the alien image. There is also a tendency to associate mainly with the elites of the host society, and to limit the learning of language and other cultural adjustments to activities directly associated with work tasks.

The Peace Corps was established in 1961 to promote international goodwill by sending volunteers to provide technical help to developing nations at the community level. It illustrates a firm policy of avoiding enclave living, association only with elites, and acculturation only in work-related areas.[30] Its program of temporary integration was designed to promote the pluralistic goal of better understanding of other peoples. Success requires close contact with the people of the host country, and living on the same level as the people in the community. This accentuates both culture shock and cultural fatigue, and many representatives have found it necessary to spend their weekends with their fellow volunteers. This pattern of withdrawal and return has enabled most of them to manage some very difficult adjustments. There have been many strains as a result of negative attitudes in the host country toward the volunteers, such as resentment of the value judgment that the society is undeveloped and needs changing, rejection of women in roles traditionally occupied by men, suspicion of Western urbanites in traditional, rural areas, and in some instances suspicion of espionage. But in spite of such problems, it appears that this international attempt at noncompetitive, equal-status contacts has had considerable success.[31]

PLURALISM AND ASSIMILATION

Pluralism in the United States is intertwined with the logically opposite process of assimilation. This perspective contrasts with an older view that all our minority groups have been or are being totally assimilated, and also the view that all have retained their original identities. The further suggestion that pluralism and assimilation form one process[32] may seem surprising at first. To say that the retention of group identity and the loss of group identity are part of the same sequence of events requires specification of what the common process is. Perhaps Gordon has come the closest in his analysis of acculturation and structural integration within the social classes (see Chapter 9).[33] In the meantime we seek knowledge of the conditions under which assimilation takes place and those under which pluralistic developments occur, and the ways in which these are interrelated.

The New Ethnicity

It is not clear whether ethnic identity has become more important to many Americans in recent years, or has just been rediscovered by social scientists. It would seem that it has become more important at least to blacks, and to other racial minorities who have borrowed the black power perspective; but it is very difficult to tell whether ethnic identity has become less or more important to European immigrant groups. But while the trend is speculative, it seems possible to document the continued existence and importance of ethnic identities.

Evidence has been marshalled to show that socially significant differences among immigrant groups in the United States do not disappear within three generations. Descendants of these groups differ from other groups in their family life, voting behavior, choice of friends, leisure-time activities, and in attitudes toward work, religion, and civil liberties.[34] In an analysis of European immigrant groups based largely on opinion survey data, the interpretation is that the effects of ethnic background have not been lost in the presumed American "melting pot." Ethnic differences are reported in political attitudes and participation, family life, occupational patterns, attitudes and behavior concerning alcohol and sex, certain personality traits, and other matters.[35] A number of studies have shown that ethnic and religious identities have continued not just in the central cities, but also (and seemingly more voluntarily) in the suburbs.[36]

Before the emergence of pride in American black culture there was abundant evidence that black subcultures existed. One analysis based on national opinion polls from 1950 to 1961, with the effects of education and region held constant, found that blacks and whites differed considerably in their attitudes on the following matters: child rearing, the punishment of juvenile offenders, political identification, the role of the United Nations, the role of the church, minority issues, and big business.[37] The interpretation was that the black subculture has been shaped by the long experience with prejudice and discrimination. This is in keeping with the larger view that minority culture and identity are modified in interaction with the dominant community.

The conviction in the 1960s that blacks could not gain equality through assimilation, the route that had been followed by so many European immigrants, apparently caused many blacks to shift to some type of pluralistic outlook.[38] Separatism had limited appeal, although it was separatist leaders who insisted on being called black, and some of them—especially Malcolm X—became widespread symbols of black pride. At the beginning of the 1970s, about three-fourths of the blacks interviewed in national surveys stated a preference for living in racially integrated neighborhoods and having their children attend integrated schools.[39] Supporting the right to be free of involuntary segregation, or personally preferring integrated housing and schools, does not necessarily indicate assimilationism. A good deal of institutional integration may be associated with considerable voluntary segregation and cultivation of group identity and political power.

The Chicago Studies

For many decades assimilation was a prominent interest in studies of racial and cultural groups. This was true of the community studies of stratification by Warner and others (see Chapter 4). Park's view of the eventual inevitability of assimilation (Chapter 2) led to many efforts to try to understand the process. Nevertheless, the Chicago studies between World Wars I and II produced much convincing evidence of ethnic pluralism.[40] Minority communities received much attention. Thomas and Znaniecki's study of the experiences of Polish immigrants, Wirth's analysis of the ghetto, and Zorbaugh's study of class and ethnic groups in Chicago all focused on the cultural adaptations and the identities of immigrant groups.[41] In his interpretation of these and other studies, Stonequist stressed the marginal position of immigrant groups,[42] and Park characterized the immigrant groups as a "mosaic of segregated peoples."[43] Myrdal's somewhat later study emphasized the way the culture of American blacks had been shaped by their cumulative efforts to cope with slavery and later with prejudice and discrimination under Jim Crow.[44]

Beyond the Melting Pot

Much of the attention to ethnicity since the mid-1960s stems from Glazer and Moynihan's comparisons of the experiences of different ethnic groups in New York City. In rejecting the idea that group differences had disappeared in the melting pot, they developed the theoretical view that as a group is assimilated it also keeps adapting and develops a modified identity.[45] Thus a Greek is different from a Greek American. Ethnic groups may lose their language and many of their traditional customs in the second and third generations, yet retain ties of family, friendship, religion, fraternal and protective associations, and economic interests. New York's ethnic groups appeared to Glazer and Moynihan to be political interest groups, participating in established political institutions to protect and advance themselves. In short, they saw the ethnic groups as culturally assimilated to a large extent, but manifesting considerable structural and political pluralism.

Dual Identity

Another attempt to conceptualize the relationships between assimilation and pluralism, apparently in large agreement with Glazer and Moynihan, is Greeley's six-step characterization of the process of acculturation and assimilation:[46]

1 cultural shock
2 organization and self-consciousness
3 assimilation of the elite
4 militancy
5 self-hatred and anti-militancy
6 emerging adjustment

The last stage involves harmonizing the ethnic and the American identities. One is comfortable being both "Irish American" and "American." This formulation appears to subordinate pluralism to assimilation, and it also seems to imply that both are inevitable outcomes for immigrant groups. Stage theories do not stand up well against the data, as we saw in Chapter 2, and the thesis of dual identity is not dependent on the idea of stages. Despite its limitations, Greeley's scheme has suggestive value for further work on the complexities of ethnic identity.

A Relational View

In the wave of enthusiasm for studying the rediscovered ethnic groups, it is understandable that the focus has been on the groups and their communities, often to the neglect of the interaction with the dominant community. Glazer and Moynihan have been criticized, for example, for concentrating on the politics and other interests of ethnic groups without taking the responses of the dominant community sufficiently into account. This may partly be why they erred in suggesting that blacks, Puerto Ricans, and Mexican Americans would follow the path taken by the European immigrants, and also failed to anticipate that blacks would not limit their protest activities to the conventional political channels.[47]

Newman has proposed a relational or interaction approach, with an emphasis on conflict, as a means of clarifying the nature of pluralism.[48] Like Greeley, and like Glazer and Moynihan, he sees assimilation and pluralism as reciprocal or twin aspects of patterns of minority-dominant relations. Conflict can arouse group awareness and unity and retard assimilation, but group pride and organization can also facilitate assimilation. Latent tensions and conflicts can activate groups that seem not just accommodated, but assimilated to a considerable degree.[49] Thus ethnicity may become important at any time, so long as there is any sense of group identity, and this may be so for generations.

CONCLUSION

Pluralism is a form of intergroup accommodation in which there are not only group differences, but in which there is mutual toleration of the differences. This does not necessarily mean mutual admiration, nor equality. Analysis of pluralism is facilitated by distinguishing its cultural, structural, and political dimensions, and keeping these three empirical aspects separate from pluralistic ideology. Noting different degrees of these dimensions aids in comparing different pluralistic structures.

There are latent tensions and conflicts in pluralism, as there are in any pattern of intergroup accommodation, and societal crises and changes can result in its modification or demise. Patterns as stable as the three-dimensional one in Switzerland are not common, but so far industrial-urban changes have apparently not disturbed it much. The Yugoslavian federal plan to ensure ethnic identities has been undermined inadvertently by the decentralizing of economic authority, yet the government keeps struggling to make pluralism work. It seems miraculous that the millet system lasted nearly seven centuries, much of the time peacefully, and that it took the decline of the Turkish Empire to shake it.

Pluralism in the United States is not new, either as ideology or reality, yet it remains a puzzle to the American people and to social scientists and historians who have attempted to understand it. Perhaps one important reason why we are puzzled by pluralism is that the rights of individuals are emphasized in our system of law and government rather than the rights of groups. Ethnic identities have apparently been changing rather than disappearing as groups are being assimilated, but it is not yet clear exactly what has been happening and why. Understanding would seem to require focusing on the interaction between groups, not just on the ethnic minority, and particularly on social conflict. Efforts to date to clarify the complex relationships among pluralistic accommodation, assimilation, and conflict have been rather exploratory, and much creative work remains to be done.

FOOTNOTES

1   Hunt & Walker, 1974, pp. 24–41.
2   Schermerhorn, 1970, pp. 122–28; Blackwell, 1975, pp. 10–12.
3   Wirth, 1945, p. 354; Shibutani & Kwan, 1965, pp. 516–25.
4   Addams, 1914.
5   Kallen, 1924.
6   Adamic, 1944; Newman, 1973, pp. 67–70.
7   Schermerhorn, 1970, p. 122.
8   Shibutani & Kwan, 1965, pp. 518–24.
9   Schermerhorn, 1970, pp. 123–24.
10   Hughes, 1943; Wagley & Harris, 1958, pp. 169–70, 195–99.
11   Van den Berghe, 1965, pp. 78–79; Schermerhorn, 1970, pp. 124–27.
12   Gordon, 1964, pp. 235–36.
13   Schermerhorn, 1970, pp. 127–28.
14   Schermerhorn, 1970, pp. 122–123.
15   Hunt & Walker, 1974, p. 7.
16   Hunt & Walker, 1974, pp. 20–21.
17   Hunt & Walker, 1974, Ch. 8.

18   Hourani, 1947, p. 17.
19   Hourani, 1955, p. 121; Coser, 1972.
20   Hunt & Walker, 1974, pp. 244–60.
21   Hunt & Walker, 1974, pp. 41–48.
22   Hunt & Walker, 1974, pp. 42–45.
23   Hunt & Walker, 1974, Ch. 12.
24   Hunt & Walker, 1974, pp. 368–97.
25   Hunt & Walker, 1974, p. 10.
26   DuBois, 1956; Basu & Ames, 1970; Ibrahim, 1970, pp. 38–40.
27   Morris, 1960, pp. 7–30; Davis, 1963, pp. 53–54; 1971, pp. 36–37; Ibrahim, 1970, p. 40.
28   Sewell & Davidsen, 1961; pp. 31–35. This was a longitudinal test.
29   Davis, 1963, p. 53; 1971, pp. 37–39.
30   Hunt & Walker, 1974, pp. 400–401.
31   Hunt & Walker, 1974, Ch. 13.
32   Pettigrew, 1976, pp. 13–18.
33   Gordon, 1964, Ch. 7.
34   Laumann, 1972.
35   Greeley, 1974.
36   Newman, 1973, pp. 77–78.
37   Broom & Glenn, 1966.
38   Glazer, 1971.
39   Goldman, 1971, pp. 179, 267.
40   Newman, 1973, pp. 74–75.
41   Thomas & Znaniecki, 1918; Wirth, 1928; Zorbaugh, 1929.
42   Stonequist, 1937.
43   Park, 1928, p. v.
44   Myrdal, 1944.
45   Glazer & Moynihan, 1963, pp. 13–23.
46   Greeley, 1969, pp. 31–37.
47   Glazer & Moynihan, 1963, pp. 310–15; Newman, 1973, pp. 81–82.
48   Newman, 1973, Ch. 4.
49   Newman, 1973, pp. 182–83.

REFERENCES

Adamic, Louis
1944   A Nation of Nations. New York: Harper and Row.
Addams, Jane
1944   Twenty Years at Hull House. New York: The Macmillan Co.
Basu, A. K., and Richard G. Ames
1970   "Cross-Cultural Contact and Attitude Formation." Sociology and Social Research 55, 1 (October): 5–16.
Blackwell, James E.
1975   The Black Community: Diversity and Unity. New York: Dodd, Mead and Co.

Broom, Leonard, and Norval D. Glenn
1966   "Negro-White Differences in Reported Attitudes and Behavior." Sociology and Social Research 50 (January): 187–200.
Coser, Lewis A.
1972   "The Alien as a Servant of Power: Court Jews and Christian Renegades." American Sociological Review 37 (October): 578–81.
Davis, F. James
1963   "Perspectives of Turkish Students in the United States." Sociology and Social Research 48 (October): 47–57.
1971   "The Two-Way Mirror and the U-Curve: America as Seen by Turkish Students Returned Home." Sociology and Social Research 56 (October): 29–43.
DuBois, Cora
1956   Foreign Students and Higher Education in the United States. Washington, D.C.: American Council on Education.
Glazer, Nathan
1971   "Blacks and Ethnic Groups: The Difference, and the Political Difference It Makes." Social Problems 18, 4 (Spring): 444–61.
Glazer, Nathan, and Daniel Patrick Moynihan
1963   Beyond the Melting Pot: The Negroes, Puerto Ricans, Jews, Italians, and Irish of New York City. Cambridge, Massachusetts: The M.I.T. Press.
Goldman, Peter
1971   Report from Black America. New York: Simon and Schuster.
Gordon, Milton M.
1964   Assimilation in American Life: The Role of Race, Religion and National Origins. New York: Oxford University Press.
Greeley, Andrew M.
1969   Why Can't They Be Like Us! New York: Institute of Human Relations Press.
1974   Ethnicity in the United States: A Preliminary Reconnaissance. New York: John Wiley and Sons.
Hourani, A. H.
1947   Minorities in the Arab World. London: Oxford University Press.
1955   "Race and Related Ideas in the Near East," in Andrew W. Lind (ed.), Race Relations in World Perspective. Honolulu: University of Hawaii Press.
Hughes, Everett C.
1943   French Canada in Transition. Chicago: University of Chicago Press.
Hunt, Chester L., and Lewis Walker
1974   Ethnic Dynamics: Patterns of Intergroup Relations in Various Societies. Homewood, Illinois: The Dorsey Press.
Ibrahim, Saad E. M.
1970   "Interaction, Perception, and Attitudes of Arab Students Toward Americans." Sociology and Social Research 55, 1 (October): 29–46.
Kallen, Horace M.
1924   Culture and Democracy in the United States. New York: Liveright.
Laumann, Edward O.
1972   Bonds of Pluralism: The Form and Substance of Urban Social Networks. New York: Wiley-Interscience.

Morris, Richard T.
1960   The Two-Way Mirror. Minneapolis: University of Minnesota Press.
Myrdal, Gunnar, et al.
1944   An American Dilemma. New York: Harper and Row.
Newman, William M.
1973   American Pluralism: A Study of Minority Groups and Social Theory. New York: Harper and Row.
Park, Robert E.
1938   "Foreword," pp. v–vii in Louis Wirth, The Ghetto. Paperback ed., 1958. Chicago: University of Chicago Press.
Pettigrew, Thomas F.
1976   "Ethnicity in American Life: A Social Psychological Perspective," pp. 13–23 in Arnold Dashefsky (ed.), Ethnic Identity in Society. Chicago: Rand McNally.
Schermerhorn, R. A.
1970   Comparative Ethnic Relations: A Framework for Theory and Research. New York: Random House.
Sewell, William, and Oluf M. Davidsen
1961   Scandinavian Students on an American Campus. Minneapolis: University of Minnesota Press.
Shibutani, Tamotsu, and Kian M. Kwan
1965   Ethnic Stratification: A Comparative Approach. New York: The Macmillan Co.
Stonequist, Everett
1937   The Marginal Man. New York: Scribner.
Thomas, William I., and Florian Znaniecki
1918   The Polish Peasant in Europe and America. Chicago: University of Chicago Press.
Van den Berghe, Pierre L. (ed.)
1965   Africa, Social Problems of Change and Conflict. San Francisco: Chandler.
Wagley, Charles, and Marvin Harris
1958   Minorities in the New World: Six Case Studies. New York: Columbia University Press.
Wirth, Louis
1928   The Ghetto. Paperback Edition, 1958. Chicago: University of Chicago Press.
1945   "The Problem of Minority Groups," in Ralph Linton (ed.), The Science of Man in the World Crisis. New York: Columbia University Press.
Zorbaugh, Harvey
1929   The Gold Coast and the Slum. Chicago: University of Chicago Press.

THREE

THE ASSIMILATION OF GROUPS

9
The Process of Assimilation

In order to understand pluralism it has been necessary to consider assimilation, to which the emphasis shifts in this chapter. *Assimilation* of a minority is the loss of group identity through merging with the dominant community. In relation to pluralism the distinction has been drawn between cultural and structural separation, and the reciprocals of these are the two basic dimensions of assimilation. *Cultural assimilation is acculturation*—i.e., the replacement of the minority group's distinctive cultural traits with those of the dominant community. *Structural assimilation is integration* of social interaction—i.e., replacing the minority group's own institutions and informal social patterns with participation in those of the dominant community. Patterns of accommodation between groups weaken and disappear as the separate identities merge. Even though acculturation or integration may have proceeded a long way, the process of assimilation is not complete so long as the group being assimilated has any sense of its own identity.

Many of the measures of assimilation are designed to trace the modification or disappearance of cultural traits, such as the foreign language, naming systems, traditional values and attitudes, and modal personality characteristics. Rates of intermarriage have been interpreted as indicators both of cultural and structural assimilation, despite lack of knowledge about which social structures mixed couples and their children become associated with.[1] Participation in political, economic, educational, religious, and leisure-time activities has been used to indicate structural integration. Low or declining social distance scores have sometimes been treated as indirect measures of structural integration. Ever since the monumental study of Polish immigrants by Thomas and Znaniecki, case histories—based on material such as letters, diaries, biographies, and interviews—have been used by some researchers to get at the process of cultural assimilation and the changing sense of group identity.[2]

ASSIMILATION VERSUS THE MELTING POT

The idea of the melting pot was both a nineteenth century explanation of what was happening when the different immigrant groups came together in America, and an ideological view of what should happen. The emphasis here is on the explanatory concept; the melting pot ideology is left to Chapter 10. The explanation was that the cultures and social patterns brought by the different groups were melting together to create an entirely new way of life.[3] From the end of the century to the 1930s the most widely accepted historical interpretation was the Turner thesis that frontier life had blended the immigrant groups together to produce a distinctly new people. The frontier was more important in creating the American character, he held, than any European culture or the ways of the eastern cities.[4]

The Order of Arrival

The different groups that migrated to America did not have an equal chance to contribute to the presumed melting pot process. The English colonists came first, and their descendants and later migrants from Great Britain predominated numerically. The cultural and social patterns of the dominant community remained British. The result was more the assimilation of the colonial English patterns by immigrants from Northern Europe than a fusion resulting in totally new ways. Likewise, the later immigrants from Southern and Eastern Europe assimilated a still largely British cultural and social pattern rather than contributing equally to a melting pot process. Cultural contact perhaps always results in some two-way borrowing, but apparently the immigrant groups have been overwhelmingly on the receiving end.[5]

The Triple Melting Pot

On the basis of a study of rates of intermarriage in New Haven, Connecticut, from 1870 to 1940, Kennedy advanced the "triple melting pot" hypothesis. She maintained that national groups were increasingly merging, but largely within the confines of the three major religious communities of Protestants, Catholics, and Jews. In-marriage among the national groups declined from 91.2 percent to 63.6 percent from 1870 to 1940, and the trend was consistently downward. But in 1940, 79.7 percent of the marriages of the Protestants (Germans, Scandinavians, and British) were among themselves, 83.7 percent of the marriages of Catholics (Irish, Italians, and Poles) were with other Catholics, and 94.3 percent of the marriages of Jews were with other Jews.[6] A later analysis showed that this basic trend continued in New Haven until 1950.[7] At least for New Haven, during the time period involved, it appears that religious pluralism was holding strong while national identities were declining.

In his widely read book, *Protestant-Catholic-Jew,* Herberg argued that as national identities declined, identification with one of the three major religious groups was becoming increasingly important.[8] In a similar vein, in a study of a large number of denominational mergers, Lee maintained that Protestantism was no longer divided by ethnic loyalties.[9] Such treatments have been considered supportive of Kennedy's hypothesis. Her use of the concept of the triple melting pot suggested that the national groups were merging to produce new and different Catholic, Protestant, and Jewish religious communities. The alternative hypothesis of a triple pattern of assimilation would imply that national groups are being absorbed by established religious communities.

Despite continuing evidence of substantial increases in ethnic intermarriage in a number of cities,[10] neither the triple melting pot nor the triple assimilation hypothesis now seems very tenable. First, as noted in Chapter 8, ethnic identities seem to be considerably more alive in the United States than appeared to be the case for some time. This applies both to European and non-European immigrant groups, and to racial minorities. Second, intermarriage between Catholics and Protestants apparently is higher in the United States as a whole than in New Haven, especially in places where the number of Catholics is relatively small.[11] So national identity seems to be stronger and the Protestant, Catholic, and Jewish identities somewhat weaker than in the triple melting pot view.

A review of the literature on intermarriage rates, intergroup friendships, group residence, occupations, and political participation has been interpreted to show that Protestants and Catholics have merged to a large extent, and that Jews have mingled with nonaffiliated gentiles. The suggestion that emerged from this is that the Protestant-Catholic-Jew categories must be replaced by a new set of triplets: (1) white Christians (Catholic and Protestant), (2) Jews and unaffiliated whites, and (3) blacks.[12] However sound this may prove to be, it is another indication of the implausibility of the single melting pot hypothesis. And, even though the triple melting pot idea also seems questionable, it appears more and more that assimilation and pluralism must be understood in relation to each other.

CULTURAL ASSIMILATION

The first, difficult adjustments to a new way of life are the beginnings of the process of cultural assimilation. New time schedules, new modes of transportation, ways of getting to work, housing and health care, even learning a new language, are among the many adjustments that cannot wait. In Chapter 7 we saw how immigrant communities develop organizations to help newcomers make these adjustments, and that further cultural assimilation is retarded for those who remain relatively segregated in their own communities.

Acculturation to new food habits is difficult for many, and immigrant groups tend to perpetuate some of their traditional foods and to encourage others to borrow them. In a study of vegetarian immigrants from India, living in a state university community, acculturation to new food habits was found to have three phases: (1) "eggetarian," (2) semi-non-vegetarian, and (3) nonvegetarian. Increases in the amount of interaction with members of the host society were associated with dropping the traditional food habits and the supporting religious beliefs.[13]

Effects of the Minority Culture

The nature and rate of a group's assimilation are affected by its culture, and it appears that similarity to the host culture facilitates acculturation. Immigrants from the British Isles, English-speaking Canada, Australia, and France have acculturated fastest in the United States; peoples from Northwest Europe have been intermediate; and those from Southern and Eastern Europe have acculturated more slowly. A strong sense of pride in the culture of origin retards assimilation, and such pride is reinforced by nearness to the homeland—as illustrated by immigrants in the United States from French Canada and Mexico. A strong written tradition, such as that of the Jews, seems to retard acculturation. So does the persistence of familism, which was found in an interview study in San Antonio to be very strong among Mexican Americans. Fatalistic attitudes were prominent only among the less educated, but at all educational levels the support for familism was significantly higher than among the Anglo interviewees.[14]

Italian Americans illustrate how some of a group's traits can retard acculturation while others seem to advance it. The "Little Italys" apparently have resisted acculturation more than most other immigrant communities have, for several reasons. Probably 85 percent of the migrants had been agricultural villagers, and they settled largely in industrial cities. Rural Italians have had a traditional fear of the representatives of three urban-centered institutions: government, the Church, and absentee landowning. Most were Roman Catholic, and they settled in what had been largely Protestant cities. Family loyalty has been strong, and the family has been the most important audience and reference group. The traditionally open display of emotions contrasts with the more reserved American style. But the Italian traits of strong individualism and an ardor for saving have often been credited with facilitating their cultural assimilation. These latter traits may have facilitated assimilation, or at least economic success, but they should not in themselves be treated as indicators of acculturation.

From a study of Japanese American students in Los Angeles County, it appears that the educational success of a minority group may be due to its own cultural values and habits rather than to its having assimilated American ones. Data came from school records of achievement and from questionnaires on aspirations and value orientations completed in 1966 by Japanese Americans in selected 6th, 9th, and 12th grades. It was concluded that Japanese culture provides strong and unambiguous incentives for success in American public schools. Subordination of individual interests to the family promotes internalization of the traditional emphasis on educational and occupational success, and on legitimate means of achieving the goals. Traditional submission to the father's will facilitates acceptance of the pyramided structure of authority at school. Peer approval among the Japanese American students, who traditionally have had a collective rather than an individualistic orientation, depends on scholastic achievement. More of them like school than is true of Anglo students, who experience some cultural conflicts about school authority and academic achievement.[15]

Effects of the Mass Media of Communication

The newspapers and magazines of the dominant community have apparently not been a strong force for acculturation, especially for the less-educated newcomers and those unable to read the language. Minority newspapers and magazines convey some information to facilitate essential adjustments. Mainly, however, they foster identification with their own group and its culture, so their chief thrust has been pluralistic. Pride in the group's activities, and in the accomplishments of its members, has been a major theme in the foreign language, black, and other minority publications in the United States.

The electronic media have evidently been a much stronger force for acculturation than the printed ones. Movies began reaching the masses after World War I, radio during the 1930s, and television during the 1950s. Even when there is maximum structural separation, minority communities cannot remain as culturally isolated as they often were before being penetrated by the electronic media. In fact, massive acculturation evidently may occur even when there is little contact with dominant groups.

Children experience acculturation at school, but movies, radio, and television reach all age groups with depictions of the life patterns of the dominant community. Dramas, advertisements, news, comedies, and other programs take minority people into the simulated homes of the dominant community, portraying social roles and the associated beliefs, attitudes, and feelings. For black adolescents, for example, the electronic media have evidently been a major means of socialization to the ways of the dominant community.[16] At the same time, the media have fostered awareness of the social separation of the minority and dominant communities.

STRUCTURAL ASSIMILATION

To clarify the distinction between cultural and structural assimilation, let us consider the social relationships between the sexes. To the extent that males and females pursue different interests there is neither cultural nor structural assimilation. Cultural assimilation means the disappearance of different interests and social norms, so that males and females become equally interested in all activities,[17] including child care, football, cooking, poker, needlework, and jogging. But if males and females pursue common interests in separate groups, assimilation is cultural only and not structural. For instance, the elimination of different physical education activities in high school for boys and girls, but still in sex-segregated classes, is acculturation only. If boys and girls are in the same classes there is also some degree of structural assimilation (integration).

Primary Group Integration as Crucial

In Gordon's analysis, the assimilation of ethnic groups consists of seven variables and subprocesses, as indicated in Table 9.1. He considers these to be steps or stages in the assimilation process.[18] Acculturation of immigrant groups usually takes place first and may continue indefinitely, whether other subprocesses occur or not.[19] Acculturation does not necessarily lead to integration, he holds; but integration does necessarily lead to acculturation, and also to the disappearance of the

TABLE 9.1

The Assimilation Variables

SUBPROCESS OR CONDITION	TYPE OR STAGE OF ASSIMILATION	SPECIAL TERM
Change of cultural patterns to those of host society	Cultural or behavioral assimilation	Acculturation
Large-scale entrance into cliques, clubs, and institutions of host society, on primary-group level	Structural assimilation	None
Large-scale intermarriage	Marital assimilation	Amalgamation
Development of sense of peoplehood based exclusively on host society	Identificational assimilation	None
Absence of prejudice	Attitude receptional assimilation	None
Absence of discrimination	Behavior receptional assimilation	None
Absence of value and power conflict	Civic assimilation	None

SOURCE: Gordon, 1964, p. 71.

separate identity of the ethnic group. Thus, structural integration—particularly into primary-group interaction in kinship, recreational, religious, and other institutions—is crucial to the entire process of assimilation. The implication is that integration into economic, political, and educational institutions does not necessarily lead to integration at the more intimate, face-to-face level.

Central to Gordon's analysis is the role of intermarriage, which he considers an inevitable outcome of the minority entrance into cliques, clubs, and other primary groups. Young people tend to marry from among those who have been in the same informal social circles. The more fully an ethnic group intermarries, the more it loses its identity, which in turn brings an end to prejudice, discrimination, and value and power conflicts involving the group.[20] To the extent that intermarried couples identify with the minority community, however, the group identity is not diminished. Estimates based on a survey in the Boston area indicated that many of the children of Jewish-gentile marriages are raised as Jews, so that the loss to the Jewish community is a good deal less than the rate of intermarriage.[21] A summary of the evidence concerning Muslim immigrants in the United States and Canada indicates that the children of those who marry outside the faith are usually reared as Muslims when they live in or near a Muslim community, but not when they are dispersed.[22]

Gordon Reconsidered

In addition to having provoked a great deal of thought, Gordon's major contribution probably has been his demonstration of the importance of structural assimilation, and of the fact that it may not occur even when acculturation has proceeded a long way. Most of the prior work on assimilation was focused on acculturation. However, some questions are in order.

First, Gordon moves from acculturation to integration into primary groups, largely passing over secondary institutions, except for the informal interaction within them. Many clues to understanding both pluralism and further assimilation apparently lie in the economic absorption of groups,[23] and in integration into schools and politics. Second, prejudice, discrimination, and conflict are impossible, by definition, when there is no longer an identifiable minority group. Thus, why not end the list of variables or subprocesses (Table 9.1) with the loss of ethnic identity, and treat it as the measure of complete assimilation?

Third, Gordon focuses on the consequences of structural assimilation to the neglect of the conditions under which it occurs. He treats discrimination more as a dependent variable than as a major obstacle to integration into primary-group activities. He notes the role of prejudice, but he emphasizes minority-group pluralism, suggesting that it is often excessive.[24] As noted in the present book, in prior discussions of "social" segregation (Chapter 6) and of the middle minority (Chapter 4), very strong barriers are often erected against a minority's integration into the informal patterns of interaction in the dominant community. Much of the minority resistance to integration is a defensive response to social discrimination. So, assimilation into primary group structures would seem to depend to a large extent on the reduction of systematic patterns of social discrimination.

Finally, there has not been a great deal of primary-group integration of the ethnic groups new to American cities in this century, so Gordon's analysis suggests a questionable image of the society. Even if his thesis about the catalytic effects of this level of structural assimilation is correct, it cannot explain the continuation of so many parallel ethnic structures. Although he indicates concern about relationships among pluralism, discrimination, conflict, and assimilation,[25] his analysis suggests that ethnic differences produce abnormal tensions, and that assimilation is the master process whereby social order is restored.[26]

THE GENERATIONS

Most international migrants are young adults. Therefore, although generations overlap, those who immigrate at about the same time are approximately in the same generation. Immigration was heavy from Southern and Eastern Europe from the 1890s to its sharp curtailment in 1921 (see Chapter 10). Most of the descendants of those who came in the 1890s are now in the family's third or fourth generation in the United States, while for those who came in 1920 or so the second and third generations now predominate.

The Foreign-Born

The more a person has been socialized in the society of origin, the more difficult it is to be assimilated in another one. Thus, other things being equal, the older the person is at the time of immigration, the more difficult both cultural and structural assimilation are. Those who migrate as small children learn the new language and new social habits readily, unless they are isolated from contacts with the dominant community for many years. Much of assimilation apparently occurs in childhood.[27] Rarely do those who migrate as adults learn a new language and new patterns of social participation well, or discard completely their traditional loyalties, beliefs, and attitudes. Since the typical immigrant is a young adult male, the assimilation of most of the foreign-born does not proceed beyond minimal cultural adjustments and sufficient economic integration to survive. For example, one must learn the daily and weekly time schedule, the system of transportation, and how to get and keep a job.

Not only do immigrant communities facilitate the early phases of assimilation while retarding the later ones, they also provide a pattern of accommodation of the group to the dominant community. This keeps alive the identity of the group, and fosters pluralistic habits of negotiation and of shuttling back and forth between the minority and dominant communities. The better-educated and occupationally successful immigrants are more likely to disperse, bringing them into closer contact with the host society and accelerating their assimilation. The less-educated tend to remain in or near the ethnic community, even though the typical shortage of women results in intermarriage for many of them. The amount of assimilation of different foreign-born groups and individuals varies considerably, and some of them have experiences more typical of the second generation.

The Second Generation

MARGINALITY   The children of the foreign-born experience a great deal of acculturation, especially at school. As this occurs, they often learn that their parents' ways are considered inferior and not American, and they question their group's traditional beliefs and norms. For example, as they learn new norms for relationships between age and sex groups, they typically challenge the traditional respect accorded by the younger to the older, and by females to males. There are countless issues for generational conflict, and the children feel caught between the parental culture and the American ways. Thus they have often been depicted as a marginal generation, caught between two cultural and social worlds, and belonging to neither.[28]

JUVENILE DELINQUENCY   The urban slum areas in which immigrant groups have first settled have long had very high official rates of juvenile delinquency. As long as Southern and Eastern European immigrants were concentrated in these areas, explanations of delinquency rates prominently included the cultural conflicts that presumably disorganized the second generation. Shaw and McKay noted, however, that the rates were high for all groups in the high delinquency areas, not just for second-generation ethnics. They proposed that delinquency results from a gap between learned (American) cultural aspirations and opportunities available for achieving them.[29] This explanation was revived in Cohen's delinquent subculture theory,[30] and in Cloward and Ohlin's theory of opportunity structures,[31] after blacks and Spanish-speaking groups had largely replaced the European ethnics in the (officially) highest delinquency areas. Such explanations of gang delinquency seem to work as well for one group or American generation as another. So, despite the logical fit of such theories to the cultural marginality and limited means of so many second-generation Americans, they apply generally to poor families in the slums and not just to ethnic assimilation.

The validity of the official delinquency rates, and thus of the differences among areas, was not seriously questioned until the 1960s. The differences are very misleading, since it is now clear that there is far more delinquency in middle-class areas than juvenile-court records indicate.[32] Middle-class offenders are more likely to be handled unofficially and turned over to their parents. Police officers patrol the poorer neighborhoods more intensively, and are more likely to handle the cases in those areas officially.[33] Stereotypes of minority groups, and of very poor people in general, apparently affect the chances that children will become official delinquents.

MONOLINGUALISM   Most second-generation Americans have become facile in the use of English, while learning very little of the parental tongue. Even though they may understand a good deal when their parents use the ethnic language, they have usually resisted speaking it because of its association with what are perceived to be the backward ways of the old country. The deliberate retention of the group's language, as among the Amish, has been rare. The resistance of the second generation to learning the language that embodies the parental culture promotes acculturation.

BILINGUALISM   Mexican Americans have been a major exception to the usual language pattern, although some in the second generation have spoken only English. Some have spoken only Spanish, but bilingualism has been most common. Spanish has been maintained in most second- and third-generation homes, among middle-class, working-class, and poorer families alike.[34] Below average performance on verbal tests given in school has been widely reported, but it should surprise no one that children who do not speak much English do not score well on tests in English. Such results were long interpreted as proof that bilingualism retards learning. Many Mexican American children within the normal range of intelligence have even been placed in programs of special education for the mentally retarded on the basis of low test scores.[35]

More recent evidence suggests that bilingual education does not retard learning, and that it may stimulate intellectual development.[36] Long-run performance is the important criterion, and it has been shown that verbal test scores are poor predictors of subsequent socioeconomic status.[37] A study of 1,129 Mexican American households in the Los Angeles area showed that bilingualism had some positive and some negative effects on status attainment. Bilingual children in the working-class and poor groups completed fewer years of schooling than those who spoke only English, but subsequently the ability to speak Spanish was a sign of ethnicity and a help in the blue-collar job market. In the middle class, bilingual children completed more years in school than the monolingual ones, but later the stigma of being identified as Mexican resulted in some discrimination in the white-collar job market.[38] The effects of bilingualism evidently vary with social class position, and they depend on group status, thus on prejudice and discrimination.

The Third Generation

Much of the evidence of the continuing strength of ethnic identities has come from observing third-generation Americans (see "The New Ethnicity" in Chapter 8). This contrasts with the view that immigrant groups are assimilated by the third or fourth generation, a view focused on cultural assimilation only. Gordon's view, of the high degree of structural separation of ethnic groups that have been largely assimilated culturally, seems to refer mainly to immigrants in their third or fourth generation in America. Perhaps more of the traditional cultures remain than has been thought, especially beliefs about the family, leisure time, work, and religion. A subculture of some strength may develop that combines remnants of the traditional culture with emerging political, occupational, and other beliefs, attitudes, and behavior patterns.

"Hansen's law" has been known to social historians for over four decades. It states that the second generation tries to escape its ethnicity while the third attempts to bring it back. The third generation experiences a crisis of identity, according to this reasoning, and returns to an awareness of the ways of its grandparents.[39] This may be a general tendency, but the responses of each generation are affected by changes in dominant attitudes and discrimination against the entire group. At a given time the third generation tends to experience less prejudice and discrimination than the first does, so ethnic identity may become more asset than liability.

Some support was found for Hansen's law in interviews with fifty Italian and fifty Irish Americans in 1966 in the same Catholic parishes in Providence, Rhode Island. Nearly 70 percent of those in the third generation said they thought of themselves as Irish or Italian, as compared with about 50 percent in the second and first generations. Yet the third generation was more removed from the ghetto neighborhood, and about 63 percent had married outside the ethnic group as compared with only 15 percent of the first generation. Very few of the third generation had joined an organization with an ethnic purpose or orientation. However, many of them indicated resentment of discrimination, anxiety about the demands for equality being made by black migrants, and a sense of a common ethnic destiny.[40] This suggests that the identities of third-generation ethnic groups have been strengthened in recent years by competition for jobs, housing, and space in schools with the more recent migrants into the ghettos.

THE NUMBER AND NATURE OF CONTACTS

Assimilation is directly related to the number of contacts with members of the dominant community and the extent to which the contacts are intimate. The more the incoming group is dispersed the more contacts there will be, since small, local groups cannot effectively maintain their own culture and social structures. The smaller the ratio of newcomers to prior residents the more frequent social contacts must be, and the greater the likelihood of very close ones. This is illustrated by a study of eighty-three Jewish migrants from cities to twelve small towns in southern Illinois. They had become so integrated and locally oriented that they considered the people of the town, rather than the small Jewish contingent, to be their primary reference group. They had as many non-Jewish as Jewish friends, and joined both Jewish and non-Jewish organizations stressing community prestige.[41]

Naturalization promotes contacts by (1) increasing employability and (2) facilitating intermarriage. Most large employers either prefer or require citizenship, or at least first papers. Some companies encourage the process by paying immigrants for time spent learning English. Many immigrants become naturalized in order to marry a citizen. The more uneven the sex ratio is, the more likely it is that intermarriage will occur. Intermarriage promotes both the frequency and closeness of contacts between immigrant and dominant groups. The very low rate of naturalization of Mexican Americans is an indication of their pluralism.[42]

PERSECUTION

Extremely harsh actions against a minority group arouse its self-consciousness and produce defensive measures. The denial of citizenship, brutal physical treatment, confiscation of property, or involuntary resettlements are actions of a type that enhance the unity of the group. The excesses of the Nazis in Germany apparently renewed a sense of identity among Jews, who were being assimilated in countries around the world,[43] and much the same thing has happened to the overseas Chinese in Southeast Asia. When harsh measures are used to force a group to become assimilated, as demonstrated in Chapter 10, the typical reaction is a renewed sense of identity and strong resistance to assimilation.

PHYSICAL DIFFERENCES

The Degree of Visibility

Even when groups that are physically different become culturally assimilated, they remain visibly different from the dominant community. Involuntary segregation can limit to a minimum the structural assimilation of racial groups, the physically handicapped, women, and the aged. Even considerable integration into secondary institutions may occur without equal opportunities for rewards. When institutionalized discrimination is otherwise minimal, barriers to the integration of racial minorities into primary-group structures in American society remain great. The more physically different the group is from members of the dominant community the greater the latter's wish to maintain social distance. Thus the dominant group's resistance to the critical phase of structural assimilation of racial groups is greatest for blacks, despite their being more acculturated than are the other racial minorities in the United States. Opposition to black-white intermarriage has been great, and the rate has been low.[44] It was still prohibited by law in twenty-eight states in 1958, but the Supreme Court declared such statutes unconstitutional in 1967.

Racial Amalgamation and Assimilation

Amalgamation does not promote assimilation for blacks in the United States, since the social definition of a black is anyone with any known black ancestry, a definition based on racist beliefs (see Chapter 5). Because more than three-fourths of American blacks are racially mixed, as a heritage of slavery and Jim Crow, their physical characteristics vary widely. "Passing" by a black still refers to persons with even the smallest trace of negroid ancestry, and leaving the black community permanently is the only way an almost all-white person can escape discriminatory barriers to the structural assimilation of blacks. The rate of permanent passing has apparently been quite low,[45] and it has therefore had a negligible effect on assimilation. The route of assimilation that has been relatively open to European immigrants—through intermarriage—is not a realistic possibility for blacks.

For the other racial minorities in the United States, however, amalgamation may promote assimilation. The physical differences are smaller than those between blacks and whites, and there is much less fear of racial mixture. Many Americans have expressed pride in Indian ancestry, at least so long as it is not more than one-fourth. Mexican Americans are perceived largely as a cultural rather than a racial minority, although the vast majority are mestizo, and some are pure Indian (or pure white). When it is recognized that a Mexican American has Indian ancestry the person is not regarded as "passing." Even for Puerto Ricans on the mainland the tendency is to treat mulattos as white, unless the person is very dark or has other distinctly negroid features. The response to partly Oriental ancestry is apparently similar to that made to Indians and Spanish-speaking groups, but few Orientals have intermarried. The route of assimilation followed by many European immigrants, although closed to blacks, seems to be possible for the other racial minorities—through amalgamation.

CONCLUSION

Both the melting pot view and the conclusion that immigrant groups have been rapidly assimilated by the host society have rested chiefly on observations of acculturation. It is now clear that barriers to integration into social structural patterns, especially into participation in primary-group networks, can prevent full assimilation. Largely acculturated groups may still experience strong prejudice and discrimination. A renewed sense of identity may be reflected in the building of parallel social structures, in measures for self-protection, in political action, or in the emergence of a modified subculture. Such responses have been made by many groups in the third generation in America.

The assimilation of immigrant groups, especially those from Southern and Eastern Europe, is far from complete. Yet it has gone much further than it has for racial minorities. As a cultural minority becomes acculturated, it loses its visibility, and its separate identity may disappear if it becomes accepted in the informal groups in the dominant community. Racial groups, no matter how fully acculturated in the United States, continue to experience discrimination because of their physical differences. Blacks evidently cannot be assimilated through amalgamation in the United States, as the other racial minorities can, at least not so long as the social definition of a black continues to be racist—i.e., a person with any known black ancestry.

FOOTNOTES

1   Gordon, 1964, pp. 130, 216; Lee, Potvin & Verdieck, 1974.
2   Thomas & Znaniecki, 1918.
3   Gordon, 1964, pp. 115–20.
4   Turner, 1920, pp. 22–23.
5   Gordon, 1964, pp. 124–29.
6   Kennedy, 1944.
7   Kennedy, 1952.
8   Herberg, 1955.
9   Lee, 1961.
10 Bugelski, 1961; Mittelbach & Moore, 1968; Fitzpatrick, 1966; Alba, 1976.
11 Gordon, 1964, p. 130.
12 Mueller, 1971.
13 Gupta, 1975.
14 Farris & Glenn, 1976.
15 Schwartz, 1971.
16 Gerson, 1966.
17 Hacker, 1951, pp. 67–68.
18 Gordon, 1964, pp. 70–71.
19 Gordon, 1964, p. 77.
20 Gordon, 1964, pp. 80–81.
21 Fein, 1971.
22 Elkholy, 1971.
23 Shannon & McKim, 1974.
24 Gordon, 1964, pp. 111–14, 235–39.
25 Gordon, 1964, pp. 241–65.
26 Newman, 1973, p. 85.
27 Teske & Nelson, 1976.
28 Stonequist, 1937.
29 Shaw & McKay, 1942, pp. 435–41.
30 Cohen, 1955.
31 Cloward & Ohlin, 1960.
32 Short & Nye, 1958, p. 297.
33 Piliavin & Briar, 1964.
34 López, 1976, pp. 234–35; Grebler, Moore & Guzmann, 1970, Ch. 18.
35 Mercer, 1973, Ch. 7.
36 Balkan, 1970; Lambert & Tucker, 1972; Mackey, 1972.
37 Jencks, 1972, pp. 220–21, 350.
38 López, 1976.

39 Hansen, 1937; 1966.
40 Goering, 1971.
41 Schoenfeld, 1970.
42 Grebler, Moore & Guzmann, 1970, Ch. 23.
43 Shibutani & Kwan, 1965, p. 221; Barron, 1946.
44 Heer, 1966; Monahan, 1970, pp. 462–64.
45 Burma, 1946; Eckard, 1947.

REFERENCES

Alba, Richard D.
1976 "Social Assimilation Among American Catholic National-Origin Groups." American Sociological Review 41, 6 (December): 1030–46.
Balkan, Lewis
1970 Les Effets du Bilinguisme Français-Anglais sur les Aptitudes Intellectuelles. Brussels: AIMAV.
Barron, Milton L.
1946 "Jewish Intermarriage in Europe and America." American Sociological Review 11, 1 (February): 6–13.
Bugelski, B. R.
1961 "Assimilation Through Intermarriage." Social Forces 40 (December): 148–53.
Burma, John H.
1946 "The Measurement of Negro Passing." American Journal of Sociology 52, 1 (July): 18–22.
Cloward, Richard A., and Lloyd E. Ohlin
1960 Delinquency and Opportunity. New York: The Free Press.
Cohen, Albert K.
1955 Delinquent Boys: The Culture of the Gang. New York: The Free Press.
Eckard, E. W.
1947 "How Many Negroes Pass?" American Journal of Sociology 52, 6 (May): 498–504.
Elkholy, Abdo A.
1971 "The Moslems and Interreligious Marriage in the New World." International Journal of Sociology of the Family 1 (May): 69–83.
Farris, Buford E., and Norval D. Glenn
1976 "Fatalism and Familism Among Anglos and Mexican American Families in San Antonio." Sociology and Social Research 60, 4 (July): 393–402.
Fein, Leonard J.
1971 "Consequences of Jewish Intermarriage." Jewish Social Studies 33, 1 (January): 44–58.
Fitzpatrick, Joseph P.
1966 "Intermarriage of Puerto Ricans in New York City." American Journal of Sociology 71 (January): 395–406.

Gerson, Walter M.
1966 "Mass Media Socialization Behavior: Negro-White Differences." Social Forces 45 (September): 40–50.

Glazer, Nathan, and Daniel Patrick Moynihan
1963 Beyond the Melting Pot: The Negroes, Puerto Ricans, Jews, Italians, and Irish of New York City. Cambridge, Massachusetts: The M.I.T. Press.

Goering, John M.
1971 "The Emergence of Ethnic Interests." Social Forces 49, 3 (March): 379–84.

Gordon, Milton M.
1964 Assimilation in American Life: The Role of Race, Religion and National Origins. New York: Oxford University Press.

Grebler, Leo, Joan W. Moore, and Ralph C. Guzmann
1970 The Mexican-American People: The Nation's Second Largest Minority. New York: The Free Press.

Greeley, Andrew M.
1974 Ethnicity in the United States: A Preliminary Reconnaissance. New York: John Wiley and Sons.

Gupta, Santosh P.
1975 "Changes in the Food Habits of Asian Indians in the United States: A Case Study." Sociology and Social Research 60, 1 (October): 87–99.

Hacker, Helen Mayer
1951 "Women as a Minority Group." Social Forces 30 (October): 60–69.

Hansen, Marcus L.
1937 The Problem of the Third Generation Immigrant. Rock Island, Illinois: The Augustana Historical Society.
1966 "The Third Generation," pp. 255–71 in Oscar Handlin (ed.), Children of the Uprooted. New York: Harper and Row.

Heer, David M.
1966 "Negro-White Marriage in the United States," Journal of Marriage and the Family 28 (August): 262–73.

Herberg, Will
1955 Protestant-Catholic-Jew. Garden City, New York: Doubleday.

Jencks, Christopher
1972 Inequality. New York: Harper and Row.

Kennedy, Ruby Jo Reeves
1944 "Single or Triple Melting Pot? Intermarriage Trends in New Haven, 1870–1940." American Journal of Sociology 49, 4 (January): 331–39.
1952 "Single or Triple Melting Pot? Intermarriage Trends in New Haven, 1870–1950." American Journal of Sociology 58, 1 (July): 56–59.

Lambert, Wallace, and Richard Tucker
1972 Bilingual Education of Children: The St. Lambert Experiment. Rowley, Massachusetts: Newbury House.

Lee, Che-Fu, Raymond H. Potvin, and Mary J. Verdieck
1974 "Interethnic Marriage as an Index of Assimilation." Social Forces 53, 1 (September): 112–19.

Lee, Robert
1961 The Social Sources of Church Unity. Nashville, Tennessee: Abingdon.

López, David E.
1976 "The Social Consequences of Chicano Home/School Bilingualism." Social Problems 24, 2 (December): 234–46.

Mackey, W. F.
1972 Bilingual Education in a Binational School. Rowley, Massachusetts: Newbury House.

Mercer, Jane
1973 Labeling the Mentally Retarded. Berkeley: University of California Press.

Mittelbach, Frank G., and Joan W. Moore
1968 "Ethnic Endogamy—The Case of Mexican Americans." American Journal of Sociology 74 (July): 50–62.

Monahan, Thomas P.
1970 "Are Interethnic Marriages Really Less Stable?" Social Forces 48 (June): 461–73.

Mueller, Samuel A.
1971 "The New Triple Melting Pot: Herberg Revisited." Review of Religious Research 13, 1 (Fall): 18–33.

Newman, William M.
1973 American Pluralism: A Study of Minority Groups and Social Theory. New York: Harper and Row.

Piliavin, Irving, and Scott Briar
1964 "Police Encounters with Juveniles." American Journal of Sociology 70 (September): 206–14.

Schoenfeld, Eugen
1970 "Small-Town Jews' Integration Into Their Communities." Rural Sociology 35, 2 (June): 175–90.

Schwartz, Audrey James
1971 "The Culturally Advantaged: A Study of Japanese-American Pupils." Sociology and Social Research 55 (April): 341–53.

Shannon, Lyle, and Judith L. McKim
1974 "Attitudes Toward Education and the Absorption of Immigrant Mexican-Americans and Negroes in Racine." Education and Urban Society 6, 3 (May): 333–54.

Shaw, Clifford R., and Henry D. McKay
1942 Juvenile Delinquency in Urban Areas. Chicago: University of Chicago Press.

Shibutani, Tamotsu, and Kian M. Kwan
1965 Ethnic Stratification: A Comparative Approach. New York: The Macmillan Co.

Short, James F., and F. Ivan Nye
1958 "Extent of Unrecorded Juvenile Delinquency: Tentative Conclusions." Journal of Criminal Law, Criminology and Police Science 49 (November-December): 296–302.

Stonequist, Everett V.
1937 The Marginal Man. New York: Charles Scribner's Sons.

Teske, Raymond H., Jr., and Bardin H. Nelson
1976 "An Analysis of Differential Assimilation Rates Among Middle-Class Mexican Americans." Sociological Quarterly 17 (Spring): 218–35.

Thomas, William I., and Florian Znaniecki
1918   The Polish Peasant in Europe and America. Chicago: University of Chicago Press.
Turner, Frederick Jackson
1920   The Frontier in American History. New York: Henry Holt and Co.

10

Assimilationist Policies

In the previous chapters we have noted the informal social controls often brought to bear on minority groups to become assimilated. An example of these ethnocentric pressures is ridicule of the accent, gestures, or other behavior of minority people. The major concern in the present chapter is with governmental policies that are assimilationist. Brief consideration will first be given to the adoption of assimilationist policy by minority groups. In prior references to minority assimilationism (in Chapter 9, especially), the consequences of that orientation have not been emphasized.

MINORITY ASSIMILATIONIST ORIENTATION

A striking example of minority assimilationism is provided by a group of nineteenth century Polish Jews that attempted to gain equal treatment for its individual members by losing the Jewish identity completely. In the 1860s there were from 200,000 to 270,000 people in this assimilationist group, about 10 percent of the Jewish population of Poland. They embraced everything Polish and rejected everthing Jewish, including their language, traditional family and community customs, and their religion. They found that the Poles were unwilling to permit the Jewish identity to disappear, and they continued to be subject to categorical discrimination. Those who were well-to-do found themselves determinedly excluded from close relationships with the families of Christian industrialists. Many of the assimilationists were also excluded from associations with Jews, because of their Polishness, so they became marginal to both communities. Eventually these people were convinced that they could not lose their traditional identity, and they returned to the Jewish community.[1]

When this experience is compared with that of groups in the United States, it appears that minority assimilationism can succeed only to the extent that the dominant community also wants assimilation to occur. Regardless of how far acculturation has gone, it is not easy for a group to lose its separate identity if the dominant community wants it retained. Discrimination can keep alive or revive a sense of group identity, and it can perpetuate the need for separate social structures. Two hypotheses seem plausible: (1) the greater the disappointment of groups that have placed their hopes on total assimilation, or at least on a large measure of integration on an equal-contact basis, the greater the likelihood that they will shift to pluralism or separatism; and (2) the extent of a return in the third (or any) generation to identification with the ethnic group is directly correlated with the degree of continuing discrimination.

ASSIMILATIONIST IDEOLOGY

Early Anglo Conformity

At the time of the American Revolution and afterwards, the prevailing view of the proper outcome of immigration was assimilation. The white population was mostly British and Protestant, and the dominant norm was that newcomers should get rid of their traditional cultures and loyalties and become good English people quickly. This assimilationism has been called "Anglo conformity," and it was expressed by Benjamin Franklin, George Washington, Thomas Jefferson, and other Founding Fathers as desirable governmental policy.[2] The British colonists had already absorbed considerable numbers of Protestants from Germany, North Ireland (the Scotch-Irish), and some from France, the Netherlands, Sweden, Switzerland, and elsewhere. Some Catholics had come from Poland, Ireland, and a few other countries, and there were a few Jews. There was to be religious liberty, but immigrants were clearly expected to adopt Anglo-Saxon ways.

Americanism v. the Melting Pot Ideology

Although it was believed that immigration was needed to develop the expanding nation in the nineteenth century, there was also strong opposition to it. Immigration became a major issue when the value of keeping America open as a land of opportunity for the poor and oppressed came into conflict with other beliefs. Extreme fears of the strange ways of Germans and other foreigners were expressed in the Native American Movement of the 1830s and 1840s. The influx of the Irish as a result of famines produced anti-Catholic movements in the 1850s. The "Know-Nothing" or American Party (unsuccessfully) demanded restrictions on immigration and naturalization, and the ineligibility of foreign-born persons for public office.[3]

It was in opposition to the midcentury nativist movements, as well as against slavery, that Ralph Waldo Emerson and others expressed the melting pot ideology. Later came Turner's thesis that different backgrounds were merging on the American frontier to produce a completely new culture and people, no more English than any other cultural tradition (see Chapter 9). The melting pot view came to mean the biological and cultural mixing of peoples, and the loss of all prior identities in the resulting fusion. Turner seemed unsure, however, about applying this view to the "new immigration" of Catholics and Jews from Southern and Eastern Europe, whose economic opportunities lay in the industrializing eastern cities rather than on the western frontier.[4] In a popular, idealistic play in 1908 entitled *The Melting Pot,* a Jewish immigrant in New York named Israel Zangwill included the new Catholic and Jewish immigrant groups, and all other nations and races.[5]

Beginning in the early 1880s, when the volume of immigration was becoming very large, anti-immigration forces became increasingly vocal and they clashed with supporters of the melting pot view. The American Protective Association, highly influential during the 1890s, was especially alarmed about the Irish Catholics. But in that same decade immigrants from Southern and Eastern Europe greatly increased and rapidly outnumbered those from Germany and other North and West European countries, and attention shifted to the newer groups.[6] In the 41-volume Dillingham Commission Report to the U.S. Congress (1907–10), it was argued that the values and occupations of the "old immigrants" were threatened by the "newer immigrants." Anglo conformity became increasingly racist, with Grant and others contending that the peoples of Southern and Eastern Europe were biologically inferior to the Anglo-Saxons and Nordics in general (see Chapter 5). These views prevailed in the passage of drastic immigration controls in the 1920s, and in the preceding Americanization drive.

The Americanization Crusade[7]

During and after World War I the Americanization movement attracted powerful mass support. The aim was to instill Anglo-Saxon beliefs and habits in the backward newcomers with great speed, so that they would be loyal, 100 percent Americans rather than labor agitators, political risks, or criminals. Business and patriotic groups undertook programs to educate the newcomers about American political processes, naturalization, patriotism, and capitalism. Many cities initiated evening schools for immigrants, with an emphasis on the English language. The pressure became very heavy on the immigrant groups to become Americanized at once, and to demonstrate their political loyalty. Government agencies were caught up in this fervor, and public schools adopted a heavy Americanization emphasis, some of which continued after the crusade ended in 1921. The foreign-born and their children had not all suddenly been Americanized, but the crusade lent support to the passage of legislation to restrict immigration.

FEDERAL CONTROL OF IMMIGRATION

Individual Selection

Immigration had been uncontrolled during the long colonial period, and there were no regulatory measures in the new nation until immigration became a major public issue. By 1830 the states began legislating to keep out undesired individuals, especially Europe's unwanted criminals and poor. Over the decades provisions multiplied to keep out the mentally ill, beggars, prostitutes, anarchists, and other undesired categories of individuals. There were also laws providing a time period during which aliens were subject to deportation, and preventing payment of transportation of immigrants under contract to perform labor.

The first federal control came in 1882, and it followed the lead of the states in beginning a series of provisions designed to select desirable *individuals,* rather than national groups. An exception to this was the passage of the federal Chinese Exclusion Act, also in 1882, in response to pressure from California. This law sharply curtailed Chinese immigration, so that for several decades there were more who returned to China than arrived from there.[8] Also, pressure in 1907 from West Coast states persuaded President Theodore Roosevelt to negotiate the Gentlemen's Agreement, according to which Japan would not issue passports for the mainland of the United States except for persons joining a parent, husband, or child, or returning to a farm or home they had left. Otherwise the "golden door" was to remain open to people of all nations, so long as individuals could meet the screening criteria.

The Literacy Test

Public demand grew for *group selection* as the only way to reduce the flow of immigrants from Southern and Eastern Europe. The number of immigrants averaged over a million a year during the first ten years of the twentieth century, more than in any decade before or after.[9] Labor unions voiced fear of cheap labor, and anxieties spread about population explosions, Roman Catholicism, alleged clannishness of the new immigrants, cultural dilution, and the racist belief that amalgamation would lower the population quality.

In response to these pressures, the Congress established a literacy test for immigrants in 1917. The statute was written in terms of individual selection, adding inability to read in English to the criteria for screening out undesired persons. However, it is clear that the aim was group restriction, by setting up a massive hurdle that entire national groups of peasants from Southern and Eastern Europe could not get past. President Wilson vetoed the measure because the real aim was to reverse the historic policy of the open door to all desirable individuals from abroad, but it was passed over his veto.[10]

The literacy test failed to achieve the poorly hidden objective, because ways were found to help people learn enough to pass it. Immigrant communities organized large-scale coaching operations at Ellis Island and other immigrant examination centers, on ships, and even back in the home countries. After the war the volume of immigration reached the prewar level, most of it from countries that had been the target of the literacy test. The Americanization movement added to the fear that these new aliens were untrustworthy, and public support grew for more effective and more explicit group selection. The result was the decision to establish national quotas to control the national sources of immigration as well as to limit the total amount.

The First Immigration Quota System

The Immigration Act of 1921 was passed as a temporary measure, in a spirit of national emergency. It permitted annual entry of quotas of 3 percent of persons born in other nations who were living in the United States in 1910. In addition to limiting total immigration to well under half of what it had been, the 1921 law reduced the proportion that could come from Southern and Eastern Europe considerably—to less than one-half the new total. Even so, Italy had the largest quota under this scheme, because so many people born there had immigrated from the 1890s to 1910. Immigration from Mexico and other nations in the Western Hemisphere was not restricted by this or later quota systems. This was the world's first immigration quota law, and the method of group restriction set a precedent that was followed by Australia and other nations.

The Immigration Act of 1924

There was dissatisfaction with the 1921 act, despite its sharp reductions of immigration. Another quota plan was worked out by 1924, one that would require time to put into practice. In the meantime it was considered urgent to have a more drastic temporary system, one that would reduce immigration from the "wrong" countries much more.

THE TEMPORARY PROVISION OF THE 1924 ACT   The emergency act of 1921 was replaced in 1924 by another stopgap measure, the provision for annual quotas of 2 percent of the natives of other nations living in the United States in 1890 (rather than 1910). This reduced the total immigration to less than half the amount allowed under the 1921 act, by using a smaller percentage and by moving back to a year when the American population was smaller. It also accomplished a large reduction in the proportion allowed from Southern and Eastern Europe, from 44.5 to 12.4 percent (see Table 10.1), since not many immigrants had come from those nations before 1890. Under this provision Germany had the largest quota, and other North European countries from which large numbers of the foreign-born had come between the Civil War and 1890 also had substantial quotas. (The peak year of immigration from Germany, Sweden, and Denmark was 1882.) The total of 20,423 allowed for Southern and Eastern Europe was actually only about 3 percent of

TABLE 10.1

Immigration Quotas under Successive Laws, United States, 1921–1952

	1921	1924	1929	1952
Northwest Europe*	197,630	140,999	127,266	126,131
Southern and Eastern Europe	159,322	20,423	23,225	23,536
Asia	492	1,424	1,423	2,990
Africa and Oceania	359	1,821	1,800	2,000
Total	357,803	164,667	153,714	154,657
Percent				
Northwest Europe*	55.2	85.6	82.8	81.6
Southern and Eastern Europe	44.5	12.4	15.1	15.2
Asia	0.1	0.9	0.9	1.9
Africa and Oceania	0.1	1.1	1.2	1.3
Total	99.9	100.0	100.0	100.0

*British Isles, Scandinavia, Germany, Low Countries, France, Switzerland.

SOURCE: Peterson, 1961, p. 105, Table 5-2. Based on President's Commission on Immigration and Naturalization, Whom We Shall Welcome. Washington, D.C.: U.S. Government Printing Office, 1953, pp. 76-77.

the immigration from those nations in the peak years before 1921, so for them the "golden door" was almost closed. These quotas were replaced by others in 1929.

THE NATIONAL ORIGINS PROVISION   The second provision of the act of 1924 was to be permanent, with quotas based on the national origins of the white American population as of 1920. Using census figures, it took from 1924 to 1929 to compute the estimates of the national ancestry of the 1920 population of the United States. Blacks and persons born in Asia were totally excluded from the computation, and all other nations outside the western hemisphere were to have a minimum quota of 100. The exclusion of Orientals was due in large part to anti-Japanese political activities in California.[11]

It was concluded that the ancestry of Americans in 1920 was 40 percent British, so Great Britain received 40 percent of the total amount of immigration to be allowed annually, by far the largest quota. On the same basis, Germany received a quota of 16 percent of the total, the Irish Free State 11 percent, and the quotas for all other countries were less than 5 percent. The countries ranking fourth, fifth, and sixth in the quotas were Poland, Italy, and Sweden. Actually, more individuals had immigrated from Germany than from any other nation, with Italy second, the Irish Free State third, and Great Britain fourth.[12] Those from Great Britain had begun coming much earlier, however, and thus had the most descendants.

The chief justification given for the national origins quota system was that the United States had a right to remain the kind of a country it had become by 1920. Newcomers ought to be Americanized, in this view, and not allowed to arrive in such numbers that they would make basic changes in the nation's way of life. A strong assimilationist, Anglo conformity view had prevailed over the melting pot idea. Some of the public and congressional support for the national origins system was based on racist beliefs, including racial interpretations of IQ test results, but there were two other sustaining ideas. One was the belief in the cultural superiority of the American version of English institutions, with no necessary biological assumptions. The other was the value judgment that newcomers should adjust to Anglo-American ways, whether superior or not, because these ways had been the framework within which the people who migrated here first had developed the nation.[13]

If our present knowledge of world population growth had been available to the American public, there might have been less fear of the large volume of migration from Southern and Eastern Europe. Making due allowance for the Irish potato famines, the coming of the railroad and the steamship, political conflicts, religious movements, and other factors, the major explanation of both rural-urban and international migration appears to be economic. The technological revolution (industrial and agricultural) came first to Great Britain, then to Germany and Northwest Europe generally, and finally to the rest of Europe. Greater productivity reduces death rates (because of more and better food, clothing, and shelter), thus causing populations to grow very rapidly, until urban motivation to practice birth control becomes widespread and brings birthrates down closer to the lowered death rates. Agricultural workers are displaced to the cities when populations are "exploding," but instead some of them migrate to other countries when the opportunities seem attractive. When the rate of population growth begins to stabilize at a lower level again, emigration comes to a virtual stop, and the nation may even experience labor shortages.[14]

Thus, migration abroad from Great Britain became large much earlier than from other nations, and it reached its peak from North European nations after the Civil War. The turn of the century brought the technological revolution to the countries of Southern and Eastern Europe. Their population explosions were much faster than ours and Great Britain's had been, because control of contagious diseases caused death rates to drop faster than from increased productivity alone. (Germs were discovered by Pasteur and Koch during the latter third of the nineteenth century, and death rates were reduced when programs of sanitation and inoculation were instituted.) Italy, Poland, and their neighbors would still have sent us a great many more people before their population growth attenuated, although the beginning of the depression at the end of the 1920s would have been an effective brake.

Had the dynamics of population growth been understood in Congress, there would have been less surprise when the large immigration quotas assigned to Great Britain, Germany, and other Northwest European nations went largely unused. Although their populations were larger and more dense than ever, they were no longer nations with many people seeking opportunities abroad. So one unanticipated consequence of the national origins quota system was an even sharper reduction in total immigration than was planned, and a failure to attain a predictable supply of newcomers almost entirely from Great Britain and Northwest Europe.

There were other unanticipated consequences of the quotas, including some difficult problems in foreign relations, especially with Asian nations. Space was opened up for other immigrants into the industrial cities, chiefly from Mexico, Puerto Rico, and from the black sharecropping areas of the American South.[15] Finally, the nearly total stoppage of immigration from Southern and Eastern Europe rapidly changed the age distribution of the *foreign-born* from those areas, sharply reducing the total crime rate for those foreign-born groups. A large proportion of the migrants in the peak years had been young adult males, so the official rates of crime for the newcomers were high before 1921. This is because very young adult males—regardless of race or ethnicity—have the highest rates of commission of felonies. The high rates for first-generation Italian Americans were especially pointed to as proof of the need for Americanization and for the control of immigration. Extremely few young adult males were admitted from Italy after 1921, and all those who had been twenty in 1920 were thirty by 1930. Thus the studies from 1930 on uniformly showed *foreign-born* Italian Americans, mostly the same persons whose crime rates had been high a decade or two before, to have quite low crime rates. If age had been statistically controlled for, the rates would not have been high before the restriction of immigration, or low afterwards.[16]

The McCarran-Walter Act of 1952

A major immigration law in 1952 continued the basic policy of group restriction by national origins quotas, still based on the 1920 census.[17] The proposal to shift the quotas to the 1950 census figures was defeated on the ground that the proportion of Southern and Eastern European ancestry had increased since 1920. A proposal to redistribute the unused quotas of Great Britain and Northwest European countries was also voted down in Congress, on the basis that American cultural traditions (as of 1920) must be maintained. It was a time of great concern about national security (the McCarthy era), and many controversial restrictions on entering and leaving the country were added to the immigration law.

The 1952 act changed the national origins quotas very little from what they had been since 1929, as Table 10.1 indicates. The small increase for Asia was added on a basis that produced strong reaction from Asian nations. A huge "Asia-Pacific Triangle" was defined, and each of the included nations was allotted the tiny annual quota of 100, plus more for China and Japan. However, persons born elsewhere, but whose ancestry was as much as one-half from one of these nations, were to be included in that nation's quota. For example, a British citizen born in England of a British father and a mother from India could gain admission to the United States only under the Indian quota of 100. In the United Nations there was strong objections to the implied racist belief that persons with Asian ancestry are genetically inferior. Three successive presidents—Eisenhower, Kennedy, and Johnson—urged the abolition of the entire quota system in the interest of better international relations.

The Immigration Act of 1965

National quotas were finally abolished in the Immigration Act of 1965, although they were not fully phased out until mid-1968. The law limited the total amount for each hemisphere, reflecting concern about high rates of population growth, but discrimination against particular nations was ended. The total was set at 170,000 per year for countries outside the Western Hemisphere, with no nation to be allowed more than 20,000. The annual limit was set at 120,000 for all nations combined in the Western Hemisphere. Political refugees and victims of natural catastrophes are included in these totals, unless special legislation is passed for particular instances.

The 1965 act gives priority to the value of reuniting families, and to professional and technical occupational skills. It recognizes that the nation's need for unskilled workers is shrinking. It also continues safeguards against admitting persons with records of crime, poor health, political subversion, or other undesired traits; but the selection is on the basis of individual rather than group merit. The law reflects an attempt to balance the values of America as a haven for seekers of new opportunities, and as a land of individual initiative, against the minimizing of job competition and unemployment. Neither the melting pot ideology nor pluralism is explicitly endorsed in the act, yet the return to individual selection implies an easing of assimilationist pressure and greater official acceptance of cultural and racial diversity.

The preference for special occupational skills gives an advantage to individuals from the more developed nations. It also attracts some of the better-educated from developing countries, producing charges of a "brain drain," and makes it difficult for the less-skilled in those nations to gain admission. However selective it may be, the 1965 law resulted in increased immigration from a number of countries even before it was in full effect.[18] Substantial numbers have been coming from Taiwan, Hong Kong, the Philippines, Italy, Greece, Portugal, India, and other countries. Americans in general are well aware of the Cuban and Vietnamese refugees, but probably less aware that the numbers of many new immigrant groups are slowly growing. One unanticipated problem is additional pressures in some of the already overcrowded Chinatowns (see Chapter 7).

Control of Immigration from Mexico

Legal entry into the United States from Mexico increased after the Mexican Revolution of 1909, totaling 174,000 from 1910 through 1919. It rose much more after immigration quotas were applied to European nations, to nearly half a million during the 1920s.[19] It almost stopped during the depression and war decades, but since the early 1950s has averaged about 40,000 a year. From 1942 to 1964 there was also an agreement between the two countries permitting temporary entry each year to agricultural workers (braceros), and often nearly half a million came in a given year. This program became highly controversial, both because of the exploitation of the braceros and competition with Mexican American and other farm laborers.

In addition to the legal immigration there has been a large amount of illegal movement across the border. Despite the absence of a quota, many have not wanted to wait for the bureaucratic procedures for screening individuals, especially during the harvest seasons when jobs have been plentiful and time important. This illegal movement was of little concern to either nation until the Border Patrol was established to help enforce the Immigration Act of 1924, and then the "wetback" became defined as a lawbreaker, subject to criminal arrest and deportation.[20] (Most of the illegal entrants have not swum the Rio Grande or any other river, but the wetback label has stuck.) In 1975 the Immigration Service estimated that there were over eight million illegal aliens in the United States, over five million of them Mexican. Publication of such estimates arouses anxiety about enforcement of immigration laws, about tax dollars being spent for the welfare and education of illegal aliens, and about their holding jobs and thus contributing to unemployment.

Cheap labor from Mexico has long been important to employers of large numbers of farm workers, especially in the Southwest. Most such workers are willing to work hard at unskilled tasks for low wages, to work long hours without overtime pay, and to risk sudden layoffs without fringe benefits. It is to the employers' interest to have a ready supply of these workers when needed, and for the volume of illegal entry to drop when crop conditions are not good. Employers make more profit than they could if they depended solely on domestic farm labor, especially since that is now becoming unionized. Legislatures, churches, schools, and law-enforcement officials cooperate with the most powerful interest group concerned—the employers. Enforcement by the Border Patrol is partial and selective, and the relationship with employers is cooperative rather than adversary. The threat of criminal arrest and deportation helps employers to control illegal entrants and to ensure their cooperation.[21]

A far larger Border Patrol would be needed to prevent illegal entry, but agricultural employers do not support proposals for major increases. Another frequent but unsuccessful proposal in Congress is to impose a criminal penalty on employers of illegal aliens, on the premise that if a crime is involved the employer is as guilty as the worker. The most powerful opposition to this has come from the American Farm Bureau Federation. In practice the worst that usually happens to the illegal entrant is deportation. Those who wish to qualify as legal immigrants are allowed to do so either by acquiring a needed skill, or by marrying a legal immigrant or citizen. Thus even those who occupy the least powerful role, the illegal alien workers, willingly cooperate with this pattern of systematic evasion of the immigration laws.

INDIAN BUREAU ASSIMILATIONISM

Forced Assimilation I: 1871–1929

When the reservation system was started the dominant policy became forced assimilation, designed to get the Indians to abandon their tribal ways and to become rapidly Americanized. For example, the Sun Dance and traditional funerals were forbidden by the Bureau of Indian Affairs.[22] Children were compelled to attend boarding schools, away from traditional influences at home, and forbidden to use their own languages, dress, hairstyles, forms of worship, and other Indian customs. Open rebellions against the early reservation conditions were put down harshly (see Chapter 2), indicating that military force stood behind the Indian Bureau policies.

The Dawes Act of 1887 decreed the breaking up of reservation lands into family plots, a strange idea to peoples accustomed to tribal ownership of land. It was assumed that the Indians would learn to work their own farms and take pride in ownership in the Anglo-American manner. Most of the tribes had not been primarily agricultural, and they lacked farm animals, seeds, tools, and credit. Much of the land was poor and unsuited to farming, and many tribes refused to cooperate with the allotment policy. Some tribes leased land to white ranchers at low rents, or sold it. White settlers were demanding land, and areas not fenced in were opened to "squatters." The tribes lost much of their best land in these ways, and by the end of the allotment period—1914—the reservation lands had been reduced from 138 million acres to 47 million.[23]

Large numbers of Indians died of disease and starvation during these first decades on the reservations.[24] Only a few tribes adjusted rapidly to forced assimilation, and some of their members left the reservations and married whites. The opposite response was extreme apathy—a state of utter confusion due to the breaking up of tribal ways. The most general pattern, however, was withdrawal from the white man as much as possible, and resistance to the policy of forced assimilation. Congress enacted a law in 1924 that made all Indians citizens of the United States, but in seven states they were prevented from voting until the 1940s.

Bureau Pluralism I

In 1929, following the publication of the Merriam Report in 1928, the first federal steps were taken to end the policy of forced assimilation. However, it was not until the anthropologist John Collier was appointed commissioner of the Bureau of Indian Affairs in 1933 that significant changes were made toward a more pluralistic policy. The tribes were encouraged to retain their own identities and cultures— their own arts, crafts, and forms of worship—to obtain and develop new land, and to improve their health and schools. The Indian Reorganization Act of 1934 included provisions for increased tribal self-government, an Indian Civil Service, a system of agricultural and industrial credit for the tribes, and the purchase of land to replace some of what they had lost under the Dawes Act. Only three million acres were ultimately reclaimed in this manner.[25]

Although the new measures were implemented slowly during the depression and war years, health and welfare conditions improved somewhat. There was still extreme poverty on the reservations, but they no longer had the atmosphere of concentration camps. Each tribe voted on whether to accept the provisions of the Reorganization Act or not, and ninety-three had voted affirmatively by 1948. Each of these tribes was empowered to organize for self-government, and to form a corporation to conduct activities. A Tribal Council is elected and run according to procedures that are more Anglo-American than Indian, with inadequate checks and balances, and councils have often been accused of corruption and of not representing tribal views. The council must work with the reservation superintendent in interpreting and making policy. However, the superintendent, who previously was the dictatorial bureau agent, must also work with the council. The council appoints a tribal court of Indian judges, and it also exercises considerable control over tribal finances, subject to veto by the superintendent.

Bureau Assimilationism II[26]

The pluralistic approach was repudiated when the administration of President Eisenhower began, and from 1952 to 1960 the federal policy was strongly assimilationist. One aim was to end tax exemption for reservation lands, but more ultimately the purpose was to disband the tribes and to end the wardship status, with its accompanying special responsibility for the welfare and education of Indians. Beginning in 1954 the Ottawas and Wyandottes of Oklahoma and a number of other tribes were pressured into terminating their tribal organization. The results were so drastic, and criticism from other tribes so strong, that the termination policy was finally abandoned. The Klamaths of Oregon and the Menominees of Wisconsin had both owned valuable timberlands and had been nearly self-supporting. A few years after the termination of their tribal status, both groups were reduced to poverty, welfare, and bitterness.

The so-called Voluntary Relocation Program was begun in 1952, the aim being to get Indians to move to cities. Tribal lands were considered inadequate for the growing Indian populations, and urban relocation and assimilation were judged to be preferable to efforts to develop the reservations. The Bureau of Indian Affairs attempted to facilitate relocation by direct employment and also by adult vocational training, programs restricted in scope by limited budgets. Those who had had the vocational training were reported to earn more than those who did not, and the total amount of education was also found to be favorable to urban adjustment.[27]

The urban migrants have typically experienced culture shock, disillusionment, substandard housing, job layoffs, and lack of coordination among the agencies with services for Indians.[28] Usually transportation to the city has been provided, plus a few weeks lodging, but return expenses have not been covered for those who could not adjust to urban life. Even so, by 1965 nearly one-third of the relocatees had returned to the reservations. Yet relocation has been successful enough so that by 1970 between one-third and one-half of all American Indians were living away from the reservations. Designed to break up the tribes, the relocation has instead produced many militant leaders and supporters of Indian causes in recent years. Some degree of intermarriage and assimilation is doubtless taking place, but both tribal and pan-Indian identities are quite evident in the cities in recent years.

Bureau Pluralism II

The relocation program received less emphasis when the Kennedy administration began in 1960, and there were no more tribal terminations. In 1961 there was a major pluralistic development—the passage of the Area Redevelopment Act, to provide aid for underdeveloped and depressed areas in the nation. Indian reservations were explicitly declared eligible for assistance, which consists of technical aid, loans, and grants. With this assistance a number of tribes have financed successful enterprises, such as a telephone system, a construction company, banks, motels, shopping centers, and agricultural businesses. During the Johnson years the conflict between assimilationist and pluralistic policies continued, and in general the antipoverty programs were administered badly on the reservations.

The main thrust of federal policy in the 1970s has been pluralistic, with considerable support for retaining tribal identities. In 1970, (then) President Nixon took a stand against tribal termination, and in 1973 the termination of the Menominee tribe was repealed. Since 1972 the expressed federal policy has been to develop the reservations, to encourage vocational training for reservation needs, to protect Indian resources, to support greater tribal control of school curricula, and to construct roads on the reservations. President Carter has expressed support for tribal self-government, for tribal determination of budget priorities and school policies, for Indian family traditions, and for fairness with respect to the distribution of natural resources.[29]

Assimilation continues to have its supporters, including those who believe Indian courts ought to be required to conform to the Anglo-American legal norms. In this view, for example, a property settlement in a divorce that differs from a typical outcome in American courts is unjust. In the same vein, criminal defendants are denied their constitutional rights as American citizens. Indian leaders have been demanding more self-government, recognition of treaty rights, reparations, and effective economic development. As Indians have become more militant in recent years, there have been major policy issues within the tribes and among them. There have also been power struggles among the Indians, and within the bureau.[30]

ASSIMILATIONISM IN THE SOVIET UNION[31]

Russian assimilationism provides interesting comparisons with the American experience. Jewish culture and identity are discouraged by Soviet hostility to religion, as noted in Chapter 1, and Jewish emigration is prohibited by anti-Zionist policy. The Soviets rejected the czarist program of forceful Russification of the varied peoples of the non-Russian half of the population, and adopted the strategy of a multinational state. The political subdivisions correspond roughly to territories inhabited by national groups. Within the fifteen "union republics" are autonomous republics, provinces, territories, and districts, each with an ethnic identity and a measure of self-government. All these units are subordinate to the central government, but are allowed considerable cultural autonomy—in language (both in schools and in government offices), in mass communications, in literature, and in the performing arts. The officially stated ideal is that of cultural pluralism, with strong concern for minority rights.

Soviet policy statements have included the right of self-determination of its peoples, even of secession. The Poles and Finns were allowed to secede early, but the Georgians and Armenians were forcibly kept within the new Soviet Union because it was not militarily expedient to let them go. Estonia, Lithuania, and Latvia seceded, but their independence was taken from them again early in World War II. In Chapter 2 we noted the Soviet fear of minorities on the western borders during World War II, and the consequent abolition of eight ethnic territorial units and deportation of large numbers of these peoples to Siberia. In brief, the leaders of the Russian Communist Party have decided when secession will be allowed and when it will not.

Cultural pluralism apparently was adopted as an evolutionary way of bridging from the traditions of the various ethnic groups to those of the dominant Russian nationality. Instead of imposing the written Russian language on illiterate peoples, a move that would seem imperialistic and would arouse separatist reactions, the national groups have been helped first to learn to read and write in their own languages. However, it has also been compulsory to teach Russian in the ethnic schools, along with the official Soviet versions of history.

While cultural pluralism is publicly supported, programs of economic development undercut it. Industrialization and mass colonizing of Far East territories are among the Soviet policies that undermine ethnic autonomy. Large numbers of people in the national groups are being moved to industrial centers, while Russians, Ukrainians, and Armenians are sent to help the less developed parts of the Union. The ethnic groups are more cooperative than they would likely be if their cultures were suppressed, yet their ways are being eroded by occupational changes, migration to urban areas, official repression of religion, and by the teaching of Russian language and history. Soviet leaders have conceived of national diversity as a transient phase in building a more uniform socialist state, so temporary cultural pluralism is a means to the ultimate end of total assimilation.

CONCLUSION

Some assimilationist policies are blatantly open, such as the nearly half century of immigration quotas in the United States and the two different periods of forced assimilation in the Bureau of Indian Affairs. The main, but usually implicit, aim in individual selection of immigrants has been assimilation, although this method is consistent as well with both melting pot and pluralistic goals. The long-range policy of the Soviet Union evidently is assimilationist, but the more immediate and announced policy is one of cultural pluralism. Allowed to keep their own languages and customs, the national groups cooperate with central government programs that are undermining ethnic autonomy. This evolutionary strategy for Russification of the other peoples in the Soviet Union contrasts with the czarist programs of forced assimilation.

Even when assimilationist policies produce a considerable degree of acculturation, minority group identities may continue. Strong assimilationist pressures arouse defensive responses and feelings of loyalty to the group. Despite a large measure of acculturation in the United States, many minority identities seem very much intact (see Chapter 9). While American minorities have been heavily pressured to become assimilated, they have also met discrimination and have been barred from full participation in community institutions and networks of primary group interaction.

FOOTNOTES

1 Heller, 1973.
2 Gordon, 1964, pp. 84–90; Cole & Cole, 1954.
3 Gordon, 1964, pp. 91–95.
4 Gordon, 1964, pp. 115–21.
5 Zangwill, 1908.
6 Gordon, 1964, pp. 96–97.
7 Gordon, 1964, pp. 98–101.

8   Davie, 1936, pp. 315–16.
9   Statistical Abstract of the United States, 1961, p. 92.
10 Gordon, 1964, p. 102.
11 Daniels, 1962.
12 Thomlinson, 1967, p. 245.
13 Gordon, 1964, pp. 103–4.
14 Landis & Hatt, 1954, pp. 446–54.
15 Yinger, 1973, p. 5.
16 Sutherland & Cressey, 1960, pp. 143–44.
17 Thomlinson, 1967, pp. 255–56; Peterson, 1961, pp. 104–9.
18 Yinger, 1973, p. 5.
19 Grebler et al., 1970. p. 64.
20 Bustamante, 1972, pp. 706–8.
21 Stoddard, 1976; Bustamante, 1972, pp. 709–18.
22 Burnette & Koster, 1974, pp. 9–13.
23 Shepard, 1942, p. 11.
24 Burnette & Koster, 1974, p. 14.
25 Burnette & Koster, 1974, pp. 15–16.
26 Burnette & Koster, 1974, pp. 16–18, 156–59.
27 Sorkin, 1969.
28 Berger, 1970.
29 Indian Affairs, 1976, pp. 5–6.
30 Burnette & Koster, 1974, Ch. 11.
31 Hunt & Walker, 1974, Ch. 3.

REFERENCES

Berger, Fred
1970   The Minnesota Indian in Minneapolis. Minneapolis: Training Center for Community Programs.
Burnette, Robert, and John Koster
1974   The Road to Wounded Knee. New York: Bantam Books, Inc.
Bustamante, Jorge A.
1972   "The Wetback as 'Deviant': An Application of Labeling Theory." American Journal of Sociology 77 (January): 706–18.
Cole, Stewart G., and Mildred Wiese Cole
1954   Minorities and the American Promise. New York: Harper and Bros.
Daniels, Roger
1962   The Politics of Prejudice: The Anti-Japanese Movement in California and the Struggle for Japanese Exclusion. Berkeley and Los Angeles: University of California Press.
Davie, Maurice R.
1936   World Immigration. New York: The Macmillan Co.
Gordon, Milton M.
1964   Assimilation in American Life. New York: Oxford University Press.

Grebler, L., et al.
1970   The Mexican American People: The Nation's Second Largest Minority. New York: The Free Press.
Heller, Celia Stopnicka
1973   "Assimilation: A Deviant Pattern Among the Jews of Interwar Poland." Jewish Journal of Sociology 15, 2 (December): 221–37.
Hunt, Chester L., and Lewis Walker
1974   Ethnic Dynamics: Patterns of Intergroup Relations in Various Societies. Homewood, Illinois: The Dorsey Press.
Indian Affairs
1976   "Presidential Candidates State Indian Policy." Indian Affairs 92 (July-November): 5–6. New York: Newsletter of the Association of American Indian Affairs, Inc.
Landis, Paul H., and Paul K. Hatt
1954   Population Problems, 2nd Edition. New York: American Book Co.
Peterson, William
1961   Population. New York: The Macmillan Co.
Shepard, Ward
1942   "Land Problems of an Expanding Indian Population," in Oliver LaFarge (ed.), The Changing Indian. Norman: University of Oklahoma Press.
Sorkin, Alan
1969   "Some Aspects of American Indian Migration." Social Forces 48, 2 (December): 243–50.
Stoddard, Ellwyn R.
1976   "Illegal Mexican Labor in the Borderlands: Institutionalized Support of an Unlawful Practice." Pacific Sociological Review 19, 2 (April): 175–210.
Sutherland, Edwin H., and Donald R. Cressey
1960   Principles of Criminology, 6th Edition. Philadelphia: J. B. Lippincott Co.
Thomlinson, Ralph
1967   Demographic Problems. Belmont, California: Dickenson Publishing Co.
United States Bureau of the Census
1961   Statistical Abstract of the United States, 1961. Washington, D.C.: U.S. Government Printing Office.
Yinger, J. Milton
1973   "Recent Developments in Minority and Race Relations," pp. 4–22 in, Edgar G. Epps, Race Relations: Current Perspectives. Cambridge, Massachusetts: Winthrop Publishers, Inc. Reprinted from The Annals 378 (July 1968): 130–45.
Zangwill, Israel
1909   The Melting Pot: Drama in Four Acts. New York: The Macmillan Co.

FOUR

ACTION
TOWARD EQUALITY

11

Economic and Educational Programs

Strategies for raising the status of minorities vary from selective ones that are limited largely to a particular method or institutional area to broad, across-the-board approaches. Much of the selective type of effort in the United States has been aimed at economic improvement or has involved education, although in recent decades these areas have increasingly been incorporated into broader strategies. For at least the first half of the twentieth century, economic and educational programs were, for the most part, gradualistic as well as selective.

ECONOMIC IMPROVEMENT

A common existential belief underlying programs of economic improvement has been that a higher economic status facilitates more equal treatment of the group in all areas of life. Going further, it has sometimes been held that economic improvement is a necessary first step, so that efforts to produce other changes first are futile. The values of equal opportunity for individuals and full utilization of individual talents have been emphasized in ideological justifications of programs of economic improvement. Since the early 1960s the value of group equality in economic outcomes has been stressed much more than before—e.g., proportional representation in desirable occupations, positions in government and administration, and equality in promotions and pay.

Education and Economic Gains

Much of the hope for minority economic improvement has been based on the American faith in education as a means of climbing the class ladder and solving problems. Most American minorities have adopted this faith, or already had it, and have placed great hope in education. This faith has pertained not only to getting a job and remaining employed, but also to obtaining better pay, promotions, and minority movement into new occupations, professions, and administrative positions. Millions of immigrants have struggled up the educational and economic ladders, as new groups have arrived to take over their old jobs and residences.[1] However, these gains have often been made in spite of unequal treatment, and upward mobility does not put an end to discrimination against the group.

VOCATIONAL EDUCATION   Very large numbers of minority people have learned work skills in classes in vocational education, mainly in city programs geared to business and industrial needs, and very often these have led to employment. Possession of a skill does not guarantee a job, or advancement, particularly when competition is keen or when a minority group has been completely barred from an occupational area. In Chapter 6 we noted Booker T. Washington's efforts toward economic improvement through vocational schools, and the general failure in those bleakest of Jim Crow years to channel blacks into the jobs for which they were trained.

Vocational training is of special value to minorities for learning skilled trades that have traditionally been entered by apprenticeship, since that route is generally open only to those who have access to the primary-group networks of the tradesmen. Most apprentices in the construction trades, for example, have obtained their training opportunities through informal contacts. Blacks, some of whose ancestors were skilled carpenters and masons during slave days, have found it extremely difficult to break through the barrier of social segregation to apprenticeships in the construction trades.[2] Women have been largely excluded from programs of apprenticeship in male-dominated occupations, since admission to training is guarded by primary-group networks of men. Notices of apprenticeships in skilled trades are often posted only in places women do not see, such as men's washrooms. Another factor is that young apprentices are preferred, between the ages of 18 and 24, and many women do not want to enter such programs until they have married and started families.[3] Getting vocational training does not guarantee entry into craft unions and skilled jobs for minority persons, but it bypasses a crucial obstacle.

Selection for programs of vocational education can be discriminatory. Training that provides significant opportunity for some members of a group, or at a given time for many of its members, may hold down persons who want a more difficult challenge and who are capable of it. Vocational training has become so identified with minorities that counselors have often discouraged minority students from college-preparatory courses, and from aspiring to occupational areas in which minority persons are absent or scarce. For instance, a black girl who wants to study nursing may be counseled to aim for business school instead, or perhaps vocational nursing. A black boy who aspires to be a dentist may be advised that he can work with his hands in auto mechanics.

Vocational training programs are more openly labeled for men and women than they are for racial and cultural groups. For example, it is still almost impossible for a girl or woman to be admitted to vocational training for plumbing, although there are now some token trainees. The female is likely to be advised that there are openings in women's fields, such as beauty specialist or dental assistant. School officials do not want to train women for skills controlled by unions that will not admit them, and union officials say they cannot find any qualified women. Yet Title IX of the Federal Education Amendments of 1972 prohibits sex discrimination in admissions, courses, and counseling in all federally funded programs of education.

HIGHER EDUCATION   For movement upward into better-paying and more secure occupations, higher education has become more and more essential. Opportunities for both undergraduate and professional training are crucial to minorities. Both inadequate facilities and group discrimination in admissions policies help perpetuate low economic status. Many colleges and universities excluded women until well into the 1960s, and many small colleges were restricted to women. Before the 1970s, professional schools that admitted women usually had informal quotas designed to keep women students at about 5 percent of the total. There have been dramatic increases in the number of women in professional schools, but the proportion admitted is still far from half. In 1974, 23.7 percent of the nation's first-year law students were women, and 22.2 percent of all first-year medical students.[4]

During the long period of *de jure* racial segregation in higher education, only a few blacks in the Southern and border states were able to go north to college. Most of those desiring higher education would have had no opportunity except for the public and private black institutions. Graduates from these colleges and universities have provided role models of achievement for black children, as well as much of the leadership for the black community. Major changes in black enrollment patterns resulted from the desegregation process, from black migration out of the South, and from the provision of federal financial support of minorities for higher education. Until 1960 the majority of black college students in the United States attended black institutions, but in less than a decade the proportion had declined to one-third, and more recently to one-fourth or less. Enrollment in the black institutions has increased, but the percentage of blacks attending college has increased far more. The percentage of whites who are attending college remains higher, and the racial differences are especially great for graduate and professional enrollment. A higher percentage of minority students require financial aid in order to go to college. Despite financial difficulties, the forty-one private black colleges associated with the United Negro College Fund continue to provide an important segment of higher educational opportunity for blacks.[5]

EDUCATIONAL AND ECONOMIC GAPS   The discrepancy between the education of whites and nonwhites, measured by years of schooling and degrees awarded, has been reduced substantially since World War II. In 1950 the median number of school years completed by the nation's nonwhites was 6.9; for whites it was 9.7. The ratio of nonwhite to white schooling was .71. By 1972 the corresponding figures were 10.5 and 12.3. The ratio had increased to .90. The nonwhite-to-white ratio of the percentage of each group attending four or more years of high school increased from .38 in 1950 to .70 in 1972, and for those completing four or more years of college from .34 to .57. Despite major educational gains for nonwhites, it is clear that a considerable gap remains, especially at the high school and college levels.[6]

The economic discrepancies between blacks and whites since mid-century have been reduced much less than the educational ones have. During the 1950s whites penetrated new occupations faster than blacks did, increasing the occupational gap.[7] During the 1960s there were large reductions in differences between nonwhite and white occupational distributions, especially for young men.[8] However, the black gains on whites in income in the 1960s were comparatively small. The ratio of nonwhite-to-white median family income increased from .54 in 1947 to only .64 by 1970, a small reduction of a still large gap. From 1948 to 1973 the gap between the nonwhite and white proportions of unemployment and poverty were widened rather than narrowed.[9] The black gains of the 1960s in education, occupations, percentage of employment, and the small gains in family and personal earnings did not disappear in the recession of the 1970s. In fact, the racial differences in these measures evidently have become smaller. Yet, despite these further reductions, the gaps remain large.[10]

The data on earnings indicate that the black gains in education have not resulted in comparable economic gains. There is evidence that the reward for a given level of education is greater for whites than for nonwhites.[11] An analysis of national census data has been interpreted as evidence that differences in the earnings of blacks and whites are due to discriminatory treatment rather than to racial differences in education.[12] To the extent that this is true, black economic progress cannot be achieved solely by reducing the racial gap in education. The same is true for women, and will remain so to the extent that they continue to be hired for different kinds of work than men are, and so long as the pay is less for "women's jobs" than for the "men's jobs" that require comparable education.[13]

Although better-educated blacks have been less likely to be unemployed, the low correlation between black gains in education and income means that many have been *underemployed.* Often they have had to take less demanding and less lucrative jobs than whites with comparable training—a heavy disappointment for the typically upward-mobile black college student. And often it has been difficult to get housing near the place of work. Thus the great increase in the proportion of blacks in high school and college has often resulted in *status incongruity*—a discrepancy between educational and economic statuses.[14] Better-educated blacks often experience *relative deprivation*— meaning that they feel deprived in comparison with an important reference group—whites with similar training, who are much less likely to experience status incongruity. Women with advanced educations also often experience incongruity between their educational and economic statuses, and have feelings of deprivation in relation to men with equivalent training.

Urban Migrant Programs

Like the helping organizations in communities of international immigrants, programs designed to assist rural-urban migrants have usually emphasized economic adjustments. The chief concern of the Urban League, formed in 1911, has been the economic welfare of black migrants to Northern cities. Its most influential role probably has been as an employment agency, but it has also provided health, welfare, housing, recreational, and delinquency-prevention services. The membership of the league has been interracial, and it has tried to promote intergroup harmony. Its leaders have generally followed the accommodative style of the racial diplomat.

The Opportunities Industrialization Center was started in the late 1960s in Philadelphia by the Reverend Leon Sullivan. With the aid of a $32 million subsidy from the U.S. Department of Labor it has spread to over a hundred cities around the nation, helping many urban ghetto residents to gain employment or to get better jobs. The philosophy is to help urban migrants to improve their job skills through individual effort. The center provides training for such urban skills as computer techniques, business education, drafting, offset printing, photography, commercial art, and cosmetology, and for the basic skills of communication, computation, and interviewing for jobs.[15]

The economic integration of urban minorities is held back by discriminatory practices. In a study in Racine, Wisconsin, the patterns of economic absorption of blacks, whites, and Mexican Americans from 1960 to 1971 were compared. Despite numerous programs of assistance to Mexican Americans and blacks, Anglos were absorbed into the economy of the city much faster. Differences remained even when a number of variables, including the amount of education, were controlled.[16] It is difficult for urban migrant groups merely to survive and gain an economic foothold, much less to make gains toward economic equality, especially when they are racial minorities.

Minority Enterprise

Most minority businesses are small, undercapitalized, family enterprises, and the rate of failure is high. In general they provide a meager or modest living, although some are more successful. Many minority businesses furnish personal or retail services not provided by the larger society for the more segregated groups. Under certain conditions, some groups develop middle minority enterprises, which tend to be new, high-risk, low-status businesses (see Chapters 4 and 6). Family enterprises are facilitated when there are informal patterns of assistance to them in the minority community, or when governmental aid to small businesses is made available. Over a hundred rural black cooperatives were formed in the 1960s—mostly in the South—to improve farm production, employment, and marketing, and to diversify agricultural enterprises.[17]

Despite some increase in governmental assistance to small black businesses during the latter 1960s, United States Census reports for 1970 and 1972 indicated that black-owned enterprises totaled less than 2 percent of the country's ventures. At that time blacks constituted 11.1 percent of the population. Businesses owned by blacks received less than one-half of 1 percent of the nation's gross business receipts. One-third of these businesses provided personal services, and another 15 percent were eating and drinking places. Most of the enterprises were individually owned, and operated by members of families. Less than one-fourth had paid employees.[18]

One ideological justification for black capitalism is the older, gradualistic view that increasing the numbers of successful black entrepreneurs raises the respectability, and thus the overall status, of the group. The more small family businesses there are, in this view, the better. A conflicting rationale emerged following the outbursts in the black ghettos in the mid-1960s, one that supports diversity in the type and size of black enterprises.[19] In this view the aim is for blacks to gain control over their community's economic institutions, including the larger, more powerful ones. The likening of race relations in the ghetto to colonialism lends support to this ideology. According to the colonial model, it is because black ghetto residents are economically powerless that they are exploited as consumers, renters, and employees by white outsiders who own the land, buildings, and businesses. It is assumed that more economic and political power will enable blacks to gain control over all of their community institutions. The economic independence of blacks is apparently a major goal of the Black Muslims, as noted in Chapter 7.

Operation Breadbasket was started in Atlanta in the latter 1960s by the Southern Christian Leadership Conference (see Chapter 12), and then the Rev. Dr. Martin Luther King took it to Chicago and it spread to Northern cities. The chief aim was employment for blacks in white businesses in the ghetto, based on the value judgment that these absentee-owned enterprises have a moral responsibility to share some of the profits with the black community. In Chicago the Rev. Jesse Jackson has used confrontation tactics (demonstrations, picketing, and boycotts; see Chapter 13), and has succeeded in persuading ghetto employers to sign agreements for jobs for blacks, for stocking black-produced commodities, and for using such black-owned business services as advertising, banking, and transportation. Operation Breadbasket in Chicago expanded such efforts in 1971 by establishing People United to Save Humanity (PUSH), resulting in some major successes. In 1972, for example, General Foods signed a comprehensive agreement that included such commitments as jobs for blacks, support for black colleges, recruitment of black college students, and the use of black business services in such areas as law, medicine, janitorial work, pest control, waste removal, banking, insurance, and advertising. Specific deadlines and dollar amounts are often written into these agreements. PUSH also sponsors trade fairs to promote black economic interests and intergroup cooperation.[20]

The Black Economic Union was started in several major cities in 1966, chiefly by a number of black athletes. One aim was to encourage blacks to take over supermarkets and other businesses vacated by whites after the outbursts of the mid-1960s. The general goal was to provide a dependable source of capital that would encourage blacks to move into new, but low-risk, areas of enterprise, and to gain and maintain control over their own businesses. The union has successfully fostered a number of black businesses, including the acquisition of seventy-five or more McDonald's franchises in New York, Cleveland, and other cities. It has also sponsored a summer program of employment for inner-city youths.

Black enterprises have had serious difficulties in the recession of the 1970s. Eighteen percent of them failed in 1974, as compared with less than 1 percent of small businesses generally. Thirteen of the nation's one hundred largest black companies in 1972 were bankrupt or out of business by early 1975. Black unemployment reached 13.5 percent in April 1975 (36 percent for teenagers), and 8.2 percent for the nation as a whole. Thus black businesses lost large numbers of their customers. Credit for capital ventures was tight, as banks became very cautious about financing small businesses. Two federal programs, the Small Business Administration's guarantee of 90 percent of bank loans (up to $350,000) and the Office of Minority Business Enterprise's training in marketing, accounting, and starting up businesses, have provided inadequate help for black businesses during the crisis years of the 1970s.[21]

EDUCATION TOWARD EQUALITY

Members of both minority and dominant communities in the United States have produced a great quantity and variety of written and spoken words designed to combat prejudice and discrimination. The volume and impact of such communications have varied greatly from one time and place to another. Such messages come into conflict with those expressing prejudice, and with discriminatory practices, highlighting the "American Dilemma." Much of this communication originates in organized programs of education toward group equality. Often the existential assumption has been that changes in beliefs and attitudes must precede changes in intergroup behavior, but much of the educational effort has accompanied economic, legal, or other strategies.

Message Content

INFORMATION   Much of this communication has been informational—concerned with conveying what are thought to be correct existential beliefs. The more formal research and teaching efforts have stressed detailed information about historical and current conditions of particular groups, and the changing knowledge about race, culture, attitudes, and intergroup relations. Such material has competed with a vast amount of stereotyped, ethnocentric interpretation—including racism—in school textbooks and other treatments of the settlement and expansion of the United States, treatment of the Indians, immigrant groups, blacks, and women. Different sets of existential beliefs thus come into conflict with each other.

Allport's dictum that giving information about minority groups does not reduce prejudice[22] has not been sufficiently challenged. The experimental studies, involving giving an attitude test before and after a one-time showing of an informational film about a minority group, have usually shown little reduction in prejudice—especially after some time has passed. Such studies are poorly designed for the purpose, however.[23] Numerous related messages may have mutually reinforcing effects over time. Informational messages in educational programs usually contain other kinds of content, and they often are used in conjunction with economic, political, legal, or other activities. Even when a message contains only information, in practice it occurs in a social context of other messages, actions, and developments. When intergroup behavior is changing in response to new laws or other factors, information and other communications may help to modify attitudes considerably.

It has been noted, especially in Chapters 2 and 3, that major changes in attitudes toward American blacks, Jews, women, and other groups have occurred in recent decades. These changes have apparently accelerated at times when public interest in relevant knowledge has been increased in response to news coverage of issues and changes in intergroup relations. It is a plausible hypothesis that the effective dissemination of new knowledge about prejudice, intergroup relations, race, intelligence testing, ethnicity, and related topics has been an important factor in changing these attitudes.

PROPAGANDA   The use of propaganda is prominent in justifications of patterns of discrimination, and it is also used in appeals against unequal treatment of groups. *Propaganda* is the use of (one-way) communications to get people to believe and act in desired ways without careful thought.[24] It depends on the psychological mechanism of *suggestion,* the use of stimuli designed to obtain an uncritical, automatic response. One suggestion device is name-calling, used heavily in antiminority propaganda (e.g., in derogatory names for groups), but also used in appeals for equal treatment (e.g., in some uses of terms such as "bigot," "racist," or "chauvinist").

The "glittering generality" device is used in antiminority propaganda in such phrases as "American character" or "solid racial stock," and in some pro-equality uses of terms such as "democratic treatment" or "decent and fair." Some of the other suggestion devices used are testimonial (identifying ideas or actions with a highly regarded, or despised, person), card stacking (distorting facts to build a one-sided case), and bandwagon (implying that almost everyone now favors an idea or action).[25]

Dramatizations of discriminatory treatment and its consequences in human lives often are intended to appeal strongly to the emotions. In some materials, suggestive appeals are made to value commitments, while relevant information is handled objectively; in others, propagandistic appeals are made on questions of fact as well as value. Whatever the purpose, propaganda does not necessarily obtain the desired response. One person's background conditioning may enhance suggestibility to a particular propagandistic theme, while another's may lead to rejection. Success is facilitated by evoking stereotypes of groups or other images that are overgeneralized and reified (see Chapter 3).[26]

PERSUASION   Many of the appeals for group equality involve interaction with an audience, or at least the feeling of some feedback. *Persuasion,* as distinguished from the one-way nature of propaganda, involves the use of feedback communications to get people to believe and act in desired ways. Persuasion has two advantages: (1) there is at least a minimal dialogue, which heightens and holds interest; and (2) arguments can be varied as questions from the audience, letters, telephone calls, or other reactions are taken into account.[27] Persuasion can be quite rational because an exchange takes place, making it possible to raise questions about statements of fact and encouraging consideration of alternatives for action. A skillful persuader can also use the process in a highly emotional manner, with effective use of techniques of suggestion as the interaction proceeds. Persuasion thus ranges all the way from reasoned, informative appeals, to adept manipulation of moods and motives in order to bypass critical thought.[28]

We turn now to selected examples of the uses of the above appeals in educational programs for combating group prejudice and discrimination.

Programs Emphasizing Information

B'nai B'rith, the Jewish fraternal organization, instituted its Anti-Defamation League early in this century to combat (then) mounting anti-Semitism. Of the three major organizations for protecting Jews in the United States (the others being the American Jewish Committee and the American Jewish Congress), the league makes the greatest use of educational procedures. It conducts and sponsors research, and publishes pamphlets and books on a nonprofit basis. The league has made significant contributions to knowledge about intergroup relations. It offers consulting services, through its twenty-six regional offices, to educational, civic, fraternal, church, labor, and other organizations working to improve intergroup relations. Each regional office maintains an audio-visual library where films, filmstrips, and recordings on intergroup relations may be rented or bought at nominal cost.

The Anti-Defamation League of B'nai B'rith has defined its task broadly, in the belief that the treatment of Jews depends largely on the societal treatment of less powerful groups in general. It uses educational programs to combat discrimination against all minorities, to expose and oppose all totalitarian trends, to promote cooperation among different religious groups, and to foster intercultural understanding. Although the league makes some use of emotional appeals to American commitments to equal opportunity, religious freedom, and fair play, its primary emphasis is information and analysis; and the tone of its communications is moderate, reasoned, and patient.

Another organization that has emphasized information and discussion has concentrated on race relations in the South. In 1919 the Commission on Interracial Cooperation was established as a joint black-white program for promoting equality for Southern blacks. It emphasized information and did not attack the system of segregation directly, but it expressed opposition to discrimination and called for racial justice. In 1944 it was replaced by the Southern Regional Council, which played a key role in desegregating the public schools. The council has sponsored research, conferences, school courses on race relations, and other activities designed to promote interracial cooperation and orderly change.

Programs Combining Educational and Other Activities

An illustration of combining a predominantly educational program with confrontation and direct persuasion is the activities of the Association of Southern Women for the Prevention of Lynching, from 1930 to 1943. Although lynchings of Southern blacks had been declining for some time, this group is credited with reducing them almost to the point of elimination. Some of the women were black, but most were rural white women from old families and established churches, most of whose husbands were important local or state leaders. These influential women challenged the belief that lynchings helped protect South-

ern white womanhood, and called for the protection of the women of
both races.

The approach of the association was primarily educational; they
used reasoned persuasion, based on information and logic. They published facts about lynchings and their consequences for the South, and
they sponsored studies, lectures, and discussions. They also brought
petitions to community leaders and asked for meetings with city councils, county boards, state legislators, and law-enforcement officials. In
these meetings they called for specific measures to protect black men
from violence. They helped clarify the lynching issue; they provided
sound information and logical arguments; they helped keep channels
of information and discussion open; and they effectively persuaded
community leaders in face-to-face confrontations.[29]

Resistance to desegregating the public schools during the 1960s
resulted in many demonstrations, and some violence, by Southern
whites. In most instances the schools were kept open and desegregated
without serious incidents, for which at least part of the credit has been
given to groups known by their acronyms as HOPE, OASIS, SOS, COPE,
and STOP. These were women's groups, predominantly white, that
used tactics similar to those of the Association of Southern Women for
the Prevention of Lynching.[30] They provided organized information
and logical arguments, insisting that the most important values were
keeping the schools operating and giving all children as good an education as possible. They backed their educational approach with re-
strained public demonstrations and meetings with school and
community leaders. Their actions were controlled and informed, but
determined and timely.

Educational activities have been important in the women's movement, sometimes as an adjunct to specific political or economic pressure
tactics, much of it designed to facilitate ongoing discussions of the
consciousness-raising variety. The ideology for the American part of
this worldwide movement was provided in 1963 by Betty Friedan in
her book *The Feminine Mystique.* The book sold over three million
copies, and the response led its author to establish the National Organization for Women (NOW) in 1966. NOW led the dramatic expansion
of the women's movement at the end of the 1960s, and it continues to
provide a rationale, persuasive ideas, information, and some degree of
coordination to a great variety of local, state, and national efforts. Much
of the discussion and support for the movement is in women's professional, academic, church, and other organizations, and evidently in
countless small, spontaneous groups.[31] The issues involved in the drive
for equality are many and complex (see Chapter 1), and supporters of the
women's movement are not fully agreed on everything. Some women
who support the position of the movement on particular issues—such

as women in politics, or abortion on demand—do not support the idea of women's liberation.[32] Much of the communication in the movement is designed to reeducate men as well as women, since male status and roles must change if equality for women is to be achieved.

CONCLUSION

Many programs for improving minority status have been limited to one institutional area or method of approach. Economic and educational strategies have often been limited or selective in this sense, but sometimes they have been combined with legal, political, or other activities. There has been an apparent tendency for the more selective economic and educational programs to be associated with gradualistic ideology—the view that the improvement of group status must be a long, slow, step-at-a-time process. Economic strategies have often been based partly on the existential belief that economic improvement must occur first, or at least that when it does it will promote a rise in overall status. Especially when this is combined with the belief that economic advances depend on formal education, economic programs become long-range or gradualistic in orientation. When economic gains lag behind advances in education, minority persons experience both status incongruity and feelings of relative deprivation. Strategies for educating society to support group equality are also gradualistic when they are based on the belief that attitudes and feelings must be changed before it is possible to change laws and behavior. This last assumption is evidently false, as we saw in Chapter 3.

Educational programs have been characterized as liberals talking only to each other, and Allport's view that information giving does not change attitudes toward groups is often added to clinch this argument. The before-after laboratory studies are not valid evidence in support of Allport's contention, and communications aimed at reeducating society may well play a major role in reducing prejudice and changing patterns of discrimination. The long-range effects of selective educational programs are difficult to determine, although major shifts in beliefs about race, culture, and intergroup relations have not happened suddenly or by chance. The effects of educational communications may be greater, or are at least more apparent, when they are combined with other tactics, in episodes of only a few months' or years' duration. News coverage of conflicts and changes in intergroup relations provides some direct information and interpretation, and it arouses interest in relevant educational communications. Whether they are selective or part of broadly conceived strategies of change, it appears that economic and educational programs may play significant roles in movements toward group equality.

FOOTNOTES

1 Handlin, 1959; Peñalosa & McDonagh, 1966.
2 Lipsky & Rose, 1971.
3 Epstein, 1976, pp. 428–29.
4 Epstein, 1976, pp. 430–31, 437–38.
5 Blackwell, 1975, pp. 124–36.
6 Squires, 1977, p. 436.
7 Hare, 1965.
8 Johnson & Sell, 1976; Featherman & Hauser, 1976.
9 Squires, 1977, pp. 436–37.
10 Farley, 1977.
11 Harrison, 1972; Weiss, 1970; Althauser & Spivak, 1975.
12 Stolzenberg, 1975.
13 Epstein, 1976, pp. 426–27.
14 Derbyshire, 1966; Geschwender, 1965.
15 Blackwell, 1975, p. 182.
16 Shannon, 1975.
17 Blackwell, 1975, pp. 181–82.
18 Blackwell, 1975, pp. 166–80.
19 Blackwell, 1975, pp. 139–50, 174–75.
20 Blackwell, 1975, pp. 182–84.
21 The Wall Street Journal, Tuesday, April 1, 1975, pp. 1, 20.
22 Allport, 1954, pp. 452–56.
23 Ehrlich, 1973, pp. 147–49.
24 Merton, 1945, pp. 38–39.
25 Lee & Lee, 1939, pp. 23–24.
26 Davis, 1970, pp. 48–53.
27 Merton, 1945, pp. 38–39.
28 Merton, 1945, pp. 178–86.
29 Laue & McCorkle, 1965, pp. 80–90.
30 Laue & McCorkle, 1965, pp. 91–92.
31 Epstein, 1976, pp. 417–19; Freeman, 1973.
32 Welch, 1975.

REFERENCES

Allport, Gordon W.
1954   The Nature of Prejudice. Boston: Beacon Press, Inc.

Althauser, Robert P., and Sydney S. Spivak
1975 The Unequal Elites. New York: John Wiley and Sons.
Blackwell, James E.
1975 The Black Community: Diversity and Unity. New York: Dodd, Mead and Co.
Davis, F. James
1970 Social Problems: Enduring Major Issues and Social Change. New York: The Free Press.
Derbyshire, Robert L.
1966 "United States Negro Identity Conflict." Sociology and Social Research 51 (October): 63–77.
Ehrlich, Howard J.
1973 The Social Psychology of Prejudice. New York: Wiley-Interscience.
Epstein, Cynthia Fuchs
1976 "Sex Roles," Ch. 9 in Robert K. Merton and Robert Nisbet, Contemporary Social Problems. New York: Harcourt, Brace, Jovanovich, Inc.
Farley, Reynolds
1977 "Trends in Racial Inequalities: Have the Gains of the 1960s Disappeared in the 1970s?" American Sociological Review 42, 2 (April): 189–208.
Featherman, David L., and Robert M. Hauser
1976 "Changes in the Socioeconomic Stratification of the Races, 1962–73." American Journal of Sociology 82, 3 (November): 621–51.
Freeman, Jo
1973 "The Origins of the Women's Liberation Movement." American Journal of Sociology 78, 4 (January): 792–811.
Geschwender, James A.
1965 "Desegregation, the Educated Negro and the Future Protest of the South." Sociological Inquiry 35 (Winter): 58–68.
Handlin, Oscar
1959 The Newcomers. Cambridge, Massachusetts: Harvard University Press.
Hare, Nathan
1965 "Recent Trends in the Occupational Mobility of Negroes, 1930–1960: An Intracohort Analysis." Social Forces 44 (December): 166–73.
Harrison, Bennett
1972 "Education and Underemployment in the Urban Ghetto." American Economic Review 62 (December): 796–812.
Johnson, Michael P., and Ralph R. Sell
1976 "The Cost of Being Black: A 1970 Update." American Journal of Sociology 82, 1 (July): 183–90.
Laue, James H., and Leon M. McCorkle, Jr.
1965 "The Association of Southern Women for the Prevention of Lynching: A Commentary on the Role of the Moderate." Sociological Inquiry 35 (Winter): 80–93.
Lee, Alfred M., and Elizabeth B. Lee
1939 The Fine Art of Propaganda. New York: Harcourt, Brace and Co.
Lipsky, David B., and Joseph B. Rose
1971 "Craft Entry for Minorities: The Case of Project Justice." Industrial Relations 10, 3 (October): 327–37.

Merton, Robert K.
1945   Mass Persuasion. New York: Harper and Bros.
Peñalosa, Fernando, and Edward C. McDonagh
1966   "A Socioeconomic Class Typology of Mexican Americans." Sociological
       Inquiry 36 (Winter): 19–30.
Shannon, Lyle W.
1975   "False Assumptions about the Determinants of Mexican-American and
       Negro Economic Absorption." Sociological Quarterly 16, 1 (Winter): 3–15.
Squires, Gregory D.
1977   "Education, Jobs, and Inequality: Functional and Conflict Models of So-
       cial Stratification in the United States." Social Problems 24, 4 (April):
       436–50.
Stolzenberg, Ross M.
1975   "Education, Occupation, and Wage Differentials between White and
       Black Men." American Journal of Sociology 81, 2 (September): 299–323.
Weiss, Randall
1970   "The Effects of Education on the Earnings of Blacks and Whites." Review
       of Economics and Statistics 52 (May): 150–59.
Welch, Susan
1975   "Support Among Women for the Issues of the Women's Movement."
       Sociological Quarterly 16 (Spring): 216–27.

12

Legal and Political Action

Attempts to combat discrimination by influencing the law and its enforcement take a variety of forms. Some are designed to affect the legislative process, by lobbying or by educational efforts to influence public opinion on relevant issues. In some activities the aim is to help determine appointments to public positions, or to influence the actions of occupants of key offices. In others, the objective is to increase a minority's political participation and power, both in voting and in holding public office. Programs that include a number of such activities may become quite broad in scope.

Some programs are limited primarily to bringing lawsuits. The purpose of such litigation is not only to protect the existing legal rights of minority persons, but also to challenge and change judicial interpretations of oppressive laws. The frequent classification of legal strategies as selective seems to refer mainly to programs of litigation, such as that of the National Association for the Advancement of Colored People. Although limited in method, such programs can have far-reaching consequences.

THE NAACP, LAW, AND DESEGREGATION

In 1903 W. E. B. DuBois began criticizing Booker T. Washington's gradualistic program. In 1905 DuBois led a meeting of twenty-nine black intellectuals at Niagara Falls, and began the first major protest against the Restoration (see Chapter 6). Black protestors had limited resources, and many felt the need of help from whites, especially after a violent riot by whites against blacks in Springfield, Illinois, in 1908. A white group, formed to protect blacks from violence and terror, was merged with DuBois's Niagara Movement in 1909 to form the National Association for the Advancement of Colored People. The goal of the NAACP has always been full equality for American blacks, and it has continued to be interracial.

The primary strategy of the NAACP has been legal, based on the existential belief that acts of discrimination can be stopped without waiting for educational processes to change beliefs and attitudes. The association has used educational procedures, but as an accompaniment to litigation and political action rather than as a prelude. Its determined efforts have been moderate in the sense that established legal procedures have been used in the drive toward equal treatment under the Constitution. Another basic existential assumption of the NAACP has been that the laws are conflicting, exposing a national dilemma rather than consensus in the dominant community about segregation and other patterns of racial discrimination. The association's lawyers have assumed that federal judges and congressional representatives, when forced to make choices, would eventually prefer equal legal treatment for blacks and other minorities.[1]

The NAACP has provided funds, materials, or lawyers for blacks in a great many lawsuits; it has pursued appeals of cases to the federal courts; and it has worked for civil rights legislation. It led the long but successful fight against the separate-but-equal doctrine and the Jim Crow laws, basing its cases on the Thirteenth, Fourteenth, and Fifteenth Amendments to the Constitution, and winning most of its several dozen appeals to the Supreme Court. In 1939 the NAACP Legal Defense and Educational Fund was incorporated to distinguish the program of litigation from the political and educational efforts. The fund's success led to the appointment in 1967 of Thurgood Marshall, the long-time chief legal counsel of the NAACP, to the Supreme Court.[2] He is the first black member of the nation's highest court. Prior to this appointment, he had served as a federal judge in the Second Circuit Court of Appeals in New York (1961–65), and as solicitor general in the United States Department of Justice (1965–67).

Developments Before 1954

THE SUPREME COURT AND THE RESTORATION   There was a variety of views about race relations after the Civil War, in the South as well as in other regions. Decisions made by the United States Supreme Court apparently tipped the balance, bringing about Jim Crow—the legally supported system of segregation in the South.[3] During the latter quarter of the nineteenth century, the Court consistently declared state and federal statutes against discrimination unconstitutional. The 1883 decision nullifying the 1875 Civil Rights Bill with regard to "personal acts of social discrimination" had the effect of turning the protection of civil rights back to the states.[4] This opened the way for the avalanche of segregation statutes and ordinances in the South. The Court upheld these state laws, and placed the whole Jim Crow system on firm legal ground with the separate-but-equal doctrine in the case of *Plessy* v. *Ferguson* in 1896 (see Chapter 6).[5] In the North, the result was the passage of civil rights laws that were rarely enforced.[6]

THE FIRST DECADES OF LEGAL ACTION   Clearly, the NAACP had its work cut out for it when it began its long, determined struggle against Jim Crow in 1909. Some of its earliest victories were facilitated by the replacement of five of the nine justices of the United States Supreme Court from 1909 to 1911. For example, "grandfather clause" laws had been passed in several Southern states to exempt persons who had the right to vote on January 1, 1867, and their descendants, from having to own property, pay taxes, and be literate in order to vote. Since blacks could not vote in January 1867, they were excluded from a privilege granted to poor whites, and thus often excluded from voting. In 1915 these laws were declared unconstitutional.[7] In 1917, and again in 1927, city ordinances requiring segregation of the races were nullified.[8] In 1927 the Court invalidated white-only primary elections,[9] but Southern whites retained control by remaining united in the Democratic party's primaries.

During the 1930s, 40s, and early 50s the Supreme Court moved closer to rejecting the separate-but-equal doctrine, in its increasing insistence that the treatment of minorities be equal. It was held that blacks had a constitutional right to a fair criminal trial.[10] Excluding minorities from juries was held to be presumptive evidence of discrimination.[11] Denial to blacks of an unoccupied dining car or Pullman car seat was rejected, and segregated public accommodations in interstate commerce was held unconstitutional.[12] The Court made a major decision on voting during World War II, going against its earlier precedents, holding that blacks cannot be excluded from party membership and political conventions.[13] The right of states to prohibit racial discrimination by labor unions was upheld,[14] and court enforcement of restrictive housing covenants was invalidated.[15]

THE HIGHER-EDUCATION CASES   Segregated public school education was the area in which the key legal breakthrough occurred, in 1954. During the two prior decades, in decisions concerning professional and higher education, the Supreme Court had moved consistently toward rejection of the separate-but-equal doctrine. In 1938 the Court held that the University of Missouri could not exclude Lloyd Gaines from its law school, paying his tuition in a neighboring state, solely because he was black.[16] After this case twelve Southern and border states began admitting blacks to postgraduate studies in previously all-white public universities.

In June 1950, two very important cases were decided. Segregated facilities for law study were being developed in Texas. The decision was unanimous that the University of Texas law school must admit Hemon Sweatt, on the ground that the separate facilities were not equal. Also in the opinion, however there was dictum (gratuitous comment not precisely relevant to the legal issue decided) to the effect that the separate-but-equal doctrine in education violates the Fourteenth Amendment.[17] Such a comment by the nation's highest court is an important indication of its thinking, and the NAACP lawyers were gratified to see their strategy succeeding.[18]

On the same day as the Sweatt decision, the Court unanimously held that G. W. McLaurin was to be admitted on a nonsegregated basis to the University of Oklahoma, for the pursuit of a Doctor of Education degree.[19] McLaurin had been kept apart from other students by such devices as a separate table in the cafeteria, special study desks in the library, and special desks in anterooms adjoining his classrooms. The Court said the separate facilities were not equal, although it might logically have held that segregated facilities are illegal even when they are substantially equal. After these two decisions, a number of Southern universities began admitting professional students without any strings attached.

The desegregation of schools in the South began at the postgraduate level, then, and was cautiously extended to undergraduate education. After the above two decisions there were court cases and public demands to desegregate undergraduate education, and the Sweatt and McLaurin cases became important precedents. By 1954 there were about a thousand blacks in integrated classrooms in previously all-white public colleges and universities in twelve Southern states, but none in South Carolina, Mississippi, Georgia, and Alabama. Facilities in most public institutions built for blacks continued to be unequal to those for whites, with restricted opportunities for professional and postgraduate studies generally.

THE NARROWING GAP   The unmistakable trend of the federal courts led Southern school districts to make major improvements in public school facilities for blacks after World War II. The aim was to show substantial movement toward equal facilities in order to have a strong stance from which to oppose the view that segregation itself is unconstitutional.[20] At any rate, a racial comparison of instructional expenditures for 1940 and 1952, in seven states (Alabama, Arkansas, Florida, Georgia, Mississippi, North Carolina, and South Carolina) showed major gains by blacks on whites. The expenditures (for teacher salaries and other instructional costs) per black pupil in 1940 were 43 percent of those per white pupil; by 1952 the corresponding figure was 70 percent, still far from equal. In these same states, plus Oklahoma, there was a great reduction in the racial gap in capital expenditures—i.e., outlays for buildings, land, and equipment. In 1940 the capital expenditures per black pupil were only 23 percent of those per white pupil; in 1952 the figure was 82 percent. Black schools had been built much faster than white ones during the latter 1940s and early 1950s. However, by 1952, the capital value of white schools per pupil was still 2.39 times greater than that of black schools.[21]

Brown v. Board of Education of Topeka[22]

Although the *Brown* case has been the focus of public attention, four other public school segregation decisions by the United States Supreme Court were announced on the same day in May 1954. The other cases originated in South Carolina, Virginia, Delaware, and Washington, D.C.[23] The NAACP pressed these cases not as a test of the quality of black educational facilities, but of the constitutionality of segregated schooling. Lawyers for the states concerned produced evidence that the racial gap in educational expenditures was being reduced, and argued that it would be eliminated. The Court treated this evidence as irrelevant to the legal issue, which it said was whether segregation of schools is inherently unequal.

The Supreme Court decided that racially separate public schools are inherently unequal. Thus a statute in Kansas that had the effect of requiring Linda Brown to attend a junior high school for blacks only was unconstitutional. More precisely, the constitutional issue was the use of race as a *legislative category* in statutes concerning public schools, and the decision in the *Brown* case was that this violates the *equal protection clause* of the Fourteenth Amendment. Racially segregated public schools, in other words, are incapable of providing equal educational opportunity. Technically, the Court said it was not overruling the *Plessy* v. *Ferguson* precedent. The facts in the *Plessy* case were different (a violation of a Jim Crow law on seating in trains), and so was the constitutional issue (reasonableness of the use of state police power). The Court said separate-but-equal reasoning was not applicable to education. Yet the *Brown* decision overruled the spirit of the Plessy case, and it heralded the end of the separate-but-equal doctrine.[24]

Justifications of resistance to desegregating the schools have emphasized the contention that the Supreme Court's decision is unconstitutional. Briefly, let us consider the arguments advanced. First, there is the view that states may "interpose" their sovereignty between themselves and the federal government, since education is left to the states. This overlooks the obligation of the states to follow the Constitution in all their actions. Second, the argument has been advanced that the Court is bound by its own case precedents. This view is a great oversimplification of the judicial process. Appellate courts usually follow precedents when there are some that are reasonably close to the facts of a case at hand, and when there are no conflicting precedents. Even such clear-cut precedents are overruled, however, when there are compelling reasons to do so. Typically, instead of clear-cut precedents, there are only conflicting lines of decisions that are more or less *analogous* to the current case.[25] Judges very often have to decide which analogy is the most persuasive, an especially difficult task when the case involves interpretation of a statute or a constitution, or both.[26] In the school segregation cases, the Supreme Court had to choose between a line of analogous decisions in the *Plessy* tradition and another that included the *Gaines, Sweatt,* and *McLaurin* cases.[27] In its brief, the NAACP cited forty-six supporting legal precedents from prior cases.[28]

A third argument to justify resistance has been that the school segregation decisions were based on psychology and sociology rather than law. In the trials in the four state courts, social scientists had been called as expert witnesses on the general effects of racially segregated schooling. The usual criticism, however, has been of the use by the NAACP of a brief prepared by thirty-two nationally known social scientists, documenting the conclusion that black children in segregated schools develop an inferior conception of self. The use of the "Brandeis Brief," a summary of information about a situation relevant to the case at hand, is well established in constitutional law. Courts have often taken "judicial notice" of professional or scientific existential beliefs, as an alternative to making their own assumptions. The material in this brief was directly relevant to the constitutional issue as the Court had defined it.[29] The Court cited this special brief as partial support for its opinion in the *Brown* case. It also cited seven of the works listed in the bibliography of the brief, three of which are publications by Kenneth Clark (black psychologist), E. F. Frazier (black sociologist), and Gunnar Myrdal (Swedish economist).[30]

The decisions in the 1954 school cases were unanimous, and so was the implementation order issued by the Court in May 1955. The latter required the desegregation of schools "with all deliberate speed," allowing for practical problems to be solved and for different situations in different school districts throughout the South. The NAACP got local blacks in 170 or so school districts, in seventeen states, to sign petitions to their boards demanding immediate school desegregation. Alarmed and angered, white segregationists took advantage of the flexible standard in the implementation order and resisted the Court's clear intention.[31] Implementation proceeded slowly and unevenly, and endless lawsuits against school districts clogged the trial courts.

Legal Extensions of Desegregation

The Supreme Court indicated in its dicta in the school segregation opinions that its holding would not be limited to education. The *Brown* decision was quickly extended by analogy to cover parks, golf courses, bathing beaches, public transportation, and other public facilities, as well as housing. The Court eventually ruled (in 1967) that state statutes prohibiting interracial marriage are discriminatory and unconstitutional. The *Brown* case became a key precedent as the Court consistently held that legislation based on racial classifications is discriminatory and therefore unconstitutional.[32] The case thus signalled the downfall of the legal support for the entire Jim Crow system.

Southern reaction to these judicial extensions of desegregation was often very strong in the area of public recreational facilities. For example, Montgomery, Alabama, closed all its city parks in 1959 rather than desegregate them, and Jackson, Mississippi, closed its public swimming pools in 1963. By the mid-1970s, both of these cities had opened new public parks and swimming pools on an integrated basis. The strong resistance to desegregating the public schools after the *Brown* decision must be understood to a large extent as action to prevent what has since happened—the demise of the whole system of *de jure* segregation.

Desegregation of Southern Schools

By the 1956–57 school year, less than 4 percent of the racially mixed districts in the South had begun even token integration. By contrast, almost three-fourths of the mixed districts had begun desegregating in the border areas (Delaware, District of Columbia, Kentucky, Maryland,

Missouri, Oklahoma, and West Virginia). Most border districts complied voluntarily, but Southern districts generally took no action until ordered to by a federal court. The Deep South states avoided the process completely for several years, but it began in Florida in 1959, Louisiana in 1960, Georgia in 1961, Alabama and South Carolina in 1963, and Mississippi in 1964. For many years there was only token compliance in these six and the five other Southern states (Arkansas, North Carolina, Tennessee, Texas, and Virginia), but there were substantial increases in the mid-1960s. This rise was due at least partly to the fact that Title VI of the Civil Rights Act of 1964 gave federal administrative officials the power to withhold federal funds from school districts not complying with desegregation orders, although enforcement actions were not strong at first.

By 1966–67, about one-sixth of the black pupils in the eleven Southern states were in schools with whites, as compared with three-fourths in the border states and the District of Columbia.[33] Then came more determined enforcement, and by 1972–73 about 91 percent of Southern black pupils were in racially integrated schools, as compared with about 89 percent in the North. The amount of change in the South in these few years was very great. However, the majority (about 54 percent) of the black pupils in the South in 1973 were still in *predominantly black* schools.

Although there was some desegregation in nearly all Southern school districts by the mid-1970s, there were continuing issues and legal struggles. In 1976 the United States Department of Justice took action to prevent *private* white schools from denying admission to blacks, since this impairs desegregation of the public schools. Several states were operating segregated vocational schools and facilities for the handicapped. In 1973 there were still ten parallel systems of higher education—i.e., with institutions for blacks meeting the same needs as schools for whites in the same cities. In 1975 the Justice Department filed suit against the State of Louisiana for operating parallel universities for blacks and whites in Baton Rouge, also in New Orleans and in Shreveport. Louisiana State University's four-campus system ranged from 89 to 97 percent white, while Southern University's three campuses and Grambling University were about 99 percent black.

Resistance to Desegregation

Much of the resistance to desegregating the schools in the South has been within the framework of law, in the sense that legal procedures have been used. These include:[34]

1   countless delays, using legal tactics
2   pupil placement laws, enabling students to be assigned to schools on the basis of individual criteria, with no mention of race

3 laws providing tuition for blacks to go to school out of state
4 closing the public schools and substituting private, segregated ones
5 legal actions to stop the activities of the NAACP in Southern states

Although many Southerners intended to use these procedures indefinitely, they were countered with unexpected speed by the Supreme Court, which continued to give high priority to matters concerning the school cases. Closing the public schools was considered by segregationists to be their ultimate and unbeatable weapon. It had to be used much sooner than expected, and in 1959 it collapsed when the Supreme Court held this action unconstitutional in Prince Edward County, Virginia. It was not until 1969, after much more obstruction, that the Court held unanimously in a Mississippi case that further delays were unconstitutional, regardless of administrative problems.[35] In 1968 the Court had declared that school boards must come forward with realistic plans that will work now.

The legal devices discussed above have been supplemented by other organized tactics. Fifty or more Southern organizations have used economic and political pressures, illegal force, or intimidation to forestall desegregation. Most influential have been the White Citizens Councils and the revived Ku Klux Klan. Such organizations contributed heavily to the slow, uncertain progress of integrating the schools in the early years, and to the accompanying tensions and occasional violence.[36] Southern sympathy for resistance declined markedly in the mid-1960s, and still further by 1970.[37]

The early integration of schools was usually peaceful, but in 1957 there was a major exception when Governor Orval Faubus of Arkansas called out the National Guard in open defiance of a federal court order to desegregate Little Rock High School. This encouraged a strong white protest against integration and precipitated a dramatic legal confrontation between state and federal officials. The outcome was that President Eisenhower ordered in federal troops to control the protesters and to oversee the integration of the school.[38] Thereafter, many Southerners accepted desegregation as inevitable, and leaders such as Governor James L. Almond, Jr., of Virginia—previously an outspoken segregationist—urged compliance with federal law. Others continued to resist, however, including some of the South's major political leaders.

The white response to admitting Autherine Lucy to the University of Alabama in 1956 was a major riot. In 1962 Governor George Wallace led statewide opposition to the first efforts to desegregate elementary schools in Alabama, and in 1963 he tried unsuccessfully to block two black students from being admitted to the University of Alabama. When the admission of James Meredith to the University of Mississippi was opposed by the governor in 1962, federal troops were needed to control the ensuing white riot. Desegregation of the public schools met a particularly violent white response in New Orleans in 1960 and in Birmingham, Alabama, in 1963.[39] Whites reacted with demonstrations and some violence in the mid-1960s to desegregating some of the schools in Mississippi, Louisiana, and Alabama.[40]

The Question of Racial Balance

The conclusion of the United States Commission on Civil Rights in 1967 was that any school that is half or more black is racially unbalanced, meaning that children in it are denied equal educational opportunity.[41] This standard received support in 1966 in the Coleman-Campbell report, a study conducted for the United States Office of Education in response to a directive in Title IV of the Civil Rights Act of 1964. In this study of the school achievement of 600,000 students in schools in all fifty states, family and neighborhood were found to be the most important influences on the conception of self.[42] Only in those schools in which the majority of pupils were white did the achievement of black children improve significantly. Black children did best in classrooms ranging from 15 to 40 percent black, but little relationship was found between racial balance and the achievement of white pupils. This has been interpreted as evidence in favor of racial desegregation of schools, but it should be noted that the study did not deal with busing or other means for achieving racial balance.

In a review in 1975 of 120 studies of the effects of racial desegregation of schools, the evidence concerning the influence on academic achievement was judged to be inconclusive. As for the effect on attitudes, prejudice had apparently been reduced in some cases, while conflict had been promoted in others. The research was inconclusive on the effects of segregation on the self-concepts of the children. The studies were made in a variety of settings, yet the conditions under which learning is improved or attitudes changed have not been illuminated much. Racial balance, as defined above, had been achieved in some of the schools studied but not in others.[43]

There have been definite increases in higher educational achievement (in degrees and years of school completed) by American blacks in the past two decades, especially by Southern black males.[44] The extent to which this is due to school integration is very difficult to determine. A number of studies have shown that educational ambition develops differently for black and white youth. In a study of Southern high school seniors, educational aspiration was closely associated with the amount of education of the head of household for whites, but only for those blacks in families with high status. The important variable for most of the black students was the perceived amount of opportunity available to them.[45] Perhaps desegregation has important influences on the minority's view of the opportunity structure, especially when "racial balance" is achieved.

The Busing Issue

Busing was used a good deal in the South in order to maintain *de jure* segregation of the schools, and desegregation has often brought a reduction of busing. In the North, and the newer areas of the South, busing is one means of reducing the *de facto* school segregation resulting from patterns of racially separate housing. The Supreme Court has extended the precedent of the *Brown* case to *de facto* segregation, and it has accepted busing as a legitimate means of accomplishing desegregation.[46] Whether voluntary or ordered by a court, busing to achieve racial balance in the schools is usually a last resort.

Rezoning—the redrawing of boundaries so that districts are as racially mixed as possible—can bring about racial balance when black and white areas are adjacent. The *pairing* plan—putting a previously black and a nearby white school in a common zone, and using one school for the first three grades and the other for the upper three grades —can sometimes work at the elementary level, but rarely at the secondary. The *"magnet school"*—one in the ghetto that is exceptionally well staffed and equipped in order to attract volunteer transfers to it from white schools—has been approved in Dallas, Boston, and other cities. Sometimes these alternatives to busing are not feasible, or they are insufficient to achieve racial balance.

The process of *resegregation* complicates efforts to achieve racial balance in the schools. White movement to the suburbs from urban districts that have been desegregated often has changed mixed areas into all-minority neighborhoods and schools. The outward movement of city populations has been taking place for decades, and the integration of schools is only one factor in this continuing process. In at least some cities, school integration has accelerated the white flight to the suburbs significantly. At any rate, the school population of Atlanta in 1973 had become 80 percent black. Washington, D.C. had become 86 percent black by 1973, and the surrounding urban areas in Maryland and Virginia were 80 percent white. In Chicago, while black students were still somewhat less than half the city's school population in 1973, many of its elementary and high schools were either all black or almost all black.[47]

The busing and other plans for desegregating city schools have generally pertained only to the central city, not the suburbs. In 1971 the Supreme Court upheld the use of busing to end the *de jure* segregation of the schools in the entire metropolitan area of Charlotte, North Carolina.[48] In 1974 the Court rejected a metropolitan busing plan for the

Detroit area, saying this was not required to correct *de facto* school segregation within the city.[49] At that time about two-thirds of the City of Detroit's school population was black, and many of its schools were all or mainly black. So long as busing to achieve racial balance is not extended to the suburbs, whites can largely escape desegregation by leaving the central city, thus adding to resegregation. By 1976–77, over 79 percent of the school enrollment of Detroit was black. Data from the schools in Kansas City, Missouri, from 1956 to 1974, showed that the white flight to the suburbs from desegregated schools was greatest from districts with 30 percent or more black students, or a recent, rapid increase in the percentage of blacks.[50]

Whether by busing or other means, desegregation of the city schools has been largely peaceful. Among several exceptions have been the burning by whites of school buses at Pontiac, Michigan, in 1971; violence and verbal abuse by whites against black children in the Canarsie district of Brooklyn, New York, in 1972; white attacks against buses and black men in South Boston in 1974; and white rioting in Louisville, Kentucky, in 1975. Even where such incidents have marked the start of desegregation, generally the plans have been operating uneventfully a year or two later. Nearly half of the plans for ending *de facto* segregation have been voluntary—i.e., they were responses to local pressures rather than to orders from the federal courts or the Department of Health, Education and Welfare (HEW).

Some of the opposition to the busing plans may be rejection only of the particular method of desegregation. No other plan seems quite so threatening to neighborhood control of its own schools, and the additional time, expense, and risk of busing arouse anxieties. Much of the criticism, however, evidently reflects opposition to school desegregation by any means. The strongest opposition to a busing plan in Richmond, California, came from working-class and lower-middle-class people who had lived in areas now occupied by blacks, and who felt that desegregation threatened the education of their own children and perhaps their own economic gains.[51] Ethnic groups have been prominent among the opponents of busing plans in a number of cities, motivated apparently by perceived self-interest to protect themselves from close competition with the city's newest ethnics.[52] People more securely located in the community structure feel less threatened by busing.

President Nixon took a stand against the busing plans, and under him both the HEW and the Department of Justice reduced their enforcement efforts. The Nixon appointees to the Supreme Court apparently swung the balance to the side of caution in the busing cases. In June 1977, when the Court said the Dayton, Ohio, school board had initiated too large a busing program, it cautioned all courts against ordering systemwide desegregation unless systemwide discrimination was proven. During the national election campaign of 1974, on the October day when rioting began in the Boston school controversy, President Ford publicly criticized the federal court order to use busing to desegregate the Boston schools. A Gallup poll just before the election showed 68 percent of the American electorate opposed to busing to achieve racial balance in the schools. Public opposition still predominates, but President Carter and his administration have cautiously supported busing as a means of desegregating the schools.

The NAACP and a considerable segment of the black community continue to support busing plans, but some blacks oppose them. The Congress of Racial Equality (CORE) has taken a strong position in favor of blacks remaining in black schools, and retaining control over their own schools. One of CORE's existential beliefs is that hostile treatment in white schools has harmful effects on the personalities of black children; another is that cooperating with the view that blacks learn better in the presence of whites lends encouragement to the racist belief that whites are mentally superior.[53] The CORE view is an application of the internal colonial model of race relations (see Chapter 6), and it calls for rejection of school desegregation by any means, not just by busing.

FEDERAL CIVIL RIGHTS ACTS

Civil rights matters were largely left to the state legislatures and to the courts for nearly two-thirds of the twentieth century. A powerful coalition of Southern Democrats and conservative Northern Republicans repeatedly blocked civil rights bills. The major breakthroughs finally came in the mid-1960s.

Legislation Before 1964

Most federal civil rights legislation until 1964 was concerned with the voting rights of Southern blacks. In 1939 the Hatch Act made it a crime to threaten, intimidate, or coerce voters in federal elections. In the Civil Rights Act of 1957, the United States attorney general obtained the power to file lawsuits to protect the voting rights of citizens in federal, state, or local elections. A Civil Rights Commission was also created by this act, and given the power to subpoena witnesses for investigations of voting rights in any election. The Civil Rights Act of 1960 required that registration forms, applications, and all other voting records be kept for twenty-two months, and made it a federal crime to defy court orders in voting cases. The act also empowered federal courts to appoint referees to ensure that qualified blacks get to register and vote, where local voting registrars are under court orders.

The Civil Rights Act of 1964

A very comprehensive federal civil rights act was finally passed in 1964, the same year in which the Twenty-fourth Amendment to the Constitution was passed. The amendment abolished the requirement of poll taxes for voting in federal elections. The 1964 act contains provisions against virtually the entire rank order of discriminations against minorities (see Chapter 6), with special emphasis on schools, other public facilities, employment, union membership, and voting registration in federal elections. The act includes discrimination based on sex.

The 1964 act has lent support to the federal courts on school desegregation. It authorizes federal financial and technical aid to help school districts to desegregate. It directs federal agencies to take steps against discrimination, and authorizes the withholding of funds from state and local agencies as a last resort, and after proper hearings are held. It empowers the attorney general of the United States to file lawsuits to desegregate schools, and also to intervene in cases initiated by private persons claiming they have been denied rights guaranteed by the Fourteenth Amendment. The act also gave legislative support to the Supreme Court's extension of desegregation to the entire area of public facilities, mentioning parks, swimming pools, stadiums, hotels, motels, restaurants, filling stations, and places of amusement if either interstate commerce or discriminatory state action are involved.

Finally, although limited to federal elections, the 1964 Civil Rights Act provides some specific guidelines to ensure voting rights. It requires the same standards to be used in registering all voters, and prohibits disqualification for minor errors in filling out applications. Literacy is to be presumed for all persons with a sixth-grade education unless proven otherwise in court by election officials. Literacy tests must be written, with copies available to applicants. When the attorney general of the United States makes a charge of discrimination in voting, a federal court of three judges must be impaneled to hear the case, with appeals going directly to the Supreme Court.

The Civil Rights Act of 1965

Several voting provisions in the 1964 act were extended to state and local elections in 1965, and the judicial enforcement procedures were simplified. Federal examiners are required whenever twenty or more complaints of voting discrimination are made in a county. Literacy tests, and other voter qualification devices, were eliminated for all

counties or states that had less than half the voting-age residents registered in November 1964. These 1965 provisions had the majority support of both parties in Congress, the long-standing coalition having
been at least temporarily broken. The same Congress voted to investi-
gate the Ku Klux Klan, and to abolish the immigration quotas (see
Chapter 10).

PRECIPITATING EVENTS   Following the passage of the Civil
Rights Act of 1964, a number of events occurred that helped convince
the Congress that the act of 1965 was necessary.[54] Encouraged by the
1964 act, the Student Non-Violent Coordinating Committee (SNCC, usually called "Snick") organized a Freedom Summer in 1964, a drive to
register black voters in the South. When over twelve hundred students
arrived in Mississippi to start the campaign they were met with hostility and harassment. In June, a Northern black worker in the drive
and two Northern whites—James Chaney, Michael Schwerner, and
Andrew Goodman—were murdered. A deputy sheriff and seventeen
others were eventually convicted of depriving the three young men of
due process of law (the most serious federal charge that could be
brought), and sentenced to terms of from three to ten years.

Early in 1965 a drive to register black voters in Alabama was
accelerated, and police harassment of registrants was encouraged by
Governor Wallace. In protest against this treatment, a nonviolent
march was organized, led by Dr. King and the Southern Christian
Leadership Conference. At a bridge at Selma the march ended when the
protesters were teargassed and assaulted with clubs by police—very
startling sights and sounds on the evening news telecast. After federal
intervention, a much-enlarged march occurred, from Selma to the state
capital at Montgomery. A white civil rights worker who joined the
marchers, Mrs. Viola Liuzzo of Detroit, was shot and killed from am-
bush as she drove on the highway. The Rev. James Reeb, a Unitarian
minister, died in Selma after he and two other Northern clergymen
were beaten by a small group of whites.

POLITICAL RESULTS   Before the 1965 act was passed the number
of registered Southern black voters had already been greatly increased,
and during the first year after passage of the act the total was more than
doubled. Not only did the numbers continue to climb in succeeding
years, but so did the percentage of Southern blacks reporting that they
had actually voted. The number of elected black officials has made
corresponding increases since 1965, nationally as well as in the South.[55]
By 1975 there were around three thousand elected blacks in the nation,
half of them in the South, mostly in city and county offices. There were
well over a hundred mayors, some of very large cities. There were over
two hundred blacks in state legislatures in 1974, and two lieutenant
governors. The sixteen blacks in the United States House of Representa-

tives in 1973 (an increase from five in 1964) included four women. Edward W. Brooke, senator from Massachusetts, was first elected in 1966. All this increased political participation is within the framework of the established political parties; a resolution for a black party was defeated at the second National Black Political Convention, held in Little Rock, Arkansas, in 1974.

The Civil Rights Act of 1968

A major part of the 1968 legislation deals with discrimination in housing. It prohibits discrimination in selling or renting federally owned housing or multi-unit dwellings mortgaged under the Federal Housing Administration or the Veterans Administration, in all apartments and other multi-unit housing, and in single-family dwellings sold or rented through realtors. The 1968 act also provides penalties for injuring or intimidating civil rights workers or blacks engaged in voting, registering to vote, jury duty, schooling, or other uses of public facilities. Indians are assured certain rights in relation to tribal governments, the courts, and all levels of government. The act defines as federal crimes the making, selling, or demonstrating of weapons for use in civil disorders, and interstate traveling with intent to incite a riot.

WOMEN, LAW, AND POLITICAL ACTION

Legislative Developments

Although there had been some improvements in the legal status of women before the 1960s,[56] the legal foundations of the current women's movement were provided in federal legislation in 1963 and 1964. The Equal Pay Act of 1963, which added a new subsection to the Fair Labor Standards Act of 1938, was passed to combat wage discrimination against women. It requires employers to pay women the same rates men are paid if both perform substantially the same work, under identical working conditions, in the same establishment.[57] Title VII of the Civil Rights Act of 1964 bans discrimination based on race, color, religion, sex, or national origin, in employment in all industries affecting commerce, employment agencies serving such industries, and labor organizations in such industries. Sex was added as a last-minute amendment in a move to get the entire 1964 act defeated, but the amendment passed and became a powerful tool for women's rights.[58] Title VII was extended and enforcement powers added in the Equal Employment Opportunity Act of 1972.

The Equal Employment Opportunity Commission established guidelines for complying with Title VII and the Equal Pay Act, and it has processed large numbers of complaints of discrimination against women in hiring and promotion. Enforcement has been sufficiently rigorous so that awards of back pay have resulted in many cases. For example, the EEOC joined a group of women lawyers in a lawsuit against the American Telephone and Telegraph Company, which employs more women than any other firm in the world. Not only was AT&T compelled to provide specific goals and schedules for hiring and promoting women and other minority employees, but it also was ordered to pay $23 million in pay increases to women and minority males who were underpaid for their job categories, and $15 million in back pay to persons who had been discriminated against in promotions. Another result was that, in its advertising and its booklets, AT&T stopped referring to telephone operators as "she" and to line workers and managers as "he."[59]

Title IX of the Education Amendments of 1972 prohibits discrimination by sex in educational programs that receive federal money. It forbids differential treatment of the sexes in curricula, counseling, rules for running schools (such as curfews), treatment of employees, and admission to all vocational, professional graduate, private undergraduate, and previously single-sex undergraduate institutions. Title IX became effective in mid-1975, and has been widely applied to programs of physical education, athletics, recruitment of students, extracurricular organizations and activities, and other matters. In the Vocational Education Amendments of 1976 there is strong wording against sex bias in vocational education.

The federal Equal Credit Opportunity Act was passed in 1974, with different provisions to go into effect over a three-year period. It bars refusal of credit or loans because of sex or marital status. A woman cannot be asked whether she plans to have children or not, and no inference about this can be made from her age. Among other regulations is the requirement that part-time income must be counted in credit ratings, that any person must be given reasons why credit is refused, and that a woman may use her maiden name (or any legal name she wishes) in applying for credit.

In March 1972 the Congress passed the Equal Rights Amendment (ERA) to guarantee women equal rights under the law. If it is ratified by thirty-eight states by March 1979, it will become the Twenty-seventh Amendment to the United States Constitution. By mid-1977, after some states had rescinded their approval, the vote for the amendment stood at thirty-five. The votes were close in some states, such as the defeat by two votes in North Carolina in 1977. Opponents have claimed that women already have gained full legal equality,[60] while supporters have pointed to sexual differences in laws concerning social security benefits, jury exemptions, maternity leaves, public educational institutions, public employment, the small private employer, and other matters.

Political Action for Women

The National Organization for Women continues to devote much of its attention to political activities. In 1971, NOW helped form the National Women's Political Caucus, which has become influential at political party conventions. The caucus promotes women's equality, both in elections and in the discussion of public issues. Other organizations that work for legislation or executive action toward equality for women include the Women's Lobby and the Women's Campaign Fund. The League of Women Voters remains nonpartisan and devoted to educating the public on political questions; but it takes stands on specific issues, and it supports equality for women.

The number of women elected or appointed to public office in the United States has never been very large. Only 8 percent of the country's state legislators were women in 1975, and in 1974 less than 5 percent of the legislators and top appointees in the nation's capital. Usually the women in high posts have succeeded their husbands or fathers, or have been appointees. In 1974, Ella Grasso of Connecticut became the first woman governor to be elected in her own right, and Mary Ann Krupsak of New York was elected the nation's first woman lieutenant governor. Women have usually not run for office before the age of forty, after a career of volunteer service in local community affairs. Now more younger women are running, usually after studying law.[61]

The Equal Rights Amendment has had high priority in women's political activities in recent years. In 1975 the American Association of University Women decided to shift its national convention out of Missouri because that state had rejected the ERA. In 1976, for the same reason, the League of Women Voters scheduled its 1978 national meeting in Ohio instead of Illinois. The AAUW estimated the financial loss to Kansas City, Missouri, to be above a million dollars; the LWV estimated the loss to Chicago at about half a million. Fifty-five organizations had joined the boycott by December 1977, causing an estimated $15 million loss to Chicago, $16 million to Atlanta, $9 million to Miami, and losses to other cities in states that had not ratified the ERA.

THE AFFIRMATIVE ACTION ISSUE

In developing guidelines for implementing the equal employment laws, the EEOC followed suggestions from the courts concerning detailed steps. At first "affirmative action" referred to nondiscrimination in advertising job openings, active recruiting among minority groups that might not know of the jobs, and helping to train minority persons not fully qualified. Widespread noncompliance by employers apparently contributed to the development of objective criteria. Also, Executive Order 11246—issued in 1965 and amended in 1972—implied a quantitative standard in requiring most major employers to develop and follow written programs to correct "underutilization" of minority and female employees in hiring and promotions. By the early 1970s, the concept of affirmative action had come to mean increasing the numbers of minority persons employed, promoted, appointed as administrators, admitted to schools, and so on. When the goal of achieving the proportion of a minority group found in the general population was added, the guidelines had become quotas.

The quota approach to equal employment for groups has been criticized as a violation of the principle that it is unconstitutional to give such categories as race and sex special legal treatment. If quotas can be used for any purpose, the argument runs, they will be used to discriminate against groups. Critics of "reverse discrimination" also contend that preferential treatment of some groups is unfair to other groups that have been discriminated against at one time or another, and that may now be kept from jobs, promotions, or school admissions for which they are qualified. This line of criticism of quotas has been extended to busing for racial balance.[62] It has also been contended that preferential treatment denies equal opportunity to equally qualified persons in the dominant community. In general, the answer in the courts has been that preferential treatment is legitimate when the purpose is to correct inequality rather than to discriminate against members of a group, but the use of quotas to achieve this end has increasingly been challenged. Whether such action is reducing inequality significantly for women and other minorities remains to be seen.[63]

OTHER LEGAL ACTIVITIES

The Southern Poverty Law Center

The SPLC was started in 1971 in Montgomery, Alabama, by Julian Bond and Joseph J. Levin, Jr. Bond became its first president, and Levin was legal director for the first six years. The aim of the center is to use the courts to gain fair and equal treatment for the poor of all races. Clients pay no fees, and most of the lawsuits are class actions, which benefit many persons other than the plaintiffs. Much of its activity has been on behalf of poor blacks in the South, often for criminal defendants.

The center compelled Montgomery to desegregate the YMCA, which had been receiving city and state support, and to reopen the city's recreational facilities to poor blacks. In 1972 the center obtained a federal court order requiring Alabama to hire one black for each white until its force of state highway troopers was one-fourth black, the percentage of blacks in the state's population. It has been instrumental in welfare and jail reforms, in stopping HEW's program of "involuntary" sterilization of poor minors and mental incompetents, and in getting Alabama to admit black children to state orphanages rather than sending them to reformatories.

The center's activity has not been limited to blacks, or to the South. It persuaded a federal court to reject the height and weight restrictions for hiring state troopers in Alabama, opening the way for the recruiting of women. It pursued a case on behalf of the handicapped against the bus system of Rochester, New York, for having buses too narrow and steps too high. It has been to court in New Mexico on behalf of "urban Indians" who have been denied the benefits of the national Indian Health Service because they are not living on a reservation.

Some landmark cases before the United States Supreme Court have been won by the center. One compelled Montgomery to eliminate recreational funds for private, segregated schools. Another resulted in equal pay and equal benefits to women in the armed services. Finally, the center forced Alabama to reapportion its state legislature, creating "one man, one vote" districts. The immediate result of the reapportionment was the election of seventeen blacks to the legislature.[64]

The American Civil Liberties Union

The ACLU was founded in 1920 to protect civil liberties—those legal rights guaranteed to all citizens by the Constitution, with emphasis on freedom of inquiry and expression, privacy, due process of law, and equal treatment in law. This includes civil rights—those rights guaranteed by the Thirteenth and Fourteenth Amendments and the civil rights laws. The major activity of the ACLU has been the conduct of lawsuits, with the help of volunteer lawyers, and only the Department of Justice has appealed more cases to the United States Supreme Court. It has also attempted to protect civil liberties in legislation and administrative proceedings at the federal, state, and local levels.

Much of the activity of the ACLU has helped protect the rights of members of minority groups. Examples include actions concerning freedom of religion, free speech, and the rights of migrant workers, voters, aliens, children and youth, criminal defendants, and prisoners. Some ACLU actions have been undertaken to help specific minority groups, such as those on behalf of Japanese Americans detained during

World War II, Jehovah's Witnesses, homosexuals, and the fishing rights of Indians of the Northwest. The ACLU has opposed segregated juries, and it provided legal support during the Southern civil rights movement of the 1960s. Among actions on behalf of women are opposition to the separate-but-equal approach to women's athletics, and to discrimination on the basis of sex or marital status in rates for health, accident, and disability insurance.

Mexican Americans and the Law

POLITICAL ACTIVITIES   The feeling of powerlessness with respect to government is apparently still widespread among Mexican Americans.[65] Political participation has increased since the late 1960s, but the level is still relatively low, despite more determined efforts in a number of organizations. The League of United Latin-American Citizens (LULAC), begun in 1929, became more political in the 1960s, pushing for favorable legislation and bringing complaints of discrimination to state and federal offices. The Mexican American Political Association (MAPA), the Political Association of Spanish-Speaking Organizations (PASSO), and the La Raza Unida party have emphasized voter registration, equal employment, and the election of Mexican Americans. The Southwest Voter Registration Education Project was begun in 1974.

MALDEF   Mexican Americans won some important appeals to the United States Supreme Court on such matters as segregated schools and juries in the 1940s and '50s, but the creation of MALDEF filled a need for a systematic program of litigation. The Mexican American Legal Defense and Educational Fund was initiated by a Ford Foundation grant in 1968, with national headquarters in San Francisco. A young woman lawyer who had worked with the NAACP in the South in 1967, Vilma S. Martinez, became president and general counsel of the fund. Although rural problems are not neglected, the emphasis is urban, since nearly nine-tenths of the nation's Mexican Americans live in urban areas. MALDEF emphasizes lawsuits, but it also conducts research projects and provides information for public education on legal issues relating to Mexican Americans and other minorities. Another purpose of the Fund is to provide financial help to Mexican American law students, with its Educational Grants program.

Most of the fund's cases have involved discrimination in employment or education, but some have been concerned with voting, land and water rights, prison reforms, or other matters. Its successes include cases on school desegregation and the right to bilingual education. In 1976, two MALDEF suits against large canning industries in California gained protection against discrimination in hiring, firing, promotions, seniority, training, and processing complaints. Cases on voter registration practices and discriminatory at-large election districts have resulted in increased representation by both Mexican Americans and blacks in the Texas State Legislature.

Indians and the Law

Although Indian Bureau policies have become quite pluralistic in recent years (see Chapter 10), the tribes have great difficulty influencing the making and administering of the federal, state, and local laws that affect their development. The range of relevant issues is wide. The National Congress of American Indians, representing the reservations, supports a modest lobbying effort in Washington, D.C. The urban-based American Indian Movement has preferred confrontation tactics (see Chapter 13) to regular political participation and systematic litigation. The Native American Rights Fund is an inter-tribal group formed to use the courts to protect Indian interests.

The National Indian Youth Council, a reservation group started in 1961, has used strategies that include political and legal action. For example, in 1976 it developed a program to oppose strip mining and the building of six coal gasification plants on the Navajo Reservation in New Mexico, a threat to the Navajo Irrigation Project. Opposition is difficult after legislation for a project has already been passed by Congress, and especially so in this instance because the action was to help meet the nation's energy crisis. The NIYC has sought funds nationally and has attempted to help educate the American public on the issue; it has helped organize Navajo communities for a petition campaign; and it has done technical and legal research in preparation for its challenge to the project in the federal courts.

The National Committee Against Discrimination in Housing

The NCDH illustrates a rarity—an organization devoted to combating discrimination in one important aspect of life, on behalf of all minority groups. It has emphasized urban housing for all poor groups. Located in Washington, D.C., since its founding in 1950, the committee has followed legislative developments closely, and has monitored the effectiveness of governmental agencies in carrying out open-housing laws. It has provided legal counsel, and has initiated lawsuits on many housing practices, including FHA mortgage loan procedures, zoning and land use, and urban renewal. It has supplemented its political and legal activities with field services for community and civil rights groups, handbooks and other publications, research to provide organized information on housing questions, and public educational efforts through the mass media.

The NCDH has played a major role in landmark federal court decisions on housing, and in the passage of the Civil Rights Act of 1968, the Housing and Urban Development Acts of 1968, 1969, and 1970, and other major open-housing legislation.[66] It appears that its specialization in the complex field of housing has facilitated these and other successes. Another factor is that the committee has increased its power to influence the law and its administration by joining in coalitions with other groups. It has cooperated with the NAACP, the Urban League, CORE, and many other minority and civil rights groups.

CONCLUSION

Law can be an effective instrument in establishing and maintaining patterns of institutionalized discrimination against minorities. It can also be effective in combating discrimination and moving toward equal treatment of groups. Significant improvements in the status of blacks, women, and other minorities in recent decades must be attributed in considerable part to landmark court decisions and legislation against discriminatory practices. The first major breakthrough occurred in the federal courts, before and during the early 1950s, as the result of a determined strategy of litigation by the NAACP. The decisions in the school segregation cases were the beginning of the end of the entire system of *de jure* segregation in the South. These legal victories sparked a national movement that produced comprehensive civil rights laws in the 1960s, and major gains for minorities in education, employment, and voting.

Legal changes usually have some unanticipated consequences.[67] Noting only a few such items in the complex chain of events following the *Brown* decision, who—in 1954—could foresee ethnic studies programs, affirmative action quotas, a militant Indian movement, the crisis in the North over school busing for racial balance, or women highway troopers in Alabama? Few people, including social scientists, anticipated the widespread changes in beliefs and attitudes that occurred, especially in the South. For some, the change in the law was apparently sufficient to change attitudes; for others, the enforced changes in behavior resulted in changes in beliefs and attitudes. Laws against unequal treatment evidently place discriminators on the defensive as law-violating deviants, and they provide minorities with legal means to defend themselves, challenge beliefs underlying prejudices and patterns of discrimination, and foster equal-status contacts and interaction.[68] Many prejudiced persons thus become less so, and unprejudiced persons have the law to help them resist pressures to discriminate.

The probability of obtaining new laws for intergroup relations, and of enforcing them, depends on how strong the pattern of accommodation is. When discriminatory practices are uniformly followed in the dominant community, and strongly supported by prejudices and underlying beliefs, the legal strategies of minorities can avail little. To the extent that there are actual or latent conflicts over minority questions, the use of political tactics and litigation can often shift the balance of interest-group power. The more the public attitudes and practices toward a minority group become inconsistent and ambiguous, the greater becomes the probability that antidiscrimination laws can be obtained and enforced by determined action.[69]

Strategies to change laws that affect group status, through legislation and/or litigation, usually have been supplemented by efforts to educate the general public about the issues. Efforts to get antidiscriminatory statutes enforced include the use of the courts, public education, monitoring and confronting governmental agencies, and providing materials and consultation for minority organizations and other concerned groups in the community. The chances of success in getting laws changed and enforced are apparently associated with the degree of realism in assessing the interests, actions, and relative power of groups in the dominant community. Success also depends on effective cooperation with other minority and civil rights organizations.

FOOTNOTES

1   Greenberg, 1959, pp. 1–78.
2   Bland, 1973.
3   Woodward, 1966, p. 108; Berry, 1971, pp. 103–37.
4   Civil Rights Cases, 109 U.S. 3 (1883).
5   *Plessy* v. *Ferguson*, 163 U.S. 537 (1896).
6   Foster, 1962 (a), pp. 176–77.
7   *Guinn & Beal* v. *U.S.*, 238 U.S. 347 (1915).
8   *Buchanan* v. *Warley*, 245 U.S. 60 (1917); *Harmon* v. *Taylor*, 273 U.S. 668 (1927).
9   *Nixon* v. *Herndon*, 273 U.S. 347 (1927).
10 *Powell* v. *Alabama*, 287 U.S. 45 (1932); *Brown* v. *Mississippi*, 297 U.S. 278 (1936).
11 *Norris* v. *Alabama*, 294 U.S. 587 (1935); *Pierre* v. *Louisiana*, 306 U.S. 354 (1939); *Smith* v. *Texas*, 311 U.S. 128 (1940); *Cassell* v. *Texas*, 239 U.S. 282 (1950).
12 *Mitchell* v. *U.S.*, 313 U.S. 80 (1941); *Morgan* v. *Virginia*, 328 U.S. 373 (1946); *Henderson* v. *U.S.*, 339 U.S. 816 (1950).
13 *Smith* v. *Allwright*, 321 U.S. 649 (1944).

14 *Railway Mail Association* v. *Corsi,* 326 U.S. 88 (1945).

15 *Shelley* v. *Kraemer,* 334 U.S. 1 (1948); *Burrows* v. *Jackson,* 346 U.S. 249 (1953).

16 *Missouri ex rel. Gaines* v. *Canada,* 305 U.S. 337 (1938).

17 *Sweatt* v. *Painter,* 339 U.S. 629 (1950).

18 Bland, 1973, pp. 60–82.

19 *McLaurin* v. *Oklahoma,* 339 U.S. 637 (1950).

20 Blackwell, 1975, pp. 103–4.

21 Pierce et al., 1955, pp. 288–90.

22 *Brown* v. *Board of Education of Topeka,* 347 U.S. 483 (1954).

23 *Briggs* v. *Elliot,* 342 U.S. 350 (1952); *Davis* v. *County School Board of Prince Edward County,* 103 F. Supp. 337 (1952); *Gebhart* v. *Belton,* 344 U.S. 891 (1952); *Bolling* v. *Sharpe,* 344 U.S. 873 (1952).

24 Blaustein & Ferguson, 1957, pp. 10–11, 95–125; Greenberg, 1959, pp. 208–74; Bland, 1973, p. 82.

25 Davis & Foster, 1962, pp. 109–34.

26 Foster, 1962 (a), pp. 149–73; Blaustein & Ferguson, 1957, pp. 54–75.

27 Foster, 1962 (a), pp. 173–92; Blaustein & Ferguson, 1957, p. 118; Rosen, 1972, Ch. 6.

28 Bland, 1973, p. 74.

29 Blaustein & Ferguson, 1957, pp. 126–37; Foster, 1962, pp. 168–70; Rosen, 1972, pp. 52–101, 134–96.

30 Clark, 1950; Frazier, 1957; Myrdal, 1944.

31 Blaustein & Ferguson, 1957, pp. 218–29; Bland, 1973, pp. 86–87.

32 Countryman, 1965; Blaustein & Ferguson, 1957, pp. 145–57, 180–209; Bland, 1973, Ch. 4.

33 Southern Education Reporting Service, 1967, pp. 1–4, 41–42.

34 Blaustein & Ferguson, 1957, Ch. 15; Greenberg, 1959, pp. 221–45; Campbell, 1961; Farley, 1975, pp. 4–7.

35 *Alexander* v. *Holmes County Board of Education,* 396 U.S. 19 (1969).

36 Carter, 1959.

37 Gallup Political Index, Report No. 12, May 1966, p. 16; Los Angeles Times, May 3, 1970, Sec. H., p. 4.

38 Record & Record, 1960; Campbell & Pettigrew, 1959; Berry, 1971, pp. 180–83.

39 Crain, 1969, pp. 250–52, 309.

40 Leeson, 1966; Wirt, 1970; Berry, 1971, pp. 190–99.

41 United States Commission on Civil Rights, 1967.

42 Coleman, Campbell, et al., 1966.

43 St. John, 1975.

44 Edwards, 1975.

45 Kerchoff & Campbell, 1977.

46 *Keyes* v. *School District No. 1, Denver, Colorado,* 413 U.S. 189 (1973).

47 Blackwell, 1975, pp. 107–8; Farley, 1975, pp. 19–21.

48 *Swann* v. *Charlotte-Mecklenburg Board of Education,* 402 U.S. 1, 29–30 (1971).

49 *Milliken* v. *Bradley,* 418 U.S. 717 (1974).

50 Levine & Meyer, 1977.

51 Rubin, 1972, pp. 64–73.

52 Glazer, 1975, Ch. 5.

53 Blackwell, 1975, pp. 119–20.
54 Berry, 1971, pp. 200–204; Blackwell, 1975, pp. 201–3.
55 Blackwell, 1975, pp. 208–15.
56 Foster, 1962 (b), pp. 247–61; Kanowitz, 1969, Chs. 2 & 3.
57 Kanowitz, 1969, Ch. 5.
58 Kanowitz, Ch. 4.
59 Epstein, 1976, pp. 420, 428.
60 Kanowitz, 1969, pp. 192–96.
61 Epstein, 1976, pp. 434–36.
62 Glazer, 1975, Chs. 2, 3, 6; cf. Gilbert & Eaton, 1970.
63 For an application of the criterion of proportionality to the ranks held by blacks in the army, see Butler, 1976.
64 Southern Poverty Law Report, January 1976; January/February 1977.
65 Welch, Comer & Steinman, 1975.
66 Blackwell, 1975, pp. 159–62.
67 Akers & Hawkins, 1975, pp. 314–19.
68 Berger, 1968, pp. 237–38; Greenberg, 1959, p. 7; Schur, 1968, pp. 137–38.
69 Davis, 1962, pp. 74–77; Schur, 1968, p. 136.

REFERENCES

Akers, Ronald L., and Richard Hawkins (eds.)
1975   Law and Control in Society. Englewood Cliffs, New Jersey: Prentice-Hall, Inc.
Berger, Morroe
1968   Equality by Statute, Revised Edition. New York: Anchor Books.
Berry, Mary Frances
1971   Black Resistance/White Law. New York: Appleton-Century-Crofts.
Blackwell, James E.
1975   The Black Community: Diversity and Unity. New York: Dodd, Mead and Co.
Bland, Randall W.
1973   Private Pressure on Public Law: The Legal Career of Justice Thurgood Marshall. Port Washington, New York: Kennikat Press.
Blaustein, Albert P., and Clarence Clyde Ferguson, Jr.
1957   Desegregation and the Law. New Brunswick, New Jersey: Rutgers University Press.
Butler, John Sibley
1976   "Assessing Black Enlisted Participation in the Army." Social Problems 23, 5 (June): 558–66.
Campbell, Ernest Q.
1961   When a City Closes Its Schools. Chapel Hill, North Carolina: Institute for Research in Social Science, University of North Carolina.
Campbell, Ernest Q., and Thomas F. Pettigrew
1959   Christians in Racial Crisis: A Study of Little Rock's Ministry. Washington, D.C.: Public Affairs Press.

Carter, Hodding, III
1959   The South Strikes Back. Garden City, New York: Doubleday and Co.

Clark, Kenneth B.
1950   Effect of Prejudice and Discrimination on Personality Development. Washington, D.C.: Midcentury White House Conference on Children and Youth.

Coleman, James, and Ernest Q. Campbell, with Carol J. Hobson, James McPartland, Alexander M. Mood, Frederick D. Weinfeld, and Robert L. York
1966   Equality and Educational Opportunity. Washington, D.C.: U.S. Government Printing Office.

Countryman, Vern (ed.)
1965   Discrimination and the Law. Chicago and London: University of Chicago Press.

Crain, Robert L., assisted by Morton Inger, Gerald A. McWorter, and James J. Vanecko
1971   The Politics of School Desegregation: Comparative Case Studies of Community Structure and Policy-Making. New York: Doubleday Anchor Books.

Davis, F. James, and Henry H. Foster, Jr.
1962   "The Judicial Process and Social Change," Ch. 4 in F. James Davis et al., Society and the Law. New York: The Free Press.

Edwards, Ozzie L.
1975   "Cohort and Sex Changes in Black Educational Achievement." Sociology and Social Research 59, 2 (January): 110–20.

Epstein, Cynthia Fuchs
1976   "Sex Roles," Ch. 9 in Robert K. Merton and Robert Nisbet, Contemporary Social Problems. New York: Harcourt, Brace, Jovanovich, Inc.

Farley, Reynolds
1975   "Racial Integration in the Public Schools, 1967–1972: Assessing the Effect of Governmental Policy." Sociological Focus 8, 1 (January): 3–26.

Foster, Henry H., Jr.
1962   (a)"Public Law and Social Change," Ch. 5 in F. James Davis et al., Society and the Law. New York: The Free Press.
1962   (b)"Family Law in a Changing Society," Ch. 7 in F. James Davis et al., Society and the Law. New York: The Free Press.

Frazier, E. Franklin
1957   The Negro in the United States, Revised Edition. New York: The Macmillan Co.

Gilbert, Neil, and Joseph W. Eaton
1970   "Favoritism as a Strategy in Race Relations." Social Problems 18, 1 (Summer): 38–52.

Glazer, Nathan
1975   Affirmative Discrimination: Ethnic Inequality and Public Policy. New York: Basic Books, Inc.

Greenberg, Jack
1959   Race Relations and American Law. New York: Columbia University Press.

Kanowitz, Leo
1969   Women and the Law: The Unfinished Revolution. Albuquerque: University of New Mexico Press.

Kerchoff, Alan C., and Richard T. Campbell
1977   "Race and Social Status Differences in the Explanation of Educational Ambition." Social Forces 55, 3 (March): 701–14.

Leeson, Jim
1966   "Desegregation: Violence, Intimidation and Protest." Southern Education Report (December): 29–32.

Levine, Daniel U., and Jeanie Kenny Meyer
1977   "Level and Rate of Desegregation and White Enrollment Decline in a Big City School District." Social Problems 24, 4 (April): 451–62.

Myrdal, Gunnar, assisted by Richard Sterner and Arnold M. Rose
1944   An American Dilemma. New York: Harper and Bros.

Pierce, Truman M., et al.
1955   White and Negro Schools in the South. Englewood Cliffs, New Jersey: Prentice-Hall, Inc.

Record, Wilson, and Jane Cassels Record
1960   Little Rock, U.S.A. San Francisco: Chandler Publishing Co.

Rosen, Paul L.
1972   The Supreme Court and Social Science. Urbana: University of Illinois Press.

Rubin, Lillian B.
1972   Busing and Backlash: White Against White in an Urban School District. Berkeley and Los Angeles: University of California Press.

St. John, Nancy H.
1975   School Desegregation: Outcomes for Children. New York: John Wiley and Sons.

Schur, Edwin M.
1968   Law and Society: A Sociological View. New York: Random House.

Southern Education Reporting Service
1967   Statistical Summary of School Segregation-Desegregation in the Southern and Border States, 1966–67. Nashville, Tennessee: Southern Education Reporting Service.

United States Commission on Civil Rights
1967   Racial Isolation in Public Schools. Washington, D.C.: U.S. Government Printing Office.

Welch, Susan, John Comer, and Michael Steinman
1975   "Ethnic Differences in Social and Political Participation: A Comparison of Some Anglo and Mexican Americans." Pacific Sociological Review 18(July):361–82.

Wirt, Frederick M.
1970   Law and Change in a Mississippi County. Chicago: Aldine Publishing Co.

Woodward, C. Vann
1966   The Strange Career of Jim Crow, 2nd Revised Edition. New York: Oxford University Press.

13

Protest and Confrontation

Some collective protests against unequal treatment are part of a strategy of group protest. Others are spontaneous, precipitated by some event at a time of unrest and uncertainty. Some are carefully controlled, even those that involve civil disobedience (selective lawbreaking), while others become riots. Even the relatively uncontrolled outbreaks may be limited by norms of restraint, as illustrated by selective damage to property rather than wholesale destruction and violence against persons.

Strategies of protest are based on two existential beliefs: (1) that the legal, political, and other formal means of changing the norms of intergroup relations are not succeeding; and (2) that, through protest, the group will have access to public channels of expression, and that the dominant community will listen and respond. Thus a minority protest must be distinguished from a rebellion, which is an attempt to bring a dominative system to an end by force, or to escape from it. A revolution is a sustained program of action to end and replace an established system. As noted in Chapter 7, minority rebellion rests on the belief that neither political action nor protest is currently effective, or possible. Protest, political action, rebellion, and revolution all require the belief that the group is not completely powerless to influence its own fate, but they differ on the means believed to be necessary.

One risk of public protest is that the dominant community may mistake it for rebellion—even for revolution. This may lead to unduly repressive reactions by social control agents of the dominant community. Restraints are more likely to be used in repressing perceived protest. Repressive control actions endanger freedom of assembly and expression, and they may also cause some protesters to resort to rebellion or revolution.

Public protest is confrontation in the sense that the general public is faced with the minority's grievances. Protest groups often confront directly such key decision makers as mayors, city councils, major employers, legislators, school boards, school administrators, or officials of public agencies. The purpose of direct confrontation sometimes is only to express protest, but it may also be designed to press for face-to-face negotiations for the changes desired.

The black protest activities since the mid-1950s is the major focus of attention in this chapter, followed by some comparisons of the recent protests of other groups. Not only has the black protest been widespread, but it has influenced the beliefs and actions of other minorities considerably. The first major actions were in the American South.

BLACK PROTEST IN THE SOUTH

Rising Expectations and the Civil Rights Movement

Improvements in the status of American blacks during and after World War II were significant enough to arouse new questions about accommodative beliefs and practices, and new hopes for more equal treatment. Then came the legal victory in the school segregation cases in 1954, which sent black hopes soaring. Federal law had shifted significantly, and the end of the entire system of legal segregation was in sight, virtually promised by the United States Supreme Court. White discriminators would become the lawbreakers. The existential belief that great changes had become possible spread widely, a phenomenon known as the "revolution of rising expectations."[1] In more precise terms, increased gains had led to a great increase in the perceived probability of gains from further efforts.[2] The belief grew that whites would respond to peaceful but determined collective actions, since they had begun major changes in the law and the majority apparently wanted to move toward equality. The sense of rightness of the value of racial equality grew, and a major civil rights movement emerged to push for new norms of race relations.[3]

In contrast to reliance only on more selective strategies, such as those of the NAACP and the Urban League, this new civil rights movement involved broad collective actions, in two senses. First, they were general confrontations of the dominant community, often involving protest and negotiation on a number of segregation issues at one time. Second, they involved a large increase in the proportion of the black community participating.[4] This meant that increasing numbers of Southern blacks were overcoming their fear of challenging the Jim Crow system. It also meant new organizations, which welcomed only the more militant white liberals, and the rise to prominence of more aggressive black leaders—"race man" types, who began to replace the accommodating "Uncle Toms" and the "diplomats" (see Chapter 7).[5] The new leaders did not advocate violence, but they were militant in the sense that they were determined and assertive.

Nonviolent Protest and Negotiation

THE MONTGOMERY BUS BOYCOTT[6]   In December 1955, Mrs. Rosa Parks was arrested in Montgomery, Alabama, for not complying with the state law requiring racially segregated seating on public conveyances. This precipitated a black boycott of city buses, originally planned as a one-day protest, but which lasted 382 days. At a mass meeting of five thousand blacks, led by a group of ministers, it was decided after the first day to continue the boycott until the officials would agree to first-come-first-served seating, courteous treatment of blacks, and black drivers for predominantly black runs. The Montgomery Improvement Association was formed to coordinate the boycott, and the Rev. Dr. Martin Luther King, Jr., was elected its chairperson. He was a 27-year-old Baptist minister, with a bachelor's degree from Morehouse College, a degree from Crozer Theological Seminary, and a Ph.D. in religion from Boston University. His conviction that resistance should remain nonviolent prevailed, and he emerged as a strong, determined leader.

The Improvement Association established a car pool, which proved effective in getting black people to work, despite police harassment for traffic violations. The blacks responded to the harassment, threats, the bombing of Dr. King's home, and other violence in nonviolent ways, and persisted in the boycott. Approximately 80 percent of the usual black patrons stayed off the buses, so the company and downtown merchants suffered severe economic losses. The NAACP took legal action, and in December 1956, the United States Supreme Court (citing the *Brown* case as a key precedent) held the state Jim Crow law on public conveyances to be unconstitutional.[7]

The desegregation of the buses precipitated Ku Klux Klan demonstrations. There were also threats, and acts of retaliation—beatings of blacks, sniping at the buses, and bombings of black homes, churches, and businesses. The arrest and trial of some of the alleged terrorists, although the jury voted for acquittal, brought an end to the disorders.[8]

THE SOUTHERN CHRISTIAN LEADERSHIP CONFERENCE   The success of the unprecedented action in Montgomery inspired large numbers of blacks to join the broadening civil rights movement. In January 1957 the SCLC was formed in Atlanta to coordinate a nonviolent movement to implement the Supreme Court's decision against segregated buses, and King was asked to be president. He continued his pastorate in Montgomery until 1960, and also began a heavy schedule of public speaking across the nation. Bus boycotts followed in Tallahassee, Atlanta, and other cities.[9] The SCLC broadened the scope of its activities, and in the next years it led or participated in other boycotts in the South, many mass meetings, voter registration drives, demonstrations, arrests, and negotiations, usually accompanied by legal steps. A decade after the Montgomery bus boycott, the SCLC led attempted boycotts of the entire states of Mississippi and Alabama.

King emerged from the Montgomery boycott with the firm existential belief that direct confrontation of the "white power structure" was necessary for major gains for blacks.[10] He also emerged with a strengthened conviction that nonviolent resistance was the only path to follow. This conviction was based on the Christian value of loving even one's enemies;[11] he rejected racism and called for integration and brotherhood. However, his approach rested also on the existential belief that blacks could win equality only if they remained nonviolent. He believed that the nation's Christian conscience could be successfully appealed to by confrontation, but only if the protesters refused to return violence for violence.[12] Apparently this approach appealed to large numbers of Southern blacks. The song "We Shall Overcome" came to a symbolize the hopes, the new unity, and the determined but nonviolent mood of King's crusade.

This kind of disciplined militancy is difficult to maintain in large groups, especially when protest is met with violence. King frequently used his access to the public to advocate and contribute to the mood of nonviolence. In 1959 he conferred with followers of Gandhi in India, and he placed increasing emphasis on training in techniques of nonviolent resistance. After moving to Atlanta in 1960—to devote more time to the SCLC and to be co-pastor of his father's church—he led many protests throughout the South. He was arrested and jailed several times, and sometimes subjected to physical violence, but he consistently set a nonviolent example. In a letter from jail in Birmingham, Alabama, in 1963, he wrote a justification for limited use of civil disobedience against "unjust laws," confrontation tactics rather than avoidance of conflict, and nonviolent resistance.[13] In his "I Have a Dream" speech at the march on Washington in 1963, he confronted the nation with its unfulfilled promises to blacks, and stressed racial brotherhood.[14]

When King accepted the Nobel Peace Prize in 1964 in Oslo, Norway, he attributed the award to his use and advocacy of nonviolent resistance.[15] Later he tried to discourage the violence that emerged in the black protest in the North.[16] In the mid-1960s he extended SCLC's Operation Breadbasket (see Chapter 11) from Atlanta to Chicago, Cleveland, and other Northern cities, and led actions against *de facto* segregation in housing and high rents in the ghetto. The policy was to try negotiation first; then, if necessary, to apply pressure by economic boycott.[17] King acknowledged the importance of power, and considered the boycott a potent weapon. He remained committed to confrontation and nonviolence, as the SCLC still is.

THE SIT-INS   The Montgomery bus boycott inspired the lunch counter sit-ins,[18] which were followed by "stand-ins" at voter registration offices, "wade-ins" at segregated pools and beaches, "kneel-ins," and other forms of boycott and demonstration. King considered the sit-ins the turning point in American race relations. Four black freshmen from North Carolina Agricultural and Technical College began the first sit-in on February 1, 1960, at the lunch counter at the Woolworth store in Greensboro. Within ten days the sit-in movement had spread to ten campus communities in North Carolina, and in two weeks to South Carolina, Tennessee, and Virginia. It then spread throughout the South, to more than sixty cities (in twelve states) by mid-April. Most participants were Southern black students, but there were some from the white campuses. Over 50,000 students eventually participated, in over a hundred cities, and over 3,600 were jailed.[19]

The sit-ins were dramatic and they received wide news coverage. They were direct confrontations of the white economic and political power structure, and the repressive responses were often violent. The SCLC attempted to keep the mushrooming movement nonviolent. The Fellowship of Reconciliation (a Northern pacifist organization) and the Congress of Racial Equality (CORE, started in Chicago in 1942 as a black pacifist group) provided training and literature on techniques of nonviolent resistance. King was the spiritual leader of the sit-ins, but the student protesters wanted an organization of their own. The Student Nonviolent Coordinating Committee (SNCC) was formed at meetings in April and May, with headquarters in Atlanta, and it played a major role in keeping most of the participants in the sit-ins nonviolent.[20] The discipline of these students in the face of arrest and (frequently) harsh treatment impressed the nation, and the courts.

The sit-ins were effective boycotts. Protesters were not served, so they sat at lunch counters for hours at a time, usually until arrested, tying up seats and causing loss of business. Student boycotts of chain stores in the North added pressure on management to issue orders to desegregate their Southern facilities. By August 1960, lunch counters had been desegregated in chain stores in 60 Southern cities, and a year later at least 126 cities had some integrated eating facilities.[21]

The sit-ins also resulted in major legal successes. In March 1960 the NAACP developed a master plan for defending the students arrested in the sit-ins. Meeting with sixty-two lawyers who were representing over a thousand of the arrested students, the NAACP lawyers announced that the use by states of the "disturbing the peace" statutes to convict the sit-in protesters would be challenged as violations of the Fourteenth Amendment. This strategy succeeded, and in 1961 the United States Supreme Court overturned "disturbing the peace" convictions of orderly demonstrators at lunch counters in Baton Rouge, Louisiana.[22]

THE FREEDOM RIDES[23]   As sit-ins continued in 1961, CORE initiated the freedom rides, in cooperation with the SCLC, SNCC, and the NAACP. The freedom riders were Northern volunteers, black and white, many from the campuses. The rides were a direct confrontation of the South with its continuing segregation on interstate buses and trains, and in the stations. CORE, knowing that this bold challenge would arouse intense anger against the Northerners, trained the volunteers in techniques of nonviolent resistance. Their behavior contrasted sharply with the violence they often met.

President Kennedy was informed by James Farmer, then director of CORE, of the itinerary for the first freedom ride. On May 4, 1961, six black and white pairs of volunteers, and a CORE observer, boarded a Greyhound and a Trailways bus for a trip from Washington, D.C. to New Orleans. At every stop the pairs of volunteers entered segregated waiting rooms and lunch counters. Arrests had occurred only twice by the time the bus arrived in Atlanta, and only in Rock Hill, South Carolina, had some of the volunteers been beaten by whites. It was in Anniston, Alabama, that riders on the Greyhound bus met major violence. A white mob smashed windows with iron bars, punctured the tires, set the bus afire with an incendiary bomb, and beat some of the volunteers as they emerged. Riders on the Trailways bus were forced to the rear of the bus by eight whites, kicked and beaten. Two hours later at the Birmingham terminal, one black volunteer and one white, Charles Person and James Peck, were dragged into an alley and beaten unconscious before the police intervened. They required surgical attention. The bus drivers refused to continue the trip, so—after threats from crowds at the bus station and the airport—the volunteers flew to New Orleans to attend a rally.

Determined that the freedom ride to New Orleans be completed, a busload of volunteers left Nashville, stayed overnight in the Birmingham terminal, and were met by three hundred Ku Klux Klansmen in Montgomery on the morning of May 20. A group of women urged the crowd to kill the first rider who emerged—James Zwerg, a white student from Wisconsin. He was savagely beaten, but he survived, as the other volunteers were clubbed and kicked. A black student, William Barbee, was hospitalized for several weeks by Klansmen wielding baseball bats. John Lewis (later chairman of SNCC), who was injured in the first freedom ride and who had flown from New Orleans to join the busload, was injured again. Several news reporters and photographers were beaten. That night a large mob attacked the First Baptist Church of Montgomery as the Rev. Ralph Abernathy and Dr. King led a meeting in protest against the lack of police protection for the freedom riders. Finally, under pressure from Robert Kennedy—then attorney general of the United States—Governor Patterson ordered the National Guard to disperse the mob.

A mobile workshop on nonviolent resistance was conducted by James Lawson, as the bus traveled to Jackson, Mississippi, with its National Guard escort. There the freedom riders were arrested and fined, but they went to jail rather than pay fines on false charges. Before the summer ended, over three hundred other volunteers had arrived in Jackson, and all in their turn were arrested and jailed. Other freedom rides continued throughout the South.

A major objective of the freedom rides was to precipitate arrests and lawsuits, so that the NAACP could file appeals in federal courts and speed the process of desegregation. Large numbers of arrests were made, on charges such as disturbing the peace, inciting to riot, or vagrancy, and the legal strategy succeeded well. By November 1, 1961, it was required that a sign be displayed on all interstate buses indicating that racial discrimination is prohibited by the Interstate Commerce Commission. Similar signs were required at bus and train stations, and the message had to be printed on all tickets. Compliance became widespread, but freedom rides continued for a time against pockets of resistance and as a continuing test.[24]

White Backlash

The black drive for desegregation was widely perceived by whites as a distinct threat to the superior status of whites—as a revolution against the "Southern way of life." The NAACP was considered a radical organization, not a moderate one dedicated to complying with the Constitution of the United States. King and the SCLC were often depicted in the South as extremists, comparable to extreme right-wing organizations such as the Ku Klux Klan and the White Citizens Council. In this polarized climate of opinion, any means whatever used to advance the civil rights movement was generally regarded as traitorous to the South.[25]

Most of the backlash to the black protest was through legal means to evade and delay school integration (see Chapter 12), and the use of economic and political power to minimize voter registration and the desegregation of public facilities. Most Southern whites did not resort to violence, and during the 1960s a great many reluctantly shifted from defiance to compliance with the federal law. However, there were also many threats and acts of violence, often encouraged or condoned by governors or other people with power. Besides the violence that often accompanied the sit-ins and the freedom rides (above), some of the more brutal responses to desegregating the schools and registering voters have been noted in Chapter 12. The most widely publicized incidents—such as the voter registration killings in Mississippi in 1964, and the murders and police violence at Selma, Alabama—became major symbols to the nation and to the world. Some further events must be noted to portray adequately the violent side of the white backlash, although space permits mention of only a small fraction of the people who were injured or killed, or whose homes, churches, or businesses were damaged or destroyed.

The SNCC voter registration project in Albany, Georgia, began with a freedom ride in the fall of 1961, and quickly became a broader confrontation against the treatment of blacks. With the help of SCLC there were mass meetings, nonviolent workshops, demonstrations, boycotts, arrests of over two thousand, and negotiations that continued for three years. Police repression included countless beatings and other brutalities. Four rural black churches were bombed and burned. Black homes were attacked with bombs and gunfire.[26]

The SCLC Voter Education Project in Mississippi listed sixty-four acts of violent terrorism against blacks in one part of the state in the first three months of 1963. These included shootings and burnings, and the mutilation and lynching of Sylvester Maxwell in Madison County. On June 12, the head of the NAACP in Mississippi, Medgar Evers, was killed in his driveway by a sniper.[27] Also in 1963, during the months-long protest led by the SCLC in Birmingham, Alabama, the police used dogs, fire hoses, and electric cattle prods against protesters who were trying to remain nonviolent. Some fought back. On September 14 a bomb was thrown through the window of a black Baptist church while Sunday school was in session. Four little girls were killed, and twenty other children injured.[28] For this, a murder conviction in an Alabama circuit court was finally obtained in 1977.

On June 7, 1966, James Meredith (who had been the first black student at the University of Mississippi) left Memphis to begin a march across Mississippi to encourage blacks to exercise their freedoms, especially to vote. Soon after crossing the state line he was shot and wounded by a white man with a shotgun. SCLC, SNCC, and CORE leaders resumed the Freedom March and walked for three weeks, sleeping in tents. Meredith survived, and rejoined the march before it ended in Jackson. Not only did this event become another major symbol of white backlash against the black drive for equal treatment; but, as they reached Greenwood, Stokely Carmichael (then heading SNCC) got the marchers to adopt the "black power" slogan. His initial reference was to voter registration. King discouraged the slogan, and he and Carmichael had their first disagreements about this, the role of whites in the black protest, and nonviolence.[29] The black protest was responding to white backlash.

GHETTO RIOTS AS BLACK PROTEST

Blocked Hopes in the Ghettos

ECONOMIC SETBACKS   Black hopes were running high as the migration into the Northern ghettos continued before and during the early 1960s. Instead of the promised land, a great many found severe housing problems, unemployment, exploitation of ghetto consumers, and a disproportionately high burden of poverty in the ghettos. The educational and occupational gains of blacks were not resulting in significant gains in income (see Chapter 11). Nationally the rate of unemployment of blacks grew to twice that of whites, and in many ghettos it was several times higher. Automation rendered many unskilled jobs obsolete, and blacks were disadvantaged in competition for the remaining ones because of discrimination in hiring. Comparing themselves with whites, many blacks felt unwanted, irrelevant, often desperate in the midst of a rich, expanding economy.[30]

IMPACT OF THE SOUTHERN BACKLASH   Many urban blacks in the 1960s had recently moved from the South, or had relatives and friends there. Daily news accounts of the widened black protest, and responses to it, were supplemented by personal communications. Legal evasion and delay of school desegregation dragged on, along with harassment of would-be black voters, and incidents of violence. Television had become widely available, and viewers often saw the repressive actions of police or white crowds toward nonviolent protesters. The existential belief grew among blacks that the Supreme Court decisions and the civil rights laws had created false hopes, and that the federal government did not intend to support desegregation and racial equality. Questions multiplied about the efficacy of both the legal and nonviolent strategies of protest, and unrest grew in the black communities of the North.

POLICE HARASSMENT AND BRUTALITY   Discriminatory and brutal treatment by white police had been complained of by urban blacks long before the 1960s, and police action had often been the precipitating factor in riots in prior decades.[31] The belief that police and the courts were means of controlling blacks rather than protecting them and guaranteeing justice was reinforced in the 1960s; police seemed to ignore crimes committed by blacks against other blacks.[32] The Black Panther Party for Self-Defense was started in 1966 to monitor the police and prevent them from mistreating blacks. They openly carried weapons until it became illegal.

Demands grew for more black police, and for police review boards as a check on police behavior. Police issues had become symbolic of the overall frustrations of ghetto life, and of black unity against discriminatory treatment by the dominant community. The precipitating incident in most of the ghetto outbursts of the 1960s was police action—perceived as brutal, or at least as unfair to blacks. Northern blacks were unafraid to fight back against the police, and were unrestrained by norms of nonviolent resistance.

CONDITIONS FOR MINORITY-DOMINANT RIOTS   When social expectations have been disrupted and there is ambiguity and great uncertainty about what to do, various forms of crowd behavior, social movements, and public discussion may occur. The norms of accommodation between dominant and minority groups may be disrupted by migration, war, legal or political changes, technological innovation, or other major changes. In order for a crowd to become a mob (an acting crowd), some precipitating incident must occur that symbolizes the shared unrest.[33] Riots are diffuse, disorderly mob actions, usually involving spontaneous attacks on property or persons.

While the Jim Crow pattern of accommodation was stable in the South, collective actions by either the minority or the dominant group were rare. The lynchings and other violence against blacks were usually semisecret actions by small groups of vigilantes against reported violators of the norms of the racial etiquette (see Chapter 6). Crowd actions occurred at that time mainly in the border states and in the North, where the norms of race relations were more ambiguous. The largest of many riots in the World War I era was in East St. Louis, where white reactions to job competition and the use of black strike-breakers resulted in the deaths of thirty-nine blacks and nine whites.[34] Large numbers of blacks migrated to war production centers during World War II, and in 1943 there were 247 racial disturbances in forty-seven cities. The largest one in 1943 occurred in Detroit, over competition for federal housing; it became a racial battle that left twenty-five blacks and nine whites dead.[35]

The form of collective response to unrest and uncertainty depends on what beliefs are shared.[36] No action will be taken if the group believes it is totally powerless to influence its status. We have seen how the *Brown* decision spread the belief that blacks could gain greater equality if they would unite and take determined action. When delay and repression brought increasing questioning of nonviolent action, the belief that blacks could gain significantly more power continued, and so did the belief in the potency of confrontation tactics.

A minority group is most likely to undertake militant confrontation that may include violent actions when a period of rising expectations resulting from significant improvements in group status is followed by a sudden, sharp reversal (or perceived reversal). When hopes are rising rapidly a sizeable gap develops between achieved status and aspirations, and a perceived, sudden downturn in status widens the gap and makes it intolerable. Originally presented as a theory of political revolution,[37] this explanation also seems to fit spontaneous rebellions and riotous, symbolic protests. Large numbers of ghetto blacks in the 1960s apparently saw white backlash actions and economic setbacks as evidence of a sudden, sharp downturn in their status, on the heels of improvements and rapidly rising expectations.[38] *Primarily, the black ghetto outbursts of the middle and latter 1960s were strong, symbolic protests,*[39] *although in some persons and groups the response to the intolerable gap was more revolutionary.*

Ghetto Outbursts: 1964–68

The first major black ghetto riot of the 1960s occurred in the Harlem section of New York City in July 1964. The precipitating event was an off-duty white policeman's killing of James Powell, a boy who had allegedly attacked him. Black protesters, led by CORE, demanded a police review board, and they attacked police who tried to restrain them and arrest their leaders. One black man was killed; 100 blacks and 12 police were injured; and looting and violence continued the next few nights. The outbreak spread to the Bedford-Stuyvesant area of Brooklyn, and similar ones occurred that summer in Rochester (New York),

Philadelphia, Chicago, and Jersey City, Elizabeth, and Paterson in New Jersey.[40]

The wave of ghetto riots in the summer of 1965 was characterized by much burning and looting, but only limited violence against white persons. News coverage probably contributed to the rapid spread of these outbursts. No evidence appeared of a nationwide plan of agitation.[41] The largest of the riots in 1965 took place in the Watts section of Los Angeles, triggered by a patrolman's handling of an apparently drunk black driver in a way that was perceived as police brutality. During this six-day insurrection 4,000 people were arrested, over 1,000 injured, and 34 killed. Police and national guards used firearms extensively, resulting in charges of excessive use of force. Looting and burning of (chiefly) white-owned businesses resulted in from 30 to 40 million dollars' worth of property damage.[42]

Police incidents continued to be the usual precipitating factor in ghetto riots in the summers of 1966 and 1967, including the one that spread from Newark to other cities in New Jersey in July 1967. The most massive one was in Detroit in July 1967, resulting in 43 deaths (33 of them black), close to 400 injuries, and estimates of as high as 7,000 arrests and 45 million dollars' worth of property damage. There was some sniping, with heavy counterattacks by the police, national guards, and army paratroopers.[43]

When Dr. King was assassinated in Memphis in April 1968, there were spontaneous riots in 138 cities in 36 states, plus many nonviolent demonstrations. More than 50,000 national guards and federal troops were called to assist police forces. After the 1967 riots the police and national guard had been trained to use tear gas and curfews, rather than guns, for most circumstances; otherwise the number of injured and killed in 1968 would have been catastrophic. As it was, 46 or more died —11 in Washington, D.C., 9 in Chicago, 6 in Baltimore, and 6 in Kansas City. There were large numbers of injuries, but many were minor.[44] There were hundreds more ghetto riots in 1968, most of them minor, but in 1969 the disorders were mainly in smaller cities.

The National Advisory Commission on Civil Disorders, which investigated the ghetto riots of the 1960s, emphasized the grievances of blacks—especially police practices, employment, and housing—and used the term "white racism" to characterize discriminatory practices. Both political conspiracy and criminal behavior were rejected as explanations, and most of the participation in the outbursts was interpreted as legitimate protest and a demand to be included in American life.[45] Other analysts have emphasized the commission's observation that the ghetto violence was quite selective. Violent action was aimed almost entirely at property rather than persons; it was aimed mainly at businesses of whites who had exploited blacks rather than at all whites; and it rarely spread beyond the ghetto. Thus the rioting was selective,

symbolic protest—urgent messages to whites about black grievances—
not totally unrestrained aggression, or all-out rebellion.[46]

An alternative interpretation is that blacks revolted against internal colonialism, in efforts to drive whites out of their territory and gain
control of their own institutions.[47] However, other studies have generally been interpreted as consistent with the National Advisory Commission's views. After the Watts riot in 1965, black interviewees who
felt the most deprived, and who were the most isolated from the dominant community's institutions and channels of communication, were
the most inclined to support violent expression of black grievances.[48]
A study of the 1967 outburst in Newark, New Jersey, found self-
reported participants to be well informed and not isolated or alienated
from community institutions, but to be very distrustful of current
governmental activities.[49]

Black Power

White repression of Southern black protesters caused SNCC and
other groups to reject nonviolence. Although the black power slogan
began with Carmichael's initial reference to voting rights in Mississippi (above), its meaning has varied widely. Some of the resolutions
adopted at the National Conference on Black Power in Newark, New
Jersey, in July 1967 (held just after the riot ended) emphasized more
participation in the political system. Demands were made for more
black elected officials and more black appointees to high federal positions.[50] Resolutions were also passed to support the Black Muslims and
other separatist groups, and to reject integration as a means of achieving equality. Two successive heads of CORE, James Farmer and Floyd
McKissick, rejected nonviolence and strategies for gaining legal equality and integrated urban housing.[51] CORE, speaking for frustrated,
newly educated blacks moving upward into the middle class, rejected
middle-class norms of restraint and the help of whites.[52]

The most radical meaning of black power emerged in 1967 when
charges spread that Carmichael was inciting riots. He was banned from
Great Britain for advocating racial violence, and he then issued a call
from Cuba for American blacks to take up guerrilla warfare and support
a hemispheric revolution.[53] Carmichael's successor as head of SNCC—
H. Rap Brown—was arrested for advocating and leading an outbreak in
Cambridge, Maryland. Congress responded in 1968 with a bill against
the use of interstate travel to incite riots, a law designed to protect both
whites and blacks from acts of violence.[54] The assassination of Dr. King
in April and of (then Senator) Robert Kennedy in June of 1968 contributed to the radicalization of black power, and to the student movement against the Vietnam War.

Dozens of reported guerrilla-style attacks on the police were reported in 1968, such as the sniper killing of three policemen in Cleveland; and many others were reported in 1969 and 1970. The facts have been disputed in many of these incidents,[55] most of which were attributed to the Black Panthers. Many blacks were killed in confrontations between the police and the Black Panthers in 1969 (including Mark Clark and Fred Hampton in Chicago) and 1970. When Eldridge Cleaver defected to Algeria rather than return to prison when his parole was revoked, the Huey P. Newton–Bobby Seale faction shifted Black Panther strategy toward community service projects and into line with the belief that the time is not yet ripe for a revolution in the United States.[56]

Although the major black nationalist and separatist leaders became powerful symbols of group pride and determination, the vast majority of American blacks continued to support major reforms rather than revolution. Along with the SCLC, NAACP, and the Urban League, most blacks embraced black unity, black pride, and the need for major changes, but agreed with King's view that totally separate economic and political institutions cannot work.[57] *Black power had become primarily a pluralistic concept at the beginning of the 1970s. That is, blacks generally were demanding equal treatment and mutual respect of all racial and ethnic groups and their cultures, and the right of voluntary integration into community institutions, but the retention of their own group identity rather than assimilation.*[58] Since blacks were disagreed, and often uncertain, it is understandable that the emerging meaning of black power was ambiguous and threatening to the dominant community.

Confrontations on Campus

Black students began moving their protests from the streets to the colleges and universities in the fall of 1968. There were racial confrontations on a large number of campuses in 1969, and again in 1970, when student protests against the Vietnam War overshadowed the black student actions. The black student leaders were tutored by older students who had been in the sit-ins. The campus protests were militant but not revolutionary, despite the frequent use of the language of the revolutionary version of black power. The leaders condoned some violence against property, occasionally allowing the few black student revolutionaries (and "anomics") to operate unrestrained. Revolutionaries seek violent repression in order to escalate violence, and they also want reforms to fail. The militant, middle-class black student leaders sought major reforms, and they retained control of the confrontations.[59]

Black student protesters usually asked for negotiations with the administration on a list of demands that included programs of black studies. Class reading materials and instruction were typically characterized as racist. Demands included more black faculty and administrators, the admission of more black students, more financial aid, black counselors, and control of black studies programs by black students. In predominantly white institutions there were demands for separate living and dining areas, and facilities for black student organizations.[60]

The white academic community was taken aback by these demands, the strong indictments of higher education, and the frequent use of the rhetoric of third-world rebellion against colonial domination. Often the confrontations resulted in the desired agreements, but many programs of black studies were later reduced in scope, submerged in programs of ethnic studies, or dropped. These programs have taken many forms and have remained controversial among both blacks and whites.[61] In general, the fundamental goals of black studies seem far from realization,[62] but many programs have survived, and there have been noticeable increases in the teaching of black history, literature, and art. There has been much frustration over other matters, including the paucity of black faculty and facilities and funds for black student activities. Through it all, it has become more clear that black power on the campus does not imply total separation; it means being proud of the black identity, and being determined not to accept any discriminatory treatment.

PROTEST AND CONFRONTATION: OTHER GROUPS

The Women's Protest

Both the rapid rise of the women's movement at the end of the 1960s and the nature of the strategies followed require explanation. Factors that had contributed to women's consciousness of their unequal treatment included their increasing participation in the labor force, participation in wars, and the increasing use and effectiveness of techniques of birth control.[63] Strong legal foundations for the movement were provided in the Equal Pay Act of 1963 and the Civil Rights Act of 1964 (Chapter 12). Friedan's ideological foundation was published in 1963, and she established the National Organization for Women in 1966 (Chapter 11), but the movement did not accelerate rapidly until later. The answer seems to lie only partly in the fact that the nation was preoccupied with the ghetto riots and the war in Vietnam.

The major court victories in the latter 1960s over discrimination in employment and promotions, especially the awarding of large amounts of back pay in the AT&T case (Chapter 12), aroused hopes for the equal treatment of women to a new level. The immediate effect was apparently not so widespread as that of the *Brown* decision on the hopes of blacks (Chapter 12), but women's leaders were inspired to greatly increased educational, political, and legal efforts. Well before this, women had been experiencing a decline in occupational, educational, and economic (income) attainments ever since World War II, relative to the gains made by men.[64] Thus, despite absolute gains in these respects, many women were feeling relative deprivation and status incongruity (see Chapter 11). Finally, women had participated in a variety of civil rights activities, but had generally been relegated to clerical, coffee-making, and other subordinate roles. The disappointment and shock were symbolized and heightened by Carmichael's statement that the only position for women in SNCC was prone. This dramatized the minority status of women, and many female students and other women turned their attention to efforts to gain equal treatment for their sex.

The timing of the rising expectations and the setbacks was different for women than it was for blacks. Instead of an extended period of escalating hopes, followed by perception of a sharp reversal of the gains, the relative deprivation preceded and coincided with major gains in status. The gap between women's expectations and their attained status became great at the end of the 1960s, but it did not become so intolerable that collective outbursts ensued. There were a few quiet sit-ins at all-male bars and clubs, and occasionally there was peaceful picketing. The educational and political activities of the women's movement have been highly visible, and leaders have used opportunities to inform and persuade, but there has been little public protest activity. There have been many confrontations between women and employers, legislators, and public officials, but they have usually taken the form of emphasizing information, persuading, and negotiating for changed policies. The confrontations have often shown strong determination, but even these actions imply the belief that equality for women can be achieved by persistent, effective use of ordinary channels of communication and influence.

The Indian Protest

There was conflict between assimilationist and pluralistic policies for American Indians during the 1960s, and continuing economic distress (see Chapter 10). During these years of marked ambiguity in Indian policies, militant new leaders emerged to challenge the accommodative "Uncle Tomahawks" and tribal diplomats, and to demand that Indians not be a forgotten minority. Belief in the possibility of bringing about improvements in their status was apparently heightened by black strategies and successes. At a meeting in 1964, leaders of the National Indian Youth Council demanded red power (also called Indian power). These NIYC leaders included founder Herbert Blatchford (Navajo), Clyde Warrior (Ponca), Melvin Thom (Piute), and Bruce Wilkie (Makah), indicating the pan-Indian nature of the new protest. Red power means retention of Indian lands and tribal identities, and maximum control of their own development.[65]

Many of the Indian protests in recent years have been symbolic actions, designed to help educate Americans to Indian problems, and to gain support for their political and legal efforts. The federal prison on Alcatraz Island was discontinued in 1969, and in November a group of Indians occupied the island and remained for two years. They were joined by tribal groups from all over the country, dramatizing Indian issues and pan-Indian unity.[66] Organized confrontations followed in several states, usually over treaty rights or the occupancy of lands. In a study made in the Seattle area in 1971, 40 percent of 269 Indians interviewed said they had participated in protest activities, and most of these protesters rejected the use of violence. Older Indians were more inclined to protest, but the younger protesters were somewhat more likely to approve of violence.[67]

The urban-based American Indian Movement (AIM) has emphasized confrontations with the public and government officials. As a result of the relocation policy of the 1950s, Indians had moved to cities and were close-up observers of the black ghetto riots during the middle and latter 1960s. Removed from the direct control of tribal leaders, many urban Indians became critical of the accommodative approach to problems on the reservations, and of the allegedly frequent corruption in tribal government. Hopes for tribal economic, cultural, and governmental development were raised by the increasingly pluralistic position of the Nixon administration from 1970 on.

Russell Means—an Oglala Sioux, director of the American Indian Center in Cleveland, and an AIM leader—has had a special flair for staging dramatic protests. In the confrontations of the early 1970s he often used guns, believing that whites are violent people and that it is necessary to create a major disturbance to gain their attention. AIM coordinated the Trail of Broken Treaties protest in Washington, D.C. in the fall months of 1972, which turned into a tumultuous occupation of the Bureau of Indian Affairs building.[68] Early in 1973, Means led some of the Broken Treaties protesters through a series of incidents in and near the Pine Ridge (Oglala Sioux) Reservation in South Dakota, against opposition from tribal leaders, BIA officials, the FBI, and United States marshals. The protesters and a contingent of Sioux occupied the hamlet of Wounded Knee for several weeks, surrendering after numerous armed clashes that produced many injuries and some loss of life on both sides.[69] Apparently a great many Indians were distressed by these events, and by the many violent incidents between AIM and tribal leaders on a number of reservations during and after the siege at Wounded Knee.[70] The predominant belief among Indians now seems to be that dramatic protest helps their cause, but that violence may do more harm than good.

Mexican American Protest

César Chávez learned how to help urban poor people gain power through organization while working for the Community Service Organization, but he remained dedicated to nonviolent methods. He became general director of CSO, having learned well the Alinsky methods of confrontation of economic and political power holders, public protest, boycott, and negotiation.[71] Chávez resigned when the CSO rejected his proposal to organize farm workers. He formed the National Farm Workers' Association (NFWA) and went to Delano, in the San Joaquin Valley of California, to organize grape workers.

In the fall of 1965 a strike broke out at Delano over minimum pay and working conditions, and Chávez appealed to union leaders, clergymen, student leaders, and others to support a national boycott of Schenley and DiGiorgio products. He received much help from students who had practiced nonviolent methods on voter registration drives in the South. The victory in La Huelga (the strike), in the spring of 1966, launched the movement to organize farm workers known as La Causa (the cause).[72] Other boycotts include the ones used in 1970 and 1972 to bring pressure on two hundred growers of iceberg (crisp-head) lettuce in the Salinas Valley of California and parts of Arizona.

La Causa has raised the expectations of Mexican Americans, and inspired the Chicano or brown power movement. The term Chicano refers especially to youthful militants. The ideology of the movement has been expounded since 1966 in *El Gallo,* the newspaper published in Denver by Rodolpho "Corky" Gonzales and his Crusade for Justice. A key symbol is La Raza (literally the race), which refers to the cultural unity of Mexican Americans, sometimes of all Latin Americans. The general goal is Mexican American control of their own economic, political, and other community institutions, culture, and lands.[73] In addition to determined political actions, the movement has involved protests and direct confrontations, sometimes violent ones. Chicanos believe they need the power of coalitions with other minority activists, especially American Indians, on particular issues.

Reies López Tijerina founded the Federal Alliance of Land Grantees (later the Federal Alliance of Free Pueblos) in Albuquerque about 1962. Membership increased in 1965 when the Hispanic (Spanish-descent) farmers and ranchers in northern New Mexico complained of severe new restrictions on grazing rights imposed by the National Forest Service. Tijerina promised that Hispanos would get back the land originally granted to them by the Spanish government, and guaranteeed by the Treaty of Guadalupe Hidalgo, using court action or any means necessary. Actions from 1965 until 1968 included burning forests, cutting fences, and releasing jailed companions from a courthouse. Despite questions about his methods, Tijerina remains a heroic symbol of resistance to Anglo domination.[74]

Chicanos conducted a boycott of high schools in East Los Angeles in March 1968, over educational issues. Many of the subsequent demands for programs of Chicano studies in colleges and universities have been traced to this boycott of the Los Angeles high schools.[75] David Sánchez and the Brown Berets, who later had many hostile clashes with the police in several cities, lent support to this school strike.[76] Other Chicano school boycotts followed in Denver and other cities. In Crystal City, Texas, a successful high school strike—along with economic boycotts—helped the Mexican Americans gain political control of the community in 1969.[77] In 1970 a similar boycott occurred at Phoenix Union High School, and a major confrontation between Chicano students and the administration took place at Arizona State University.[78]

A final illustration will help further to convey the range of brown power activities, and also the influence of the black power movement on them. In 1970 there were three Chicano riots in East Los Angeles, and another in January 1971, all resembling the black ghetto riots of the 1960s. Police incidents precipitated them, and most of the violence was to property, mainly to businesses owned by Anglos.[79]

Puerto Rican Protest

In 1969, Cha Cha Jiminez turned the Young Lords in Chicago from street gang activity to political protest, and the Young Lords Party was also started in New York and other cities. Although they used the third-world rhetoric of overthrow of capitalist governments for a time, they concentrated on better health conditions and municipal services for the barrios. They had a breakfast program for schoolchildren, similar to that of the Black Panthers, and a campaign against lead poisoning in children from eating chips of peeling paint. The Young Lords Party represents a type of protest that is unusual for Puerto Ricans, and it has contributed to their political awareness.[80] Also, groups working for political independence for Puerto Rico often issue statements about the repression of Puerto Ricans living in the United States.

The Puerto Ricans have participated heavily in city politics, evidently believing that they can improve their status within the existing institutional framework. Herman Badillo, United States congressman, has run for mayor of New York City. Puerto Ricans have also joined a large number of occupational, civic, religious, and fraternal organizations, in the pattern of the earlier immigrants from Europe. Rather than trying to retain their own culture and identity, most Puerto Ricans seem more interested in assimilation, in individual opportunities to climb the status ladder. One effect of this is to reduce the pool of potential protest leaders. Perhaps barriers to assimilation will eventually produce a more pluralistic outlook among Puerto Ricans, more protest, and possibly a common cause with La Raza.

Japanese American Student Protest

The black power movement has also influenced the Oriental minorities, as illustrated by the findings of a 1971 study of Japanese American university students in California.[81] Most of these students were third generation (Sansei), but some were fourth (Yonsei). The first generation of Japanese Americans (the Issei) had been industrious, nonresentful, and conformist. They retained their Japanese identity, a self-image reflecting the values of hard work, obedience to authority, and self-control—all based on the central Japanese value of harmony or quietness. They resigned themselves to relocation during World War II. The second generation (the Nisei) learned their parents' values, and most of them accommodated to life in the relocation centers and helped run them. Evidently there is a considerable generation gap between the Nisei and a large majority of the Sansei, many of whom were born in the camps.

Most of these Japanese American students were classed as "liberated." They raised questions about their identity, and actively supported programs of Asian studies; but they generally favored retaining the traditional values. The more militant students rejected the traditional expression-controlling cultural style as a weakness rather than a strength; they demanded the expression of strong protest against discrimination, in the spirit of yellow power. A pluralistic assertion of group identity seems to be emerging to replace the assimilationist implication of working hard to climb the class ladder and not expressing grievances.

CONCLUSION

Minorities resort to public protest and direct confrontation when they believe that the usual institutional means for influencing their status are unavailable or not working, and that channels of expression through protest are open and that the dominant community will listen. Protest thus implies the belief that reforms are possible, and the value judgment that they are overdue. Groups that believe they are totally powerless to influence their destiny neither protest nor rebel. Those that believe they can influence their fate, but that see no hope within either ordinary channels or those of protest, rebel to change the social system or to escape from it. Sustained actions to end the system and replace it are revolutions, not protests.

A society that has not been accustomed to protest activities, even when the rights of public assembly and freedom of expression are legally guaranteed, is likely to overreact when there is resort to such actions. A major risk of the more militant forms of protest and confrontation is that the dominant community will mistake them for rebellion, even for revolution, and respond with heavily repressive actions. Repression occurs against perceived protest too, but then social control agents are more likely to practice restraints than when the actions are considered rebellions. Even nonviolent protest may be misunderstood, especially when it involves determined confrontation and attracts widespread participation and support. When protest takes more violent forms it is even more likely to be perceived as all-out rebellion, especially when there are at least a few small groups trying to escalate violence and defeat reforms, or at least using revolutionary rhetoric. Yet recent American experience suggests that the police and political leaders can learn to differentiate and to respond to protest actions with some restraint.

The thesis that rapidly rising expectations greatly increase minority inclination to protest for further improvements seems borne out by the Southern civil rights activities of the 1950s and 1960s. Throughout this century some blacks have acted on the belief that the group's status can be improved by legal, educational, or economic actions. Major legal victories in the 1950s impelled large numbers of blacks into strong protests, because hopes had been aroused by the legal breakthroughs, and visions of much more progress toward equality seemed realistically possible. The strategy of nonviolent confrontation and resistance fit the initial mood of high hopes and goodwill, and training and discipline kept large numbers of protesters nonviolent in the face of years of repression that often became violent.

The ghetto riots of the 1960s support the thesis that the most probable condition for violent minority protest (and revolution) is the perception by the group of a sharp reversal after a period of rising status and rising expectations, creating an intolerable gap between aspirations and achieved status. Just as segregationists had used strong rhetoric and frequent violence to convey their determination, a great many frustrated blacks concluded that they had to use both strong language and some violence to communicate their outrage and determination to gain equal treatment. Many supporters of the use of violent protest adopted the belief that nonviolent protest and legal and political strategies do not work—that only violence gets results. Legal and nonviolent methods had actually accomplished a great deal of change (especially in the South) by the mid-1960s, despite the backlash; but people act on what they believe is true. Many of those who acknowledged that there had been significant gains believed they were being nullified, and that only drastic actions could produce further gains.

The protests of other minorities in recent years also indicate the effects of rising expectations, relative deprivation, and in some instances the perception of reversals after significant improvements. It is also apparent that the black protests of the 1950s and 1960s have influenced the outlooks and actions of other minorities. Cooperation among different groups has been minimal, but observation of the strategies, tactics, and treatment of another group apparently affects beliefs about the possibilities of change and the potential of various methods. Groups act on their existential beliefs about the prospects for influencing their statuses.

FOOTNOTES

1   de Tocqueville, 1856, p. 214.
2   Blalock, 1967, p. 189.
3   Williams, 1965.
4   Killian, 1965.
5   Killian & Grigg, 1964, p. 133; Lomax, 1962, pp. 78–111.
6   King, 1958; Reddick, 1959, Chs. 8, 9, 10; Bennett, 1965, pp. 57–76; Miller, 1968, pp. 46–68.
7   *Gayle* v. *Browder,* 352 U.S. 903 (1956).
8   King, 1958, pp. 151–57.
9   Smith & Killian, 1958; Miller, 1968, pp. 62, 85.
10 Bennett, 1965, pp. 77–80.
11 King, 1958, Ch. 6.
12 Lomax, 1962, pp. 93–111; Vander Zanden, 1963; Oppenheimer, 1965; Bennett, 1965, pp. 68–73.
13 King, 1964, Ch. 5.
14 Bennett, 1965, pp. 130–33; Miller, 1968, Ch. 8. The march was organized by Bayard Rustin, black pacifist leader, and directed by A. Philip Randolph, president of the Brotherhood of Sleeping Car Porters.
15 Bennett, 1965, pp. 153–56.
16 King, 1967, Chs. 1, 2, 6.
17 King, 1967, pp. 143–46; Miller, 1968, pp. 261–69.

18 Reddick, 1959, pp. 133–35; Lomax, 1962, pp. 133–59; Bennett, 1965, pp. 100–101; Miller, 1968, 98–103.

19 Vander Zanden, 1960; Zinn, 1965, Ch. 2; Edwards, 1970, pp. 17–20.

20 Bennett, 1965, pp. 71–72, 101–2; Miller, 1968, pp. 103–8; Edwards, 1970, pp. 20–25.

21 Vander Zanden, 1960; Miller, 1968, p. 109.

22 *Garner* v. *Louisiana,* 368 U.S. 157 (1961); Bland, 1973, pp. 114–16.

23 Zinn, 1965, Ch. 3; Miller, 1968, pp. 114–23; Blackwell, 1975, pp. 200–201.

24 Miller, 1968, p. 121; Bennett, 1965, p. 111.

25 Wilson, 1973, pp. 128–29; Killian, 1975, pp. 61–63.

26 Bennett, 1965, pp. 113–15; Zinn, 1965, Ch. 7; Miller, 1968, Ch. 6.

27 Zinn, 1965, pp. 92–93; Miller, 1968, pp. 165–67.

28 King, 1964, Chs. 3 & 4; Bennett, 1965, pp. 117–30; Miller, 1968, Ch. 7; Berry, 1971, pp. 196–97.

29 King, 1967, pp. 23–32; Miller, 1968, pp. 253–61; Edwards, 1970, pp. 54–56.

30 Willhelm & Powell, 1964; Blackwell, 1975, p. 204.

31 Berry, 1971, p. 210; Killian, 1975, p. 91.

32 Fogelson, 1971, Ch. 3; Blackwell, 1975, pp. 204, 255–60.

33 Turner & Killian, 1972, Chs. 1–6.

34 Berry, 1971, Ch. 11.

35 Lee & Humphrey, 1943; Berry, 1971, pp. 164–68.

36 Smelser, Ch. 5; Davis, 1970, pp. 15–21; Turner & Killian, 1972, pp. 47–48.

37 Davies, 1962; 1971; pp. 133–47.

38 Wilson, 1973, pp. 132–36.

39 Fogelson, 1971, Ch. 1.

40 Berry, 1971, p. 211; Wilson, 1973, p. 136; Blackwell, 1975, p. 204.

41 National Advisory Commission on Civil Disorders, 1968, pp. 7–9; Fogelson, 1971, Ch. 2, pp. 175–77.

42 Berry, 1971, p. 212; Blackwell, 1975, p. 204.

43 Berry, 1971, pp. 215–20.

44 Berry, 1971, pp. 221–23; Blackwell, 1975, p. 205.

45 National Advisory Commission on Civil Disorders (the "Kerner Commission"), 1968.

46 Fogelson, 1971, pp. 16–17.

47 Blauner, 1969.

48 Ransford, 1968.

49 Paige, 1971.

50 Blackwell, 1975, pp. 206–8. Congressman Adam Clayton Powell convened the first black power conference in Washington, D.C., in September 1966.

51 Los Angeles Times, July 3, 1967, I, 3; July 24, 1967, I, 1, 14; August 1, 1967, I, 7.

52 Leventman, 1966.

53 Los Angeles Times, July 28, 1967, I, 18–19; Allen, 1970, pp. 247–56.

54 Title 18, U.S. Code, Ch. 102, Riots (1968).

55 Knopf, 1969.

56 Berry, 1971, pp. 222–30; Howard, 1974, pp. 52–53; Blackwell, 1975, pp. 291–95.

57 King, 1967, pp. 32–66.

58 Killian, 1975, pp. 6–7, 110–28, 161–75.

59   Edwards, 1970, Chs. 1, 2, 4, 6, 7.
60   Edwards, 1970, Chs. 5, 8, 9.
61   Ford, 1973, Chs. 11, 12, 13.
62   Orum, 1974, pp. 76–83; Carey & Allen, 1977.
63   Epstein, 1976, pp. 416–17.
64   Knudsen, 1969.
65   Josephy, 1971, pp. 1–2, 37–40, 53–57, 71–77.
66   Josephy, 1971, pp. 7–8; Howard, 1974, pp. 116–17.
67   Stauss, Chadwick, & Bahr, 1971.
68   Burnette & Koster, 1974, Ch. 9.
69   Burnette & Koster, 1974, Ch. 10.
70   Burnette & Koster, 1974, Ch. 11.
71   Alinsky, 1946; Owen, 1975.
72   Dunne, 1967; Howard, 1974, pp. 95–100; Ransford, 1977, pp. 114–20.
73   Rendón, 1974, pp. 167–70, 327–37. There are other ideological publications.
74   Knowlton, 1971.
75   Briegel, 1974.
76   Marín, 1974.
77   Shockley, 1974, Ch. 5.
78   Adank, 1974.
79   Morales, 1976; Ransford, 1977, pp. 108–14.
80   Howard, 1974, pp. 106–8.
81   Maykovich, 1972.

REFERENCES

Adank, Patricia A.
1974   "Chicano Activism in Maricopa County—Two Incidents in Retrospect,"
       pp. 246–66 in, Manuel P. Servín, An Awakening Minority: The Mexican–
       Americans, 2nd Edition. Beverly Hills, California: Glencoe Press.
Alinsky, Saul D.
1946   Reveille for Radicals. Chicago: University of Chicago Press.
Allen, Robert L.
1970   Black Awakening in Capitalist America. Garden City, New York: Double-
       day.
Bennett, Lerone, Jr.
1965   What Manner of Man: A Biography of Martin Luther King, Jr., Abridged
       Edition. New York: Pocket Books, Inc.
Berry, Mary Frances
1971   Black Resistance/White Law. New York: Appleton-Century-Crofts.
Blackwell, James E.
1975   The Black Community: Unity and Diversity. New York: Dodd, Mead and
       Co.
Blalock, Hubert M., Jr.
1967   Toward a Theory of Minority-Group Relations. New York: Capricorn
       Books.

Bland, Randall W.
1973 Private Pressure on Public Law: The Legal Career of Justice Thurgood Marshall. Port Washington, New York: Kennikat Press.

Blauner, Robert
1969 "Internal Colonialism and Ghetto Revolt." Social Problems 16, 4 (Spring): 393–408.

Briegel, Kaye
1974 "Chicano Student Militancy: The Los Angeles High School Strike of 1968," pp. 215–25 in Manuel P. Servín, An Awakening Minority: The Mexican-Americans, 2nd Edition. Beverly Hills, California: Glencoe Press.

Burnette, Robert, and John Koster
1974 The Road to Wounded Knee. New York: Bantam Books.

Carey, Phillip, and Donald Allen
1977 "Black Studies: Expectation and Impact on Self-Esteem and Academic Performance." Social Science Quarterly 57, 4 (March): 811–20.

Davies, James C.
1962 "Toward a Theory of Revolution." American Sociological Review 27 (February): 5–19.
1971 When Men Revolt and Why. New York: The Free Press.

Davis, F. James
1970 Social Problems: Enduring Major Issues and Social Change. New York: The Free Press.

de Tocqueville, Alexis (trans. by John Bonner)
1856 The Old Regime and the French Revolution. New York: Harper and Bros.

Dunne, John Gregory
1967 Delano: The Story of the California Grape Strike. New York: Farrar, Straus and Giroux.

Edwards, Harry
1970 Black Student. New York: Free Press.

Epstein, Cynthia Fuchs
1976 "Sex Roles," Ch. 9 in Robert K. Merton and Robert Nisbet, Contemporary Social Problems, 4th Edition. New York: Harcourt, Brace, Jovanovich.

Fogelson, Robert M.
1971 Violence as Protest. New York: Doubleday Anchor Books.

Ford, Nick Aaron
1973 Black Studies: Threat or Challenge? Port Washington, New York: Kennikat Press.

Howard, John R.
1974 The Cutting Edge: Social Movements and Social Change in America. Philadelphia: J. B. Lippincott Co.

Josephy, Alvin M., Jr.
1971 Red Power: The American Indians' Fight for Freedom. New York: McGraw-Hill Book Co.

Killian, Lewis
1965 "Community Structure and the Role of the Negro Leader-Agent." Sociological Inquiry 35 (Winter): 69–79.
1975 The Impossible Revolution, Phase II: Black Power and the American Dream, 2nd Edition. New York: Random House.

Killian, Lewis, and Charles Grigg
1964   Racial Crisis in America. Englewood Cliffs, New Jersey: Prentice-Hall,
       Inc.
King, Martin Luther, Jr.
1958   Stride Toward Freedom: The Montgomery Story. New York and Evans-
       ton: Perennial Library, Harper and Row.
1964   Why We Can't Wait. New York: Signet Books (published in 1963 by
       Harper and Row).
1967   Where Do We Go From Here: Chaos or Community? New York: Harper
       and Row.
Knopf, Terry Ann
1969   "Sniping—A New Pattern of Violence." Trans-Action (July/August): 22–
       29.
Knowlton, Clark S.
1971   "Tijerino, Hero of the Militants." The Journal of Mexican American
       Studies 1, 2 (Winter): 91–96.
Knudsen, Dean D.
1969   "The Declining Status of Women: Popular Myths and the Failure of
       Functionalist Thought." Social Forces 48, 2 (December): 183–93.
Lee, Alfred McClung, and Norman D. Humphrey
1943   Race Riot. New York: Holt, Rinehart and Winston, Inc.
Leventman, Seymour
1966   "Class and Ethnic Tensions: Minority Group Leadership in Transition."
       Sociology and Social Research 50 (April): 371–76.
Lomax, Lewis E.
1962   The Negro Revolt. New York: Signet Books, The New American Li-
       brary.
Marín, Christine
1974   "Go Home Chicanos: A Study of the Brown Berets in California and
       Arizona," pp. 226–46 in Manuel P. Servín, An Awakening Minority: The
       Mexican-Americans, 2nd Edition. Beverly Hills, California: Glencoe
       Press.
Maykovich, Minako Kurokawa
1972   Japanese American Identity Dilemma. Tokyo, Japan: Waseda University
       Press.
Miller, William Robert
1968   Martin Luther King, Jr.: His Life, Martyrdom and Meaning for the
       World. New York: Avon Books.
Morales, Armando
1976   "Chicano-Police Riots," Ch. 6 in Carrol A. Hernández, Marsha J. Haug,
       and Nathaniel N. Wagner, Chicanos: Social and Psychological Perspec-
       tives. St. Louis, Missouri: The C. V. Mosby Co.
National Advisory Commission on Civil Disorders
1968   Report of the National Advisory Commission on Civil Disorders. Wash-
       ington, D.C.: U.S. Government Printing Office.
Oppenheimer, Martin
1965   "Toward a Sociological Understanding of Nonviolence." Sociological In-
       quiry 35 (Winter): 123–31.

Orum, Anthony
1974 Black Students in Protest: A Study of the Origins of the Black Student Movement. Washington, D.C.: American Sociological Association.

Owen, Raymond E.
1975 "On Rubbing Raw the Sores of Discontent: Competing Theories and Data on the Effects of Participation in a Black Protest Group." Sociological Focus 8, 2 (April): 143–59.

Paige, Jeffrey M.
1971 "Political Orientation and Riot Participation." American Sociological Review 36, 5 (October): 810–20.

Ransford, H. Edward
1968 "Isolation, Powerlessness, and Violence: A Study of Attitudes and Participation in the Watts Riot." American Journal of Sociology 73 (March): 581–91.
1977 Race and Class in American Society. Cambridge, Massachusetts: Schenkman Publishing Co., Inc.

Reddick, L. D.
1959 Crusaders Without Violence: A Biography of Martin Luther King. New York: Harper and Row.

Rendón, Armando B.
1971 Chicano Manifesto: The History and Aspirations of the Second Largest Minority in the United States. New York: The Macmillan Co.

Shockley, John Staples
1974 Chicano Revolt in a Texas Town. Notre Dame, Indiana: University of Notre Dame Press.

Smelser, Neil J.
1963 Theory of Collective Behavior. New York: The Free Press.

Smith, Charles U., and Lewis M. Killian
1958 The Tallahassee Bus Protest. New York: Anti-Defamation League of B'nai B'rith.

Spilerman, Seymour
1970 "The Causes of Racial Disturbances: A Comparison of Alternative Explanations." American Sociological Review 35, 4 (August): 627–49.
1971 "The Causes of Racial Disturbances: Tests of an Explanation." American Sociological Review 36, 3 (June): 427–42.
1976 "Structural Characteristics of Cities and the Severity of Racial Disorders." American Sociological Review 41, 5 (October): 771–93.

Stauss, Joseph H., Bruce A. Chadwick, and Howard M. Bahr
1971 "Red Power: A Sample of Indian Adults and Youth," pp. 90–96 in Rudolph O. de la Garza, Z. Anthony Kruszewski, and Thomas A. Arciniega, Chicanos and Native Americans: The Territorial Minorities. Englewood Cliffs, New Jersey: Prentice-Hall, Inc.

Turner, Ralph H., and Lewis M. Killian
1972 Collective Behavior, 2nd Edition. Englewood Cliffs, New Jersey: Prentice-Hall, Inc.

Vander Zanden, James W.
1960 "Sit-ins in Dixie." The Midwest Quarterly 2 (1960): 11–19.

Willhelm, Sidney M., and Edwin H. Powell
1964 "Who Needs the Negro?" Transaction 1 (September/October): 3–6.

Williams, Robin M., Jr.
1965   "Social Change and Social Conflict: Race Relations in the United States, 1944–64. Sociological Inquiry 35 (Winter): 8–25.
Wilson, William J.
1973   Power, Racism, and Privilege: Race Relations in Theoretical and Socio-historical Perspectives. New York: The Free Press.
Zinn, Howard
1965   SNCC: The New Abolitionists, 2nd Edition. Boston: Beacon Press.

14

Dilemmas of Change: Goals and Means

ATTEMPTS TO CHANGE SYSTEMS OF DISCRIMINATION

The more thoroughgoing patterns of discrimination involve inter-locking institutional arrangements.[1] It is difficult to know where to begin in efforts to change such systems, and whether to attack one piece at a time or larger segments. We have seen how one complex pattern, the Jim Crow system of *de jure* segregation, involved the whole fabric of life in the South. Many varied and monumental efforts have been necessary to bring about fundamental change in that system, and the costs of the attendant conflicts have often been great.

We have also seen that *de facto* patterns of discrimination may become institutionalized, and strongly resistant to change. Even when there is considerable disagreement in the dominant community about the discriminatory practices, they are difficult to change if the major holders of economic and political power support or condone them. Segregation in urban housing is linked not only with segregated schooling, but also with discrimination in employment, labor unions, political participation, and membership in voluntary organizations. Administrative law provisions for individual complaints about discrimination in housing and employment do nothing to change a metropolitan structure of discrimination.[2] Reduction of institutional discrimination in a large urban area requires comprehensive metropolitan strategies.[3]

Institutional Discrimination and Racism

Racism is defined in Chapter 5 as a set of beliefs about race groups, used to justify actions toward groups. Patterns of discrimination based on racist beliefs are defined as racist practices, or institutional racism. The main alternative definition of institutional racism, often stated with reference to blacks only, includes all practices that work to the relative disadvantage of the racial minority.[4] In this latter definition, both ideological justifications of discrimination and awareness that practices are detrimental to the minority are irrelevant. This eliminates the distinction between other institutional discrimination and that for which racist justifications are offered.

The main value of the concept of institutional discrimination is its reference to the systematic way in which discriminatory practices are interrelated and enmeshed in social structure. The advantage of using the term racism to refer only to that institutional discrimination for which justifications are put forth in terms of racist beliefs is that the meanings attached to discriminatory actions are specified. The meanings make a difference in weighing the probabilities, and the strategies, of change.

Institutional discrimination is practiced against national and religious minorities as well as against race groups. and there are other supporting ideologies besides racism. When an ethnic group is confused with race, and systematic discrimination against it is justified by racist beliefs, the pattern is institutional racism. Such was the case in Nazi Germany, and in the American control of immigration by national quotas. Racist beliefs have been demonstrated to be capable of justifying the most bestial kinds of treatment of minorities, including extermination. Institutional discrimination is also practiced against women and other minorities. There are parallels between racist beliefs and the sexist beliefs used to justify systematic discrimination against women, but there are important differences (Chapters 3 and 5).

Knowledge of ideological conflicts in the dominant community can be very useful in strategies of change, as illustrated by the legal efforts of the NAACP, MALDEF, and the Southern Poverty Law Center (Chapter 12), and the confrontations of the SCLC (Chapter 13). There was a marked decline in the acceptance of racist beliefs in the South in the 1960s (see Chapter 3), a dramatic part of a national decline since World War II. This does not necessarily portend the end of racial discrimination, or of ideological justifications of it. It appears that a major replacement for the racist belief that blacks are lacking in capacity to get ahead is the belief that they lack the motivation, or will, whether because of a subculture of poverty or other reasons. Lack of motivation is at least believed to be changeable. Not many white Americans tend to explain the status of blacks or other minorities by referring to the effects of institutional discrimination,[5] although it has been stressed and called racism in official reports, including the 1968 report of the National Advisory Commission on Civil Disorders.[6]

Prejudice and Patterns of Discrimination

Most of the prejudice held by people in institutional patterns of discrimination is the conforming type—learned attitudes that reflect expected behavior toward other groups. The most effective way to change conforming prejudice is to change intergroup behavior, by láw or other means (Chapter 3). Changed patterns of interaction raise questions about the value and existential beliefs underlying prejudice and the ideology of the old pattern, thus apparently increasing susceptibility to educational efforts designed to change beliefs and attitudes (Chapter 11). Even the most rigid stereotypes may change when social pressures go strongly against them, except in those personalities in which prejudice is deeply rooted.

Apparently most prejudiced discriminators (see the Merton typology in Chapter 3) do not have deep-seated needs for prejudice against groups, but are mainly holders of conforming prejudice. A major shift of social pressure, causing many such people to change their behavior and for a time to be prejudiced nondiscriminators, eventually reduces their prejudice. Those who were unprejudiced discriminators quickly and gladly conform when law or other social norms go firmly against discrimination. The first concern is not with attitude change in strategies designed to end discriminatory behavior. In programs for changing attitudes, the target audience consists of people with the most prejudice, whether they are discriminating or not.

THE ULTIMATE GOAL: ASSIMILATION OR PLURALISM?

If the goal of having the minority group become dominant is ruled out, assimilation and total separation are the polar opposite outcomes (Chapter 7, and Part III). Separatism is ruled out if the groups are to remain in contact, leaving a choice between assimilation and pluralism —between the merging and the retention of separate identities. The ultimate goal of minority groups is equality, and from that standpoint assimilation and pluralism are instrumental rather than ends in themselves—alternative paths for attaining equal treatment.

The Issue of Integration

The traditional route to equal treatment in the United States has been for individuals to climb the class ladder and become assimilated. The pressure has been heavy for immigrant groups to become Americanized in as few generations as possible—that is, to give up their separate identities and conform to Anglo-American values (Chapter 10). Strategies of racial integration have often implied that this is the route to equality for blacks and other racial minorities. This assumption has been implicit in much of the analysis by social scientists, including Park's race relations cycle (Chapter 2). The assimilationist implication is strong in the work of Frazier, one of Park's foremost black students, as illustrated by his statement that the result of total desegregation would be "the dissolution of the social organizations of the Negro community as Negroes are integrated as individuals into the institutional life of American society."[7]

Desegregation of the schools and other public facilities in the South has meant the integration of blacks into white facilities, so the terms desegregation and integration have often been used interchangeably. The idea that another alternative to compulsory segregation is some measure of voluntary segregation has not readily occurred to people in that setting. In this book, integration has been used to mean minority participation in the institutions and informal groups of the dominant community. So defined, *integration should not be confused with the total process of assimilation, which includes integration, acculturation, and loss of the group's separate identity* (Chapters 8, 9, and 10). Gordon's concept of structural assimilation is limited to primary groups, unfortunately omitting integration into institutional structures (Chapter 9).

Not until the black power developments of the middle and latter 1960s was there widespread questioning of the desirability of integration, usually with explicit reference to the determined barriers put up by whites, and the inference that assimilation is not a possible goal for blacks. In the polarized climate of the early years of this debate, black power was often equated with separatism, and integration with assimilationism. Although there were some separatist activities, *the chief significance of black power became the development of group pride as a foundation for gaining the implicit goal of equalitarian pluralism* (Chapter 13). Evidently the vast majority of American blacks have remained committed to integration as the way to equality and individual freedom,[8] apparently in agreement with the view that racial equality is impossible without a great deal of integration in the labor force, housing, schools, and other institutions.[9] However, most have also adopted some version of the black power approach for gaining equal treatment, and pride in the black identity rather than assimilation.

Implications of Different Analytical Models

According to the *ethnic group model,* urban racial minorities have been following the path taken earlier by European immigrants—settlement of mainly lower-class migrants in the inner city, movement upward in the class structure and outward to better housing, even though usually still segregated.[10] Apparently there has been considerable upward mobility, despite discrimination. Quite aside from discrimination, the prospects for rapid and continued upward mobility are far smaller than they were for the European ethnics, for the reasons discussed in Chapter 4. Also, the competition is great among various minorities that are demanding improvements simultaneously, and with the blue-collar ethnics who are anxiously protecting their gains. Finally, the barriers to structural assimilation, especially at the primary-group level, are far greater than for European ethnic groups.

In the model of *internal colonialism,* comparisions of racial status are made with peoples exploited by outside, colonial powers (Chapters 2, 6, and 13). This suggests that changes in status require the economic and political power to control their own living areas and institutions, since colonials continue their economic exploitation as long as they have the power to do so. Maximum racial separation is called for in terms of this model, in contrast to the socioeconomic integration and assimilation implicit in the ethnic group model. Marxist versions of the colonial model imply either political rebellion and separation, or joining with white revolutionaries to gain political control.

In the *dual economy model,* the minority is characterized as a group that does low-paying, unskilled service work that is separate from the major economic system. The group need not occupy a special territory, or be oppressed by an intermediary elite, both of which are specified in the internal colonial model. Especially for Mexican Americans, who are rarely in the ghetto pattern, the dual economy model is a much better fit than the colonial one.[11] The usual suggestion in relation to the dual economy model is that the minority ought to be integrated into the dominant economy. In the Marxist version, however, the *marginal underclass* can never be integrated into a capitalist economy because the activity of its members benefits both the owners and the labor aristocracy.[12] Similar to this is the *split labor market* model, stressing exploitation and the high rates of unemployment and underemployment of the minority, and held to be applicable to black-white relations in the United States since World War I.[13]

None of these models satisfactorily accounts for all the data on urban blacks or other minorities, but each seems to have elements of truth. There is upward mobility for some, but many remain very poor (see Chapter 4). There is economic exploitation by white owners, but their control of the minority community is not so absolute as that of an occupying colonial power. These analytical models, with their contrasting beliefs on the questions of economic integration, assimilation, and separation, are used in ideological justifications for programs of change. Both for analysis and action, a good model of pluralism is lacking.

Coalition Issues

Within minority action groups issues are debated about what kinds of coalitions are desirable, and under what conditions they ought to be formed. Among the questions are who the allies should be, and whether a coalition should be formal or informal, temporary and for a single issue, or more permanent and general.[14] Among Mexican Americans, for example, many questions were raised about coalitions as the protest became more militant in the latter 1960s. The older tendency to cooperate with any group or agency that put itself forward was criticized, especially government agencies that could claim they were assisting but that were perceived as not providing any real help. Support grew for the view that Chicanos had to be more concerned with power, and to take the initiative for ending unproductive alliances and building new ones that advance La Raza.[15]

The black power developments in the latter 1960s raised fundamental questions about coalitions, including those between blacks and whites (Chapter 13). Carmichael stressed what he called the treachery of labor unions and other so-called white allies of blacks. He held that the leaders, policymakers, and most of the staff of black organizations should be blacks, with whites occupying only a few specialized, supporting roles. In his view, most whites have no guilt about racial discrimination—no American dilemma—and their only interest is in superficial reforms. Coalitions should be only with the poor whites, who share with blacks the interest in questioning and changing the racist, colonial structure of the whole society.[16]

Bayard Rustin, one of the chief contenders against the Carmichael view, favored maintaining alliances not only with white civil rights groups, but also with the Democratic Party, labor unions, and other groups supporting civil rights. Blacks, he argued, could never have gotten the major civil rights laws of the 1960s passed without coalitions with white organizations.[17] Rustin, King, Roy Wilkins (long-time head of the NAACP), and Whitney Young (then head of the Urban League) explicitly favored strategies of maximum integration, and their views on coalitions implied an ethnic group model. However, in eventually accepting the desirability of pride in the black identity, they implicitly endorsed pluralism rather than assimilation.

Equal Opportunity or Preferential Treatment?

Debate of programs of affirmative action, discussed in Chapter 12, implies disagreements about the ultimate goal of change. Elimination of discrimination in education, employment, promotions, and pay seems consistent with the right of equal opportunity to use one's individual talents to climb the class ladder. This implies the ethnic group model of assimilation into American society, a process presumed gradually but surely to eliminate inequalities among groups. Affirmative action quotas have been justified mainly as a means of speeding up the process, thus ensuring equal opportunity from now on. However, demands for preferential treatment have also been made in terms of doing justice, by making reparations to minorities for past wrongs. It is not easy to get the dominant community to acknowledge that it has badly misused its power over minorities, and especially that its members should sacrifice some opportunities to right the wrongs of the past. In effect, this view compels the dominant community to accept a colonial (or perhaps a dual economy) model of what has happened, and to make tangible amends. The issue is even sharper when Indian tribes demand payment for lands appropriated in violation of treaties.

The other major issue in the affirmative action debate is the identity of minority persons. The United States Supreme Court took a "color-blind" position in nullifying legislation about race or other minority categories, but later accepted affirmative action quotas as constitutional because the aim was to correct for inequalities rather than to discriminate against a group (Chapter 12). This implies that neither the loss nor the ignoring of group identity is necessary in order to gain equal treatment. Women cannot lose their identity any more than blacks apparently can (Chapter 9), and Mexican Americans, Indians, French Canadians, and many other groups do not wish to. Discussion of affirmative action issues has helped bring emergent pluralism into somewhat clearer focus.

Conflict or Consensus?

Some type and degree of conflict accompanies change in patterns of minority-dominant accommodation. The more powerless a group feels, the less likely it is to support strategies of change that increase the risk of conflict, especially of violence. Strategies limited to public education, and the gradual improvement of economic status (Chapter 11), tend to stress equal opportunity, responsible effort, and other points on which there is presumably national consensus. Legal strategies for changing the norms of intergroup relations, while based on the assumption of conflicting values and beliefs in the society, limit conflict to the institutional procedures of the courts (Chapter 12). Political strategies involve efforts to gain and use power, but (except for revolutionary activity) limit conflict to established political channels and processes. Willingness to make political coalitions with groups in the dominant community implies a desire to emphasize wider consensus and to minimize conflict.

Strategies of public protest and direct confrontation bring grievances and demands for major change into the open, in the belief that the chances for significant change are thereby increased, even though these actions increase the risk of conflict. Nonviolent confrontation indicates willingness to face conflict but not to start it, and nonviolent resistance is unwillingness to return violence. We have noted differences between nonviolent and violent protest in values and existential beliefs about conflict and power. We have also noted the risk of heavy repression if control agencies confuse a symbolic protest involving selective property violence with a total rebellion (Chapter 13). Extreme repression is assumed by Marxist strategists to be essential for the massive conflict that brings revolutionary change.

CONCLUSION

Consideration of the issues involved in change touches on the major aspects of minority-dominant relations that have been emphasized in this book. The patterns are varied and often complex, and cannot be reduced to a single concept or slogan. Attempts to eliminate discrimination call attention to conflict and unequal group power, the institutional structure of the more stable patterns, the variety of responses to group domination, the frequency of change, and the role of values and beliefs in conforming prejudice, ideologies, and the different strategies of change. There are similarities in the issues of change for race groups, cultural groups, women, and other minorities, and some important differences.

Minorities take no collective action unless they share the belief that they can materially affect their own statuses. The action taken depends on what values and existential beliefs are shared. The probability of changing a pattern of discrimination apparently is correlated with the extent to which the dominant community is divided on minority issues. Major changes are facilitated by the combined contributions of different strategies of change, as illustrated in 1960 and 1961 by the orchestration of the Southern sit-ins and freedom rides, systematic litigation, economic boycotts, political action, and education (Chapter 13). Laws can be changed without waiting for the elimination of prejudice; laws can effect major changes in intergroup behavior; and the most efficient way to change attitudes is to change behavior. Although people with little or no prejudice conform readily to antidiscrimination laws, enforcement often requires a great deal of sustained effort, and the contributions of different kinds of action.

Much of the change in minority-dominant relations in the United States in the past two decades has revolved around the issue of assimilation, although—unfortunately—the term of reference often is integration. The ethnic group model of upward class mobility and assimilation has been rejected by blacks as unattainable and undesirable. There are other minorities that also wish to retain their own identities, whether through their own preference or because of exclusion from the organizations and informal groups of the dominant community. Since discrimination at the club and in primary group structures is a major means of guarding dominant power (Chapters 6 and 9), groups that are not included must concentrate on other avenues to sufficient power to reduce other inequalities.

Although some blacks and some members of other groups have accepted the colonial model, and separatism, most apparently believe that equal treatment cannot be achieved without a large measure of integration into the institutions and groups of the dominant community. Black power and related slogans have mainly come to mean determination to strengthen and use the group's power base to gain equal treatment, and also to retain and be proud of the group's identity. The balance between integration and a degree of voluntary segregation remains problematic, although groups such as Jewish and Chinese Americans provide a background of relevant experiences. The development of clearer ideologies for minority action toward pluralism, clearer national policies, clearer conceptual models, and a clearer term of reference than pluralism all remain for the future.

FOOTNOTES

1 Friedman, 1975.
2 Mayhew, 1968.
3 Stafford & Ladner, 1973.
4 Stafford & Ladner, 1973, pp. 358–59; Friedman, 1975. p. 386.
5 Schuman, 1969.
6 National Advisory Commission on Civil Disorders, 1968.
7 Edwards, 1968, p. 323.
8 Campbell & Schuman, 1968, p. 6; Blackwell, 1975, p. 286.
9 Pettigrew, 1971; Van den Berghe, 1976.
10 Banfield, 1968, pp. 66–87.
11 Moore, 1976.
12 Tabb, 1971, p. 438.
13 Bonacich, 1976.
14 Rothman, 1977, pp. 169–72.
15 Florez, 1971.
16 Carmichael & Hamilton, 1967, pp. 58–84.
17 Rustin, 1966.

REFERENCES

Banfield, Edward C.
1968 The Unheavenly City. Boston: Little, Brown and Co.
Blackwell, James E.
1975 The Black Community: Diversity and Unity. New York: Dodd, Mead and Co.
Bonacich, Edna
1976 "Advanced Capitalism and Black/White Race Relations in the United States: A Split Labor Market Interpretation." American Sociological Review 41 (February): 34–51.
Campbell, Angus, and Howard Schuman
1968 "Racial Attitudes in Fifteen American Cities," in The National Advisory Commission on Civil Disorders, Supplemental Studies. Washington, D.C.: U.S. Government Printing Office.
Carmichael, Stokely, and Charles V. Hamilton
1967 Black Power. New York: Random House, Inc.
Edwards, G. Franklin (ed.)
1968 E. Franklin Frazier on Race Relations. Chicago: University of Chicago Press.
Florez, John
1971 "Chicanos and Coalitions as a Force for Social Change." Social Casework 52 (May): 269–71.
Friedman, Robert
1975 "Institutional Racism: How to Discriminate Without Really Trying," Ch.

27 in Thomas F. Pettigrew (ed.), Racial Discrimination in the United States. New York: Harper and Row.

Mayhew, L. H.
1968   Law and Equal Opportunity: A Study of the Massachusetts Commission Against Discrimination." Cambridge, Massachusetts: Harvard University Press.

Moore, Joan W.
1976   "American Minorities and 'New Nation' Perspectives." Pacific Sociological Review 19, 4 (October): 447–68.

National Advisory Commission on Civil Disorders
1968   Report of the National Advisory Commission on Civil Disorders. Washington, D.C.: U.S. Government Printing Office.

Pettigrew, Thomas F.
1971   Racially Separate or Together. New York: McGraw-Hill.

Rothman, Jack (ed.)
1977   Issues in Race and Ethnic Relations: Theory, Research and Action. Itasca, Illinois: F. E. Peacock Publishers, Inc.

Rustin, Bayard
1966   " 'Black Power' and Coalition Politics." Commentary 42 (September): 35–40.

Schuman, Howard
1969   "Sociological Racism." Trans-Action 7, 2 (December): 44–48.

Stafford, Walter W., and Joyce Ladner
1973   "Comprehensive Planning and Racism," pp. 354–68 in Edgar G. Epps, Race Relations: Current Perspectives. Cambridge, Massachusetts: Winthrop Publishers, Inc.

Tabb, William K.
1971   "Race Relations Models and Social Change," Social Problems 18 (Spring): 431–44.

Van den Bergh, Pierre
1976   "The African Diaspora in the United States." Social Forces 54, 3 (March): 530–45.

Name Index

Subject Index